Advocacy in Practice

Advocacy in Practice

Creating a Culture of Social Change
in the Human Services

Shelley Rempel

OXFORD
UNIVERSITY PRESS

OXFORD
UNIVERSITY PRESS

Oxford University Press is a department of the University of Oxford.
It furthers the University's objective of excellence in research, scholarship,
and education by publishing worldwide. Oxford is a registered trade mark of
Oxford University Press in the UK and in certain other countries.

Published in Canada by
Oxford University Press
8 Sampson Mews, Suite 204,
Don Mills, Ontario M3C 0H5 Canada

www.oupcanada.com

Library and Archives Canada Cataloguing in Publication
Rempel, Shelley, author
Advocacy in practice: creating a culture of social change
in the human services/Shelley Rempel.

Includes bibliographical references and index.
ISBN 978–0–19–900841–4 (paperback)

1. Social advocacy. 2. Human services. 3. Social change.
I. Title.

HV40.R44 2017   361.3'2   C2016-907309-2

Cover image: © iStock/exdez

Oxford University Press is committed to our environment.
Wherever possible, our books are printed on paper which comes from
responsible sources.

Printed and bound in Canada

1 2 3 4 — 20 19 18 17

For Annie, Lucas, and Myron, with love

Contents

3   Historical, Conceptual, and Contextual Developments   43

**4   An Anti-oppressive Advocacy Development Model:
Structure, Process, and Strategy Considerations   68**

Figures, Tables, Boxes, and Case Studies

Figures

Tables

Boxes

Case Studies

Preface

Welcome to *Advocacy in Practice: Creating a Culture of Social Change in the Human Services*. The goal of this book is to help foster the potential to do anti-oppressive advocacy and to provide support, encouragement, and practical information for people who want to bring positive change to their communities. The book brings together aspects of anti-oppressive theories, now familiar to students in the human services, and advocacy, a well-known skill. Anti-oppressive advocacy in this text is viewed as an ethical and moral obligation of all human service practice from the front line to the executive director. Advocacy, then, is not only the right thing to do when service providers see an injustice; it is also expected of us as professionals in human service organizations. In fact the obligation to do advocacy is specified in professional codes of ethics and standards of practice.

I have been teaching and practising advocacy for more than 25 years and for the most part used American and British literature to guide my students and me. These texts were very helpful, offering useful advocacy techniques and strategies employed in other parts of the world. In both the field and the classroom we fused our knowledge of the Canadian context with the advocacy we read about, as practised in other places. This book, however, situates anti-oppressive advocacy practice in Canada. Anti-oppressive advocacy work is highly politicized—from everyday interactions and choices to large-scale mass movements. Therefore, it is important to study advocacy within the social and political contexts in which it is practised—Canada.

I have found that most students in the human services are eager to challenge inequality and bring about greater social justice. Sometimes, early enthusiasm results in initial efforts that are poorly conceived and end with disappointing results. These early failures may leave students hesitant, insecure, and uncertain. In this book, I try to bring back hope and confidence to those who have been turned off of advocacy and to add support to the efforts of those actively using advocacy in their day-to-day practice.

With the advent of anti-oppressive practices in the human services all service providers are challenged to reflect, examine, and change, even eliminate, practices and theories that create and recreate oppression. At first it was thought that anti-oppressive theory could just be layered over existing theories to provide a type of moral guidance. However, it was soon discovered that theories grounded in oppression, power, and privilege need more than moral guidance, they need a complete overhaul or even to be discarded entirely. The past 20 or so years have been lively with dialogue, debate, research, publications, and, most importantly, application of new ways of doing social work using anti-oppressive theory. I am grateful to be working on this book at this point in time because there is so much excellent literature from which to draw. Especially helpful was the work of Bob Mullaly, Donna Baines, Ben Carniol, Lena Dominelli, Allan Johnson, and Bill Lee—most of these writing from a Canadian context. This book contributes to this ongoing conversation by bringing anti-oppressive theory to the practice skill of advocacy. Different from some of my colleagues in other areas of practice I had an easier time bringing anti-oppressive theory to advocacy practice in particular, as it is more easily compatible with anti-oppressive theory than with other theories and practices in the human services. My efforts focused on drawing linkages between the compatible elements and defining an advocacy model and practice consistent with anti-oppressive theory—a model and a practice that are discussed over the following chapters.

I am also grateful to the many inspiring advocates who practise advocacy every day, sometimes at great risk to themselves. The eight activists profiled in Chapter 6 advocate for positive changes on behalf of women, workers, Aboriginal people, the LGBTQ community, the environment, racialized groups, and people who live in poverty. Current social movements such as Idle No More, Black Lives Matter, No One Is Illegal, as well as numerous environmental groups, are demanding social, economic, and political changes in Canada and around the world. There are also new collaborations between groups with common causes such as the environment, human rights, and poverty. Information and communication technology is fueling the convergence and inspiring new advocates—a generation that is knowledgeable and politicized—to join and actively participate, working at the personal, cultural, and structural levels. Advocacy attitude abounds as formerly oppressed people find their voices and join existing advocacy efforts or start new ones, demonstrating the courage that is so necessary to pursuing social justice.

I have been researching and teaching anti-oppressive theory and practices for more than 15 years at a community college and also briefly at a local university. Prior to this, for more than 10 years, I was the executive director of a small not-for-profit agency engaged in practicing anti-oppressive advocacy at the personal, cultural, and structural levels. Like some of the advocates in Chapter 6, I believe my advocacy attitude was smouldering for many years. As a child growing up in a small Mennonite farming community in southern Saskatchewan, I learned how poverty and isolation could take a toll, but also how families and community could provide support and comfort—I hardly knew how poor we were because everyone was poor. Throughout the years I was always outraged by injustice and inequality. I saw differences between the way men and women, rich and poor, were treated. However I seldom found the courage to voice my concerns and when I did it was often ill-conceived, awkward, poorly planned, and usually ineffectual. I enrolled in university as a mature student and started to explore sociology, philosophy, women's studies, and psychology, receiving my doctorate in education in 2009. Studying helped me to find my voice, to challenge, in a more articulate way, the injustice I saw around me. I continue to be active in advocacy cases and causes with my union and in the community. It has been an honour and a privilege to be offered the opportunity to research and write this book. I hope it is useful and encourages you to be an active participant with others in creating a culture of social change.

How This Book Is Organized

Each chapter begins with a summary of the chapter objectives. All of the chapters include case studies intended to highlight a specific aspect of advocacy. The case studies in Chapters 1–4 comprise Lessons Learned sections that critically analyze the advocacy case as well as questions designed to facilitate additional analysis. All the numbered case studies present hypothetical situations and people, inspired by real experiences. Each chapter also closes with critical thinking questions based on the chapter content. Also included at the end of each chapter are recommendations for further reading and a list of interesting websites and videos. Key terms are boldfaced throughout the chapters and defined in the Glossary at the end of the book.

Readers will notice that this text uses a gender-neutral singular *they/their* pronoun in place of the standard *she/he*. This choice was made in an attempt to use language that is as inclusive as possible and *she/he* does not adequately cover people who identify as non-binary, gender diverse, intersex, gender non-conforming, gender fluid, or Questioning. This book emphasizes inclusiveness and an anti-oppressive approach and it is my hope that it can be a tool and resource for all readers.

Chapter 1 provides a discussion of the need for advocacy in the social services, a definition of advocacy, and a description of the anti-oppressive advocacy model employed in the book. Chapter 2 highlights four important considerations for advocacy, small "p" and big "P" politics, sources and relations of power, conflict types, and analysis and ethical concerns. In Chapter 3 the historical origins of advocacy and anti-oppressive theory are examined, as well as a critical review of the current context in which advocacy is practised.

Chapter 4 provides a detailed discussion of an advocacy development model including useful boxed inserts, outlines, examples, and case studies. As a companion to Chapter 4, Chapter 5 focuses on advocacy action at the personal, cultural, and structural levels using three detailed case studies. Chapter 6 features the inspiring stories of eight experienced advocates from diverse backgrounds, advocating in very different contexts for their causes.

The final chapter, Chapter 7, provides a discussion of three current and emerging trends in advocacy. In addition it provides an overview of significant advocacy strengths and skills and an affirmation of the importance of relationships in advocacy practice. The chapter concludes with a call to human service workers to assume an advocacy attitude that makes and finds everyday opportunities to advocate for equality and social justice.

An Appendix at the end of the book includes templates, instructions, and examples of commonly used forms, letters, and other tactical means used in advocacy action. The examples are based on the case studies in the chapters. The Appendix examples include information to help advocates complete an advocacy agreement form, a letter of case advocacy, a letter of cause advocacy, a letter to the editor, an op-ed piece, a media release, a petition, posters for events, demonstration signs, and demonstration chants. I hope these chapters and the Appendix offer support, encouragement, and inspiration for advocacy practice.

Acknowledgements

I would not have been able to complete this project without the generous support of many people. I would like to start with a heartfelt thank you to Myron Kramar, my partner in life, who read all of the chapter drafts and provided important criticism and positive suggestions. He also made dinner and poured the wine when it was necessary. Also a very special thank you to my dear friend and colleague Bob Wood who read all of the drafts and provided invaluable feedback. A sincere expression of gratitude to Leah-Ann Lymer, Developmental Editor, Higher Education, at OUP for her ongoing support and meticulous guidance with this project. In addition, thank you to Stephen Kotowych, Acquisitions Editor, at OUP for his ongoing interest and early encouragement. Thank you as well to Amy Hick, copy editor, for her keen eye for detail and numerous helpful recommendations. Special thanks to Oxford University Press for still valuing and caring about books as a way to share information and promote social justice. I am indebted to Mary L., Cole G., Elizabeth G., Ali C., Vivene, Ken S., Nora L., and Meaghan for generously sharing their advocacy stories. Thank you all, you are truly inspiring advocates.

Finally, I would like to express my sincere thanks to the peer reviewers, both named and anonymous, who at the beginning and final stages of the writing provided astute commentary and positive reinforcement when it was dearly needed: Mark Gallupe, Loyalist College; Robert Harding, University of the Fraser Valley; Aamir Jamal, St Thomas University; Jeff Karabanow, Dalhousie University; Brigette Krieg, University of Regina; Sirena Liladrie, Sheridan College; Elaine Spencer, Red Deer College; and Natalie Wood, George Brown College.

1 Introduction to Advocacy Using an Anti-oppressive Framework

Chapter Objectives

After reading this chapter you should be able to:

1. Define advocacy
2. Discuss why advocacy is needed in the social services
3. Use privilege and oppression models of analysis
4. Explain the main elements of anti-oppressive advocacy practice

Introduction

Chun, weakened by cancer and ravaged by medical treatments, is pressured to return to a demanding job by her employer's insurance company.

* * *

Fida is 16 years old and she and her family have just arrived in Canada from a refugee camp. She has not attended school for the past two years and knows very little English. The thought of attending high school terrifies her.

* * *

Christine, a young single-parent mother has been living in a campground all summer with her two children. The family is homeless but the children think they are on an extended camping trip. The family was evicted from their subsidized housing apartment in the spring because Christine's abusive partner didn't pay the rent. It is now September and her children should be enrolled in school but she can't find an affordable place to live.

* * *

A low-income neighbourhood located in the north end of the city is home to many Aboriginal families. The city administrators have decided to locate a hazardous waste incinerator in their community.

Injustice is pervasive in everyday life, as illustrated in the brief examples above. Individuals and families enter the doors of social service agencies in Canada hoping for some type of help with their problems, assistance that may come in the form of counselling, financial support, food, clothing, household goods, housing, or services. Service providers[1] make use of their training, education, and personal qualities to provide assistance within the mandate and resources of their agency. This same process repeats itself on a regular and predictable basis many times each day in the many thousands of social service agencies across the country. The majority of assistance is provided more or less straightforwardly using **conventional social work practices** such as interviewing, counselling, assessment, planning, referrals, and follow-up (discussed further below). While effective for many of the problems presented to service providers each day, this conventional practice has faced criticism and will not have a significant effect on changing the root causes of the problems experienced by **service users**[2] (Carniol, 2005; Mullaly, 2010). For instance, Omar, a counsellor at a seniors' drop-in centre, using the conventional approach, helps Annie find a food bank and hot meal program because her pension is well below what is needed to live each month. Omar has helped Annie in an immediate and critical way—now she will not need to face hunger when her food supply runs out. However, the conventional approach used here has not solved the underlying problem of seniors' poverty, and Annie and others like her will continue to face poverty and hunger. This is an example of the limitations of the conventional approach. It is often effective in meeting the immediate needs of service users but does not have an impact on the cause(s) of the problem. That cause can usually be traced to policy or legislation at the structural level. In the example above the cause may be traced to inadequate federal pension programs for seniors.

The conventional approach has been the primary method in human service work for more than a century in Canada. Chapter 3 details the development and gradual domination of the conventional approach in the social services. At the same time alternative and more challenging ways of working with service users have developed and flourished outside of official social work academic and professional institutions. One of these alternative methods is **anti-oppressive theory and practice** (AOTP). Briefly, human service workers using AOTP have a responsibility to recognize the social, economic, and political institutions that result in oppression. Anti-oppressive service providers have an obligation to provide relief of suffering, but ultimately the goal is to bring about transformative changes at the structural level to policies, regulations, and laws (Morgaine & Capous-Desyllas, 2015). "[S]ocial workers should aim to provide direct assistance to individuals affected by oppression, while engaging in change to transform oppressive systems" (Morgaine & Capous-Desyllas, 2015, p. 24). Anti-oppressive theory is now skilfully used in a variety of settings including some of the most oppressive: large health care institutions, child welfare services, and government **welfare** offices (Fay, 2011; Smith, 2011; Strega, 2007). In addition, the literature developing this theory and documenting the application of anti-oppressive practices is also flourishing (Baines, 2007, 2011; Morgaine & Capous-Desyllas,

2015; Mullaly, 2010). A fuller description of AOTP is provided later in this chapter and also in Chapter 3.

Anti-oppressive theory is having a growing influence on many areas of practice in the field and service providers are examining their practices through the lens of the theory and are making changes in everything from types of documentation and forms to interviewing techniques and counselling. The use of anti-oppressive theory has brought changes to skills and practices in a variety of social service settings and the process of examining current practices in the field in light of anti-oppressive theory continues. Some skills used by service providers, such as **advocacy** and community organizing, are more compatible with anti-oppressive theory. This is especially true of those advocacy and organizing practices that focus on systemic change. This text presents advocacy practices in the social services within the anti-oppressive framework, with an aim to encourage students and service providers to find opportunities for advocacy at all levels of practice.

Defining Advocacy

A simple definition of advocacy is the work, through vocal support and promotion, of bringing about a change to some condition with, or on behalf of, an individual, family, group, or community. A more complete understanding of advocacy as used in this text encompasses a strong theoretical and ethical standpoint, in order to be more meaningful and useful for service users and service providers. In fact, the skill of advocacy is used in many different **contexts**, some of which most service providers and users would find deplorable. For instance, a large developer might advocate to build a four-lane expressway through an urban wilderness area in an economically depressed community lacking in parks and recreation. Or city bureaucrats may advocate pesticide use without concern for the impact on human health. It is important to remember that many different individuals and groups use advocacy techniques to further their causes. Read or listen to the news on any given night and you will find advocacy used by individuals, groups, and governments to try to get the public to believe, follow, or support their positions. Advocacy was used in Nazi Germany, by the Apartheid government of South Africa, and more recently is used by the Islamic State of Iraq and the Levant (ISIL), to name some of the most notorious suspects. In these extreme examples incorrect and biased information was used to convince large numbers of people of the superiority of certain groups and individuals, while others were silenced by racism, anti-Semitism, violence, and extreme poverty. So advocacy can be used to do terrible things.

Conversely, advocacy can be used by people who are oppressed and their allies to bring about change to oppressive circumstances. Sometimes the change is structural, such as new or amended legislation, or even the overthrow of a repressive regime. Recent examples of broad social movements advocating for change include Idle No More, Black Lives Matter, the Occupy movement, and 350.org. Therefore, advocacy as a skill and strategy set is a relatively standard process when pared away from the theoretical, ethical, social, political, and economic contexts in which it is performed. The advocacy practice outlined in this text, however, is not pared away or devoid of context. Instead the practice of advocacy is set within AOTP. This chapter and the following chapters will discuss a contextualized practice that recognizes the complexity of advocacy work in the social service field in terms of power, politics, and conflict. Advocacy as it is discussed in this text may be used to provide relief to the immediate problems of service users, but the ultimate goal of anti-oppressive advocacy is equality, social justice, and structural change.

Several definitions are provided in the advocacy literature for social service providers (Dalrymple & Boylan, 2013; Ezell, 2001; Hoefer, 2012; Kirst-Ashman & Hull, 2006; Lee, 2001; Lee, Sammon, & Dumbrill, 2014; Schneider & Lester, 2001; Wilks, 2012). While there are differences depending on the focus, five common elements emerge from the various definitions. The first is that the advocate takes a position on the side of the service user (individual, family, group, or community). The advocate does not attempt to maintain a neutral position as is sometimes encouraged in other forms of practice, and instead tries to see the problem from the perspective of the service user. The second common element is the need to bring about a change as defined by the service user, perhaps reinstating social assistance or fighting an illegal eviction. The third element assumes there is an injustice, that the service user has a right or a need that is being denied by someone with greater power. The fourth is the anticipation of a power imbalance between the service user and an individual or institution. Greater power rests in the hands of those with higher status, more wealth, and larger numbers. Generally, the people coming to social service agencies for help are lacking in these three areas. The fifth element is the view that advocacy involves conflict (Lee, 2001). Advocates in the social service field can expect that they will encounter individuals and institutions that do not want to back down or change. Therefore, there inevitably will be conflict between advocates and their opposition (Lee, 2001).

I add to these five commonly understood elements the need to include an analysis of **privilege** and oppression using AOTP. The privilege analysis, the **P/C/S (personal/ cultural/structural) analysis model**, and anti-oppressive theory will be discussed further in the next section. A summary of the elements of the role of an advocate is as follows:

- Takes the side of the service user
- Recognizes that change is needed
- Appreciates there is injustice
- Anticipates power imbalances
- Understands that conflict is involved
- Analyzes privilege and oppression
- Applies anti-oppressive theory and practice

Whenever power imbalances exist there is a potential need for advocacy, as in Case Study 1.1.

Case Study 1.1   A Case of Discrimination in Public Housing: Advocacy Defined

Many years ago, before most provinces in Canada had made it illegal to discriminate on the basis of sexual orientation (1996), I was working at a small not-for-profit social service agency doing case advocacy. One day a same-sex couple came in to see me. They were living in a small one bedroom subsidized public housing apartment. They had recently applied to the housing authority for a larger unit for themselves and four children—one of the women had a shared custody agreement with the father of her children. The housing authority denied their request for a larger unit stating that the custody arrangement was unclear about how much time the children would be with the couple and that the couple would be over-housed if the two of them lived in a large three- or four-bedroom unit alone much of the time.

The couple felt that the custody arrangement was clear and that the housing authority was denying their transfer request because they were a same-sex couple. Further, their circumstances required immediate attention. The current apartment was located far from parks, playgrounds, and public transportation. When the children came to stay, the couple slept in the living room and the four small children slept on bunk beds in the bedroom. They had been unsuccessful in their attempts to get the housing authority to change its decision and feared the worker at the housing authority would alert Children's Aid because of the overcrowded conditions. In addition, the partner from the previous relationship was considering using the overcrowding concern to gain full custody of the children. I worked with the couple over several weeks and eventually the housing authority offered them a three-bedroom unit, appropriate accommodation for their family size.

Lessons Learned

It is important to see the injustice in this case from the perspective of the women involved. Their experience of discrimination, had it not been challenged, could have had dire consequences for their family. A simplistic analysis of the problem is that the social housing provider complied with regulations and this couple did not fit the official definition and therefore there was nothing that could be done. However, rules and regulations (legislation, in a government context) are written at a particular point in time, by people who bring their values and beliefs to the writing process. The regulations may have been written at a time when same-sex couples were not even considered a family type and divorce and shared custody arrangements were rare. Sometimes advocates need to challenge the interpretation and fairness of official rules.

continued

Critical Thinking Questions

1. What other forms of oppression are impacting on this couple?
2. What might an advocate do to confront these other forms of oppression?
3. Who writes and interprets policy, rules, regulations, and legislation?
4. What is the process for challenging and changing official regulations?
5. How is this case connected to other legislation such as human rights and child and family law?

Anti-oppressive Advocacy Practice Model

Building on the definition discussion above, the following section will outline an anti-oppressive advocacy model for practice in the human services, which provides the framework of practice for the remainder of the book. Privilege, P/C/S analysis, and anti-oppressive theory form the basis for the advocacy practice model; the model draws on the relatively new wealth of literature in those areas of study. This section begins with a brief discussion of privilege and the P/C/S analysis model and is followed by a discussion of anti-oppressive theory. Chapters 4 and 5 in particular will provide case-study–based discussions of planning and action in advocacy.

Analysis of Privilege

Privilege and oppression are two sides of the same coin, yet in the human services more emphasis has traditionally been placed on the analysis of oppression. Service providers help service users examine how oppressive forces such as racism, classism, sexism, and ableism impact their lives. Service providers are even adept at analyzing the oppression in their own lives as workers in a marginalized service sector. Often though, human service workers are less comfortable or capable of analyzing the privilege that makes oppression possible, including their own privilege as service providers. Johnson (2006), McIntosh (1990), and Mullaly (2010) point out that oppression cannot exist without privilege and therefore it is important to examine both in practice. The analysis of privilege helps to ensure that service providers are aware of their privilege and use that power to further social justice goals. "I am convinced that studies of oppression will not go anywhere toward ending oppression unless they are accompanied by understandings of systems of privilege that cause the systems of oppression" (McIntosh, 2012, p. 204).

Generally, privilege is handed to us; it is not something we need to earn or struggle for. Privilege, for the most part, is apportioned at birth based on characteristics that fit certain valued social categories in our society. In Canada these characteristics—the ones that form a mythical, default "norm"—are white skin, male, heterosexual, and able-bodied. People with white skin are born that way and have privilege because of this; they did not earn their whiteness but their skin colour gives them advantages and allows them to more easily acquire and earn other privileges such as income and education. The closer an individual aligns with the privileged norm the more likely they[3] are to acquire un-earned advantages. White, heterosexual, able-bodied women, for example, will struggle under the unearned oppression of gender but will secure many other unearned privileges. Essentially, advantages that are not earned form privilege and conversely disadvantages that are not earned are forms of oppression (Mullaly, 2010).

Privilege is generally invisible to those who have it. When pressed, people with priv-ilege will likely find that they believe they earned their good fortune or obtained it due to special talent. They have high-paid and high-status employment and they believe they have this elevated standing because they are smarter, more disciplined, have persevered, or have taken astute risks. According to Mullaly (2010), privilege is solidly based on be-liefs that support both oppression and privilege, beliefs such as

> . . . the myth of scarcity, of objective information, of might is right or the belief in the majority rule even if it tyrannizes the minority, the supremacy or the belief in a superior culture, of class, of equal opportunity or meritocracy, of stereotyping or the belief that all members of a group are the same, blaming the victim or the belief that individuals are responsible for their own oppression, and of competi-tion and hierarchy. (Mullaly, 2010, p. 290)

Mullaly adds to the list above the myth that things have always been this way and they always will be, because the structure is too difficult to change. These myths conspire to justify privilege and oppression as fairness. The myth is that if oppressed people just tried harder they too could become privileged (even though the system is stacked against them).

McIntosh (2012) cautions against the oversimplification of the analysis of privi-lege. She explains that it is wrong to think about privilege and oppression as a binary, black and white, rich and poor. Privilege is better viewed as a web with intersections that support the privilege and the oppression. As an example examine income in-equality in Canada. According to a CBC report, "the richest of the rich in Canada are married, middle-aged, white men" who have income 10 times greater than that of the average Canadian ("Wealthiest 1% Earn," 2013). The composition of the top one per cent—largely middle-aged, white, male—is virtually unchanged from 50 years ago ("Who Are Canada's," 2013). There are women among the top one per cent, as there are no doubt racialized people, but middle-aged white men predominate because they benefit from multiple intersections of privilege (male + white + heterosexual + able-bodied). Those factors intersect to create opportunities for great wealth for a few, while others are excluded. The implication for advocacy in the social services is the importance of taking the time to develop a detailed analysis of privilege that consid-ers the complexity of history and context. Eliminating one form of privilege such as race will not eliminate other forms of privilege based on income, gender, or disability.

The interconnections allow privilege and oppression to continue even if one form is eradicated.

Advocates in the human services need to understand their own privilege. Like others, advocates may be blind to their own privilege. The majority of workers in the human services are female and white. They also generally have diplomas or degrees from colleges or universities and work for reputable organizations from which they receive regular pay as well as social benefits such as pensions and dental and health care plans. It is widely believed that workers in the human service field are undervalued and not adequately compensated for their work and qualifications. This is arguably true, but compared to the people who are coming to them for help, service providers have much more privilege. This privilege allows workers to have a great deal of influence over the amount and type of provisions that service users receive; as a result service providers can use their privilege to help service users or they can be involved in reproducing oppression. To avoid recreating oppression, advocates need to analyze how they contribute to privilege and oppression. Mullaly (2010) emphasizes the importance of using privilege, and the power associated with it, to work for social justice rather than trying to deny or minimize it.

Oppression and the P/C/S Analysis

Related to the understanding of privilege is the analysis of oppression. Advocates in the social services should be familiar with the P/C/S oppression analysis model. P/C/S is the basis of anti-oppressive practices in the human services including advocacy practice. Thompson (2001) and Mullaly (2010) make use of the P/C/S analysis model as a way to examine oppression faced by individuals, families, and groups. According to the P/C/S model, oppression occurs at three levels. P stands for the personal level, C for the cultural level, and S for the structural level. "These three levels or locations of oppression are in a dynamic interaction with one another, with each level supporting, reinforcing, and influencing oppression on the other two levels and, in turn, being supported, reinforced, and influenced by the other two levels" (Mullaly, 2010, p. 61).

New and experienced advocates start their advocacy by trying to understand how oppression has impacted the service user coming to them for help. For instance, Charvi comes to a social service agency to see a worker because she has become depressed trying to cope with her family situation, a young son with severe autism and a husband unable to work because of chronic mental illness. A worker using a P/C/S analysis of oppression will help Charvi to understand how her private troubles are related to personal, cultural, and structural oppression. Charvi will come to understand that racism, poverty, and the lack of adequate social programs are having an impact on her family problems. She may not have the time or energy at this point to join a campaign to bring about structural level change, but, understanding this, Charvi will feel less responsible and be relieved of the shame and blame associated with her circumstances. In addition to helping Charvi, the service provider will make efforts to bring about changes at the cultural and structural levels. In contrast, a worker not making use of oppression analysis may focus on helping

Charvi to develop better coping strategies and make a referral to a doctor to see if medication would be beneficial. Of course, those efforts are well-intentioned and often helpful in the short term but closer observation reveals that Charvi continues to feel responsible for her less than adequate coping skills and subsequent depression. Her immediate problems may have been lessened, but the underlying issues remain. The alternative is a careful analysis of oppression and the use of AOTP with an aim to contribute to equality and social justice.

The P/C/S analysis model is depicted in Figure 1.1 (Mullaly, 2010, p. 62; Thompson, 2001, p. 22). In this model, the personal (P) level represents an individual's "thoughts, actions, and feelings"; these are unique but are also influenced by the surrounding cultural (C) level (Thompson, 2001, p. 22). For instance, at the P level a young woman graduating from high school may say she has freely chosen to become a social worker. However, cultural (C) influences that include gender-role stereotyping have influenced her decisions from the day she was born. Though, fortunately, gender stereotypes are having less influence on the career choices of women, she might not even have considered other possible careers such as engineering.

According to Mullaly, cultural level oppression "consists of those values, norms, and shared patterns of seeing, thinking, and acting" (2010, p. 63). Those individuals and groups with greater influence and power in society, through position, financial circumstances, or greater numbers, collaborate to form a **dominant culture**. The dominant culture is then popularized and reproduced in the media, arts and entertainment, and other means, through stereotyping and marginalization. Women have been and continue to be stereotyped as sensitive caregivers rather than as business leaders, firefighters, or other ostensibly more skilled positions.

To complete the model, the C level is surrounded by the structural (S) level. Oppression is not only evident at the personal and cultural levels; oppression is protected and

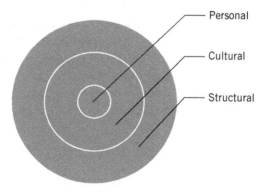

Figure 1.1   P/C/S Analysis Model

Source: Adapted from Mullaly, 2010, p. 62 and Thompson, 2001, p. 22.

nurtured by structural level social, economic, and political institutions and organizations. Oppression is legitimized, legalized, and institutionalized in legislation, regulations, and policies. For example, the Immigration Act of Canada requires immigrants to undergo a medical exam before admission to Canada. If a potential immigrant is found to have a medical condition that could result in "excessive demand" on Canada's health care system, they may be found inadmissible. The Council of Canadians with Disabilities, a disability rights group, is advocating for a change to this legislation, in part because the "Immigration Act perpetuates long held stereotypical views of persons with disabilities as being less deserving and a burden on society" (Council of Canadians with Disabilities, 2013). This is an example of discrimination embedded in legislation, resulting in S-level oppression.

The description of the P/C/S analysis discussed above may appear at first glance rather deterministic and fundamentally hopeless. However, looking at that same immigration legislation hints at possibilities for change. In fact, immigration advocates and disability advocates have brought about changes to immigration legislation and to the culture that marginalizes people with disabilities as dependent and burdensome. Individuals are active participants in changing (and maintaining) the composition of oppression at the personal, cultural, and structural levels. Individuals, through their own actions and in concert with others, can have a powerful impact on the current cultural and structural conditions. This reality is well articulated by the famous activist and cultural anthropologist, Margaret Mead.[4] "Never doubt that a small group of thoughtful, committed people can change the world. Indeed, it is the only thing that ever has" (Institute for Intercultural Studies, FAQ, 2009, para. 1).

The P/C/S model challenges the conventional social work practice that focuses on helping individuals with personal problems on a case-by-case basis. (Casework and the conventional approach are discussed further in Chapter 3.) Conventional casework would have service users adjusting to and coping with injustices such as poverty, homelessness, and racial discrimination, while the P/C/S model provides an analysis upon which to base advocacy and action to transform the structural, cultural, and personal levels. The P/C/S analysis helps to reveal how individuals are impacted by, and can also impact, personal, cultural, and structural oppression. Services users, who come through the doors of social service agencies each day trying to cope with hunger, homelessness, and mental illness, will find the roots of many of those problems at the cultural and structural levels, not in stereotypical "causes" such as lack of willpower, ignorance, or laziness. AOTP is grounded in an understanding of the P/C/S analysis of oppression.

Anti-oppressive Theory and Advocacy Practice

The advocacy proposed in this text is practiced using anti-oppressive theory grounded in the analysis of privilege and the P/C/S model. This section provides a brief overview of anti-oppressive theory as it is used to carry out advocacy work with individuals, families, groups, and communities at the personal, cultural, and structural levels (anti-oppressive theory is discussed further in Chapter 3). AOTP is increasingly the subject of social work literature (Baines, 2011; Carniol, 2005; Dominelli, 2002; Hick, 2010; Morgaine & Capous-Desyllas, 2015; Mullaly, 2010). It is discussed as a set of interconnected principles consistent with the goal of social justice. Baines (2011) explains that anti-oppressive theory is not meant to be seen as the authority on every social problem, instead it should be seen as a flexible, evolving, politicized practice that analyzes and challenges oppression at all levels.

Anti-oppressive theory is not prescriptive at any level of practice; it does not provide a specific formula, method, or step-by-step process with precise outcomes. Instead, discussions of anti-oppressive theory provide a general framework that features themes or principles firmly grounded in social justice and transformation. A social worker for the Children's Aid Society told me that using anti-oppressive theory was "a way of life" for her. She had incorporated the principles and values into her thinking and behaviour in every respect inside and outside of work. Baines identifies "core insights" that offer support for anti-oppressive practice in the social service field (2011, p. 4). These insights highlight the importance of understanding how human experiences are shaped by multiple and intersecting oppressions and that everyday interactions reproduce and challenge oppression from the micro to the macro levels (Baines, 2011, p. 4–8). She explains that service providers in social service agencies need to understand that their work is not neutral but highly politicized and that workers need to join with service users to build social movements and fight for social justice. Finally, workers need to be vigilant about critically examining their own practices and to actively incorporate approaches that further the aim of social justice and transformation (Baines, 2011). Advocates using anti-oppressive theory partner with service users to understand social inequality and to develop ways to challenge injustice.

Dominelli (2002) offers an insightful critique of conventional practices that focus narrowly on client problems, and encourages a practice that is empowering, holistic, and transformative using anti-oppressive theory as a basis. Mullaly (2010) provides a detailed analysis of privilege and oppression and illustrates how anti-oppressive social work practices can affectively fight inequality and transform society. Thompson (2001) makes use of P/C/S analysis to provide specific insight into working against racism, sexism, ageism, ableism, and other forms of oppression in the field of social work. An analysis of privilege and oppression and ally-work is featured in Bishop (2002). She makes a strong case for the type of efforts oppressors must make to be allied with people facing oppression. Common among these approaches is the analysis of privilege and oppression, allying with service users, and a goal of transformation and social justice.

In previous research, I did in-depth interviews with social workers who use versions of anti-oppressive theory in their work and students on field placement (Rempel, 2009). Three important elements emerged from the research: **reflexivity, critical analysis**, and action. Each of these will be discussed further below and a case will be made for their particular relevance to the practice of advocacy. The three elements are discussed separately; however, in practice they work together. For example, reflexivity helps to shape critical analysis, which in turn changes action. Table 1.1 provides a brief definition of the three advocacy elements. A fuller discussion of each element follows the table.

Table 1.1 Key Elements for an Anti-oppressive Advocacy Model for Human Services

Reflexivity	Reflecting on how the personal characteristics you were born with or developed through life experiences influence advocacy, then understanding how your characteristics are an advantage in some advocacy situations and a disadvantage in others. Finally, considering the best strategy for the advocacy action in light of your characteristics and the advocacy situation.
Critical Analysis	Systematic examination of power, political, conflict, and ethical considerations in the advocacy context. The systematic approach is based on the P/C/S model, privilege analysis, and anti-oppressive theory. Advocacy planning, strategy, and action emerge from the analysis.
Action	Selection of strategies and actions based on reflexivity and critical analysis. Actions range from individual, indirect, subtle acts of resistance to large, collective, public advocacy demonstrations.

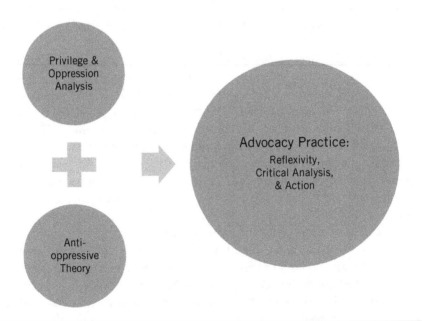

Figure 1.2   Anti-oppressive Advocacy Practice Model

Reflexivity

In the literature reflexivity is described as a systematic process of reflection, self-assessment, and the consideration of action possibilities (Smith, 1990; Stega, 2007; Tierney & Rhoads, 1993). Likewise, in advocacy reflexivity is an intense analysis of context combined with a sharp awareness of self, all with a focus on action. It is important for advocates to make reflexivity part of their ongoing work. Part of reflexivity means advocates need to examine their **social location** with regards to privilege and oppression.

> Social location refers to a person's affiliation or categorization within webs of oppression and privilege. Strands of the webs include race, age, gender, sexual orientation, class, religion, and so forth. People are shaped, but not determined, by their social location. That is, individuals have the capacity to make change and to understand the world independently of the storylines provided to them by society. While people are influenced by their social location, the sum total of who they are, and what they chose to do within this, is always changing and offers huge potential for personal transformation. (Baines, 2007a, p. 24)

For instance, Rada is aware of the privilege she has as a white woman with a university degree in psychology and a diploma in social service work. She has a secure, well-paying job as a legal advocate at a women's centre. She is an experienced advocate with an excellent understanding of the law and resources relevant to her advocacy work. She is also aware that as a woman with a Russian accent, she may face discrimination in some circumstances, such as with male lawyers in court. Rada knows that her personal characteristics can be an advantage or disadvantage as the circumstances of her advocacy change. She is alert to the changing context of her advocacy work and uses her privilege to fight for social justice for abused women. Rada assesses the context of her work with an awareness of her personal privilege and oppression.

Briefly, for this discussion, context is the circumstances in which advocacy is taking place. It includes the setting—such as a social service agency, government office, or meeting with a landlord—as well as the political and power structures inherent to the setting. In a government office a worker, supervisor, or manager has decision-making power over a service user's appeal. In a social service setting the front-line worker has the power to deny the homeless person a bed for the night in a shelter. Some services will not provide birth control or abortion referral services because of their politically conservative social orientations. Context analysis also means considering what the advocate and the service user bring to the advocacy setting in terms of privilege, oppression, power, politics, and other variables that become relevant in the advocacy process. The advocate may have an excellent reputation, years of experience, academic credentials, and the support of an upright employer, or in other words, the advocate is endowed with power in various settings. The opposite may be true of the service user. They may have little or no power in most advocacy settings. These are a few examples of context that need to be considered in advocacy. Context is discussed further in Chapters 2 and 3.

Successful advocacy action depends on reflexivity and context analysis. The reflexive advocate uses her or his analysis of self and context to determine advocacy strategy and action. Rada is advocating for Ava, who has to find a place to rent before her child will be returned to her. The Children's Aid Society took Ava's child into care because she suffered a fractured wrist when Ava's partner became violent one night after heavy drinking. Ava has no last-month-rent deposit and her social assistance has not yet come through so Rada has some challenging advocacy to do with prospective landlords. However, Rada knows some sympathetic landlords and one in particular, a Russian, likes Rada because of their similar ethnic backgrounds. Rada understands that this gives her an advantage and she knows it creates a context in which she is more likely to succeed in her advocacy for the young abused woman with no money. So Rada's accent and ethnicity is a disadvantage in some contexts and an advantage in others. In every advocacy context it is important to use reflexivity to develop strategy and action possibilities.

Critical Analysis

The second element important to anti-oppressive advocacy practice is critical analysis. Sammon (in Lee, Sammon, & Dumbrill, 2014) defines critical analysis as a process of exploring underlying "assumptions, values, and knowledge bases" (p. 10). In advocacy critical analysis means looking beyond what is at first apparent and digging into the causes, power structures, and history of an advocacy problem. Advocacy contexts can be very complex so it is important for the advocate to make critical analysis part of the ongoing advocacy process.

Gil (1998) describes the development of critical analysis "as a medium for critical reflection, and as a source for innovation of ways of life, based on alternative perceptions of needs and interests. Such transformations of consciousness can be communicated to others, and can lead to collective actions aimed at social and cultural transformations" (p. 41). Freire (2003) and Giroux (2001) describe the development of critical analysis as a necessary prerequisite for involvement in social change. Butler, Elliott, and Stopard (2003) as well as Coates and McKay (1995) explain that critical analysis is never complete or finished but instead is continually improved and strengthened through use and concerted effort. Advocates using anti-oppressive practices will need to continue to develop, maintain, and improve their critical analysis skills, skills that should be applied to all advocacy decisions and actions. In Case Study 1.2, Amaro describes how he maintains and improves his critical analysis for advocacy work.

Case Study 1.2   Amaro's Efforts to Improve His Critical Analysis

Amaro is a counsellor and advocate at a centre providing services to refugees from South and Central America and Africa. He has a degree in political science and has also taken courses in economics, sociology, and cultural studies. He does a lot of reading about the political, economic, and social conditions in Canada and around the world. He pays attention to what mainstream media such as CBC and CTV report but he knows that this is only one perspective and so he explores numerous online sources that help to provide other angles, especially those of the people most effected by violence, war, drought, and poverty. The multiple standpoints presented in the media and online and in discussions with his family, friends, colleagues, and the refugees coming to him for assistance help Amaro to continually develop his critical consciousness and his ability to do critical analysis. Amaro uses his critical analysis to examine the advocacy he does with, and on behalf of, refugees. He skilfully and effectively develops advocacy strategy and action to improve their lives at the personal, cultural, and structural levels.

Lessons Learned

Critical analysis is not a natural trait or talent. It is learned and can be improved with study and practice.

Critical Thinking Questions

1. Is there anything else Amaro could do to improve his critical analysis?
2. Does the privilege/oppression experienced by Amaro have an influence on the development of his critical analysis?
3. How would you assess your ability to do critical analysis?
4. What steps can you take to improve your critical analysis?

Amaro's critical analysis skills will remain sharp if he continues to study and research the context of advocacy problems. Anti-oppressive advocates will also want to help service users improve their own critical analysis skills as part of the advocacy process. The service user's perspective on the advocacy problem, their lived experience, contributes to the critical analysis. For instance, Idis, a gay man, recently fled Nigeria in fear for his life. Nigeria is one of seven countries in the world where homosexuality is punishable by the death penalty (Withnall, 2014). How the terror feels and the ways it impacts his life can only really come from Idis. In anti-oppressive advocacy the advocate partners with the service user and together they use critical analysis to develop a more complete view of the problem that includes the perspective of the service user as well as the social, political, economic, and historical perspectives on the advocacy. It is a type of mutual education that can result in "new interpretations" (Belenky et al., 1987, p. 221). The discussions between the service user and the advocate help to interpret the service user's experiences within a "social, historical, and political context" (Sands & Nuccio, 1992, p. 491). It is through these shared discussions and the development of a strong mutual relationship that a service user's subjective experiences are explored through critical analysis (Mullaly, 2007; Freire, 2003). Case Study 1.3 shows the benefits and use of critical analysis in advocacy practice.

Case Study 1.3   Amaro Uses His Critical Analysis

Idis is afraid of being sent back to Nigeria, where he may be killed because he is gay. He has made an appointment with Amaro for help filling out forms and preparing for his hearing with Immigration Canada. Amaro has an excellent understanding of immigration policy and many years of experience helping refugees complete forms and gather documentation for their hearings. He works closely with the lawyers at his agency to ensure that Idis receives the best possible representaion. Amaro listens carefully and documents Idis' story of dentensions, beatings, and of losing many gay friends to murder and imprisonment.

Amaro knows that the human rights atrocities comitted against gay people in Nigera are well documented by international human rights organizations and in the mainstream and online media. This information supports Idis' claim as a "person in need of protection" under the Immigrant and Refugee Protection Act Canada, S.C. 2001, c. 27 ("Immigrant and Refugee," 2001). Together Amaro and Idis complete and file the Basis of Claim form, which is then checked by the agency's lawyer. Amaro then helps Idis prepare for the hearing that will determine if he can remain in Canada. Amaro knows that it is important to gather as much evidence as possible to substantiate Idis' story for the hearing. Idis finds copies of police and medical records that document his arrests and beatings. He also has photographs and emails from friends in Nigeria that can confirm his persecution. Amaro gathers reports from international human rights organizations and credible media sites about the persecution of people from LGBTQ communities in Nigeria. An expert in international LGBTQ human rights, who has knowledge of the conditions for a gay man in Nigeria, has agreed to testify at the hearing. Amaro also arranges for testimony from a gay man who had previously fled Nigera because of persecution.

To prepare for the hearing Amaro and Idis meet with the agency lawyer to critically analyze the stories, reports, and documentation gathered, in light of current immigration and refugee legislation, to determine the best way to present Idis' case at the Immigration and Refugee Board.

Lessons Learned

This case shows the importance of critical analysis for advocacy. In this case critical analysis helps to determine what evidence should be included and how it should be presented in order to provide strategic advantages for the service user. The availible evidence is viewed against the policy, procedure, or legislation in question. The table below summarizes the evidence from the case study and a definition from the relevant legislation.

Government of Canada refugee status definition	Summary of evidence to support advocacy for a refugee claiment
"A person in need of protection is a person in Canada whose removal to their home country or country where they would normally live would subject them personally to: • a danger of torture; • a risk to their life; or • a risk of cruel and unusual treatment or punishment" ("Determine your Eligibility," 2012).	• Idis' story • arrest and medical records • photographs of injuries • emails from friends in Nigeria confirming persecution • reports from international human rights organizations and credible media • testimony from an international LGBTQ human rights expert • testimony from a gay man who had recently fled Nigeria

Critical Thinking Questions

1. How is this advocacy problem related to other issues, concerns, or disputes at the personal, cultural, or structural levels?
2. What are the official explanations of the advocacy problem? Are these believable, why or why not? What are alternative explanations of the problem?
3. Historically how did the problem evolve, where did it come from?
4. What are the underlying values, beliefs, and assumptions?
5. Where is the information about the problem coming from (knowledge base)?
6. What is the structure of privilege and oppression?

Action

Advocacy action in the field is discussed further in Chapters 4 and 5. In this section it is discussed briefly as an element in anti-oppressive advocacy. Without action there is no advocacy. However, effective advocacy, based on anti-oppressive theory, also needs reflexivity and critical analysis. In the anti-oppressive literature action is integral to practice. Several of the 10 themes discussed in Baines (2011) pertain to action and resistance (p. 6–8). "Every action we undertake is political and ultimately about power, resources, and who has the right and opportunity to feel positive about themselves, their identities, and their futures (Baines, 2011, p. 6). Mullaly (2010) explains that it is not enough to "theorize and analyze from a distance." Anti-oppressive practices including advocacy connote an active participation in transforming the world.

Action takes many forms in anti-oppressive advocacy and advocates are continually looking for opportunities to contribute to positive changes for service users and the community. Advocacy action is expressed in a range of undertakings from subtle interactions between individuals to participation in mass demonstrations. The type and level of action an advocate takes on is dependent on many variables including the training and experience of the advocate, their personal characteristics and attributes, and the circumstances or context of the advocacy.

Advocates themselves must decide what type and level of advocacy is possible in their particular situations. For example, a social worker in a large health care institution is very limited in the type of advocacy she can do because her supervisors, the doctors and other medical professionals, do not like to have their decisions questioned. They expect that their orders will be followed, period. The social worker has seen other staff punished with transfers, demotions, and termination because they questioned the decisions of those in authority. Examples of the types of advocacy action in which this social worker might engage are listed in the upper half only of Table 1.2.

In other contexts, advocacy is welcomed and encouraged. At a social service agency, all the staff are expected to do advocacy on behalf of people who are homeless or in danger of losing their housing. In fact, staff were hired because they had experience doing advocacy and once employed they work hard to improve their skills through additional training. They are also responsible for participating in and helping to organize public protests. These advocates are expected to contribute to the policies and the decision making of the agency. Examples of the types of advocacy action in which these advocates might engage are listed in all of Table 1.2.

The two social service contexts described briefly here are close to opposite ends of a spectrum. There are of course many agency contexts that fall between them and skilled advocates will continually be pushing the possibilities for advocacy action within the contexts of their work. Advocates immersed in social service agencies are in the best position to know what can be accomplished given the situation.

Table 1.2 provides brief examples of a range of advocacy actions that are consistent with the anti-oppressive advocacy model used in this text and might be used in various

Table 1.2 Examples of Advocacy Action

Advocacy Action	Examples of Action
Personal Level	• The following can be used to show disagreement: facial expressions and body language, silence, non-participation, absence • Use inclusive language that does not label or oppress • Reframe oppressive language and analysis used in professional social situations so that it is inclusive—in team/staff meetings, supervision, case management, conferences, and informal gatherings
Cultural Level and Structural Level	• Use inclusive, non-oppressive language in all records and documentation including: case notes, assessments, consultations, reports, research, briefs, appeals, complaints, and proposals • All presentations to small and large audiences should be inclusive and use non-oppressive language • Use official processes, procedures, forums, hearings, proceedings, and courts in order to file appeals, complaints, grievances, and objections • Use unofficial but legal action: work-to-rule, watchdog, whistle-blower • Use mainstream media and online information and communication media • Participate in and organize coalitions, networks, social action groups, and social movements • Use campaigns, newsletters, action research, demonstrations, workshops, petitions, letter writing, public education, political work, lobbying, girl(boy)cotts, civil disobedience, sit-ins, occupations, encampments, and blockades

social service contexts. Advocates working in agencies that discourage or punish any dissent may be confined to the actions at the personal level, while advocates working in contexts that allow or even encourage advocacy may engage in more public forms of action at the cultural or structural levels. Examples in the upper half of the table may involve only one or two other people. For instance, using facial expressions to show disagreement, rather than maintaining a neutral expression or nodding in agreement, when a colleague makes sexist comments in the lunch room. Examples in the bottom half of the table will involve working collaboratively with small to large groups depending on the cause and the strategy. As you move down the list of examples on the right side of the table the advocacy actions become more public, involve greater numbers of people, and more organization.

Conclusion

This chapter brings together the practice skill of advocacy with AOTP in the human services. Service users arrive at social service agencies each day presenting a range of needs. Advocacy is one in a number of skills service providers may use to give assistance. Advocacy alone can be effective, however, when combined with an analysis of privilege and oppression and anti-oppressive theory, it provides powerful opportunities for progressive, meaningful change. The analysis of privilege provides helpful insights for advocates into their own privilege and connections to oppression. The P/C/S model reveals just how common and widespread oppression can be for certain individuals, groups, and communities. Oppression exists at the personal, cultural, and structural levels and the three levels interact and compound one another. Yet it can also be alleviated and perhaps eliminated completely through concerted efforts at change, using AOTP to reverse, push back, and improve the effects of oppression. Three concepts are discussed in this chapter as pertinent to the practice of advocacy within an anti-oppressive framework and as forming the basis for practice—reflexivity, critical analysis, and action. Theories, models, and concepts are sometimes deemed to be too academic for service providers who are eager to *practice* advocacy rather than to *study* advocacy. Enthusiasm, passion, anger—or, as was said in a recent SSW class I was teaching "being really pissed off"—is essential for effective advocacy, and I concede that plenty of people do advocacy without having read a single book or taken a single class on the subject. However, I believe advocates want to continue to improve and be the best and most competent advocates they can for the service users needing their help. So you may find this chapter and this text useful and helpful; you may also disagree and argue against some of what is said. All of this dialogue is healthy and invigorating for advocacy in the social services and consistent with the analysis of privilege and oppression and AOTP. Continue to study, reflect, and discuss, but most of all continue to resist and act. "If we are genuinely to assist people in their suffering, radicalism is necessary" (Baines, 2007b, p. 191).

Critical Thinking Questions

1. There are different definitions of advocacy in the human services. What are the common elements to the definitions? Develop a definition of advocacy for a human service organization with which you have had some experience as a volunteer, student, or employee.
2. Review the section in this chapter on the analysis of privilege and write down all of the ways that you benefit from your privilege.

3. Explain racism, sexism, classism, ageism, ableism, homophobia, transphobia, and biphobia using the P/C/S model of oppression.
4. Consider an experience you have had personally with oppression. How did you react to the injustice? Would you respond differently after reading this chapter? How?
5. What steps can you take in your practice to include service users in advocacy?

Suggested Readings

Baines, D. (2011). *Doing anti-oppressive practice: Social justice social work*. D. Baines (Ed.). Winnipeg: Fernwood Publishing.

Bishop, A. (2002). *Becoming an ally: Breaking the cycle of oppression in people*. Halifax: Fernwood Publishing.

Johnson, A. (2006). *Privilege, power and difference*. Toronto: McGraw-Hill.

Mullaly, B. (2010). *Challenging oppression and confronting privilege*. Toronto: Oxford University Press.

Suggested Videos and Websites

Tim Wise, anti-racist essayist, author, and educator www.timwise.org/

The Anti-oppression Network https://theantioppressionnetwork.wordpress.com/

Shameless Magazine, Blogs, and Podcasts http://shamelessmag.com/

Qallunaat! Why White People Are Funny. Mark Sandiford, 2006 National Film Board Canada www.nfb.ca/film/qallunaat_why_white_people_are_funny

Notes

1. *Service provider* is used in this text as a general term for the person or persons delivering a program in a human service organization. Other examples of the terminology used in the literature and in the field include: human service worker, social worker, social service worker, child and youth worker, counsellor, advocate, therapist, case manager, caseworker, and support worker.

2. There are many different terms used in the field and in the literature to refer to people who come to social services for help. Common terms are: client, patient, consumer, survivor, and, more recently, participant. This text uses the term *service user*. I like this term because it is a reminder that we are all service users throughout our lives—sometimes we sit on one side of the desk as a professional and sometimes we sit on the other side of the desk as a service user in a social service agency or health care facility. All Canadians will benefit from various services and programs during their lives, paid for through the tax system. The following list includes some of the most frequently used programs: health care, education, social services, the Canada Child Tax Benefit, employment insurance, worker's compensation, the Old Age Security program, the Canada Pension Plan,

welfare, and subsidized housing. The income tax system also provides tax credits and deductions that deliver additional income benefits to some individuals and families based on factors such as disability or family status.

3. This text uses a gender-neutral singular *they/their* pronoun in place of the standard *she/he*. This choice was made in an attempt to use language that is as inclusive as possible and *she/he* does not adequately cover people who identify as gender diverse, intersex, gender non-conforming, gender fluid, or Questioning. This book emphasizes inclusiveness and an anti-oppressive approach and it is my hope that it can be a tool and resource for all readers.

4. According to the Institute for Intercultural Studies (2009), the original date and place this famous quote was published is unclear. It is believed that Margaret Mead said it spontaneously and it was then spread by print media. The sentiment expressed in the quote is said to reflect her beliefs and the quote exists in various forms.

2 Politics, Power, Conflict, and Doing the "Right" Thing in Advocacy

Chapter Objectives

After reading this chapter you should be able to:

1. Explain why all advocacy is political
2. Discuss sources of power
3. Understand the role of conflict in advocacy
4. Describe the main elements of ethical decision making in advocacy

Introduction

Sarah, an Aboriginal woman, is very concerned about her 15-year-old daughter, Maddie. Maddie has not been home for three days, and she is not responding to any texts or calls. The police refuse to do anything.

* * *

Raago, a refugee from Somalia, is being harassed by her landlord. He has demanded rent above the legal increase and comes to her apartment at all hours saying he needs to do an inspection. An advocate knows that Raago could get the overpaid rent back and stop the un-scheduled inspections but Raago is too afraid to confront the landlord.

* * *

An anti-poverty advocacy campaign becomes very heated with both sides using strong language and citing the media to discredit the other side. A member of your side is infuriated by the dispute and wants to leak information to the media that would "out" a prominent opposition leader and politician as gay, in hopes it will hurt his campaign and chances at re-election.

The brief scenarios above highlight challenges in advocacy practice. In the first scenario racism and oppression play a key role in police apathy towards the family crisis of a missing child. In the second scenario issues of power and conflict are of particular concern—the advocate knows how to help but the service user's fear of authority is an obstacle. Politics and ethical concerns feature more prominently in the final scenario where intense struggle has inflamed rage on both sides and the potential to do something morally reprehensible is a real possibility. This chapter focuses attention on four important considerations in advocacy work: politics, power, conflict, and ethics. Advocates, regardless of the level or context of the advocacy, will face these important considerations.

Engagement with both **small "p" and big "P" politics** is an essential feature of advocacy work. Essential for success is an analysis of the sources of power in an advocacy context for all parties: service users, advocates, and the opposition. Everyone deals with conflict situations differently and advocacy always involves conflict. A good advocate will have an understanding of their personal responses and experiences with conflict, and will also help the service user to develop their own understanding. And finally, all advocates will be challenged with the need to make ethically sound decisions in fast paced, complex advocacy practice situations.

All Advocacy is Political

> [P]olitics is not something that happens "out there" and that we can choose to ignore or "be into" or not. Rather politics always shapes our personal lives. Because of this, it is important that we be aware of it and be capable of seeing and reflecting upon the ways in which the lives of people, groups, and institutions possessing different levels and types of power are affected by political processes.
> (Stanbridge & Ramos, 2012, p. 164)

I have spoken to many students and service providers over the years who care deeply about the people coming to them for help. They really want to change unjust policies and practices. However, in the next breath they say they find politics uninteresting, they really don't understand politics, and they really don't see a political connection to their lives or the lives of service users. But politics matter. Stanbridge and Ramos (2010) put forward a compelling argument for making political analysis a part of our everyday lives. They argue for a companion phrase, "the political is personal" to go with the Carol Hanisch (1970) phrase "the personal is political" (Stanbridge & Ramos, 2012, p. 164). "Politics is personal" may also be referred to as small "p" politics.

Baines (2011) explains that social work is an "active political process" and "that every action we take is political and ultimately about power" (p. 6). Advocates in the human services need to make political analysis a part of their ongoing work. The service user who comes to the food bank because they do not receive enough welfare to buy food for an entire month is on the receiving end of a political decision. Politicians and policy makers in each province decide how much individuals and families will receive for welfare. And generally the decisions do not take into account the actual cost of housing, transportation, food, and other basic needs. A Caledon Institute study found some welfare rates in Canada were more than 60 per cent below the **poverty line or low income cut-off (LICO)** (Tweddle, Battle, & Torjman, 2013, p. 50). Living at or around the LICO is a constant struggle and the further below the LICO a recipient's income falls the more difficult life will be. So, the act of providing food at a food bank can clearly be linked to political decisions.

Advocates then, need to understand the political nature of their everyday lives and continually analyze the problems and experiences of service users using political analysis. It is also important to examine official political processes. Follow closely the decision making practices of the municipal, provincial/territorial, and federal governments. It is important to learn about the policy platforms of Canadian federal political parties such as the Green Party, Bloc Québécois, New Democratic Party, Liberal Party, and Conservative Party. For a complete official list, see Election Canada's website List of Registered Political Parties. Many of these parties will also be found at the provincial level of government. Depending on the province you live in, it is also important to follow the workings of, for example the Parti Québécois, the Saskatchewan Party, or the Wildrose Party in Alberta.

Find out which parties support the types of policies that will improve the lives of the people coming to social service agencies for help. Through advocacy efforts these political parties can be pressured to improve welfare incomes and consequently the lives of many service users.

Further, it is important for advocates to develop an understanding of the political process. Timing is especially important in advocacy efforts aimed at changing legislation. There are numerous excellent government websites providing clear, accurate information on how a **bill** (legislation) moves through parliament, from the Order Paper to Royal Assent. A similar process is followed at the provincial level of government. The timing of elections is also important for advocates, as politicians must run for election or re-election about every four years.

Elections at the municipal, provincial, or federal levels are an excellent time to get involved in the political process, learn more about party platforms, and work to promote policies that will benefit service users. For example, during an Ontario provincial election campaign housing advocates developed a pamphlet for tenants encouraging them to become informed about, and involved in, the political process. The pamphlet was dropped at the doorsteps of hundreds of tenants in a low-income neighbourhood.

Finally, it is very important for advocates to understand how responsibilities are divided between the various levels of government. If a service user needs help because they have been cut off employment insurance it is important to know that this is a federal responsibility and that an option may be to contact the constituency office of a federal Member of Parliament. Likewise if a service user needs help with a social housing issue, a landlord–tenant issue, or a subsidized daycare issue, we must know which level of government is responsible for the legislation and institutions that manage these programs.

The point here is to inspire advocates to view the context of their lives with a political analysis that makes use of the P/C/S model discussed in Chapter 1. At the personal level, advocates along with service users need to analyze, through a political lens, their everyday

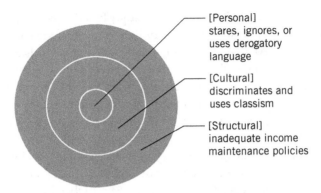

[Personal]
stares, ignores, or
uses derogatory
language

[Cultural]
discriminates and
uses classism

[Structural]
inadequate income
maintenance policies

Figure 2.1   Poverty Example Using P/C/S Model

Source: Adapted from Mullaly, 2010, p. 62 and Thompson, 2001, p. 22.

interactions. For instance, consider how homeless youth begging for money are treated. You may observe that sometimes a passerby will speak kindly and give change or small bills, some people look away and walk by quickly, and still others swear and berate homeless youth. This analysis should also include the interactions between service providers themselves and service users. That is, are advocates working in partnership with service users? Are advocates treating service users with dignity and respect?

Consider this same example at the cultural level: An advocate may find that homeless youth attending a drop-in centre are facing discrimination when they try to find employment or housing. And at the structural level, examine the impact of **social policy legislation** on homeless youth and how those big picture forces have personal and the cultural results. Remember from the discussion in Chapter 1 how these levels are interrelated and influence one another. Figure 2.1 captures the political analysis of the example of homeless youth.

Related to the political analysis above is thinking about how power is used and how to use it in advocacy. For instance, politicians are exercising their power when they pass legislation that will cause great hardship to people receiving welfare. Service providers and service users also have power but they have different types of power than a politician. Good advocates are constantly mindful of their own power and the power dynamics of an advocacy situation. The next section will delve into power considerations in advocacy.

Power Considerations

You can't be neutral on a moving train.

(Zinn, 2002)

Advocacy requires the use of power but not all service providers understand the power they have, nor are they comfortable using it. In fact, some social workers even see power and politics as inappropriate or unethical (Jansson, 2003). That may be because it is still sometimes the case that human service workers are not trained to use power *on behalf of* service users; instead they are trained to use power *over* service users. Service providers are trained to make decisions and exercise judgment in many circumstances where re- sources are limited and the need is great, such as drug treatment programs, mental health facilities, and specialized programs for children with disabilities. In other words, they have power over service users who need programs, goods, or money.

While service providers use their power and make political decisions in the course of their everyday activities, they are often under the illusion that they are neutral (not using power and not making political choices). Dominelli (2002) explains that a professional is often expected to appear to be neutral, that is, not take the side of the service user and to enforce and abide by agency regulations. The result is that service providers are accus- tomed to using decision-making powers to manage programs, services, and service users but not to advocate for service users.

The valuing of neutrality on the part of service providers comes from the close cur- rent and historical connections between government and social services. According to Dominelli (2002), "the profession has jealously guarded its alleged neutrality in the face of demands that it acknowledge its close ties to the nation state, its being driven by social control considerations, and its rationing of resources to those in need" (p. 71). Typically, social services are funded directly or indirectly by the state or conservative foundations that have a record of valuing a neutral stance. Neutral in this context usually means a po- sition that is consist with the values of the government or foundation. Service providers who assume a neutral stance will not challenge the institutions, policies, and practices that contribute to inequality. The neutral standpoint is most often associated with con- ventional practices in the social services, and political practices such as anti-oppressive advocacy are considered unprofessional by many service providers. They argue that the neutral stance is "in the best interests" of the service user, a key value in the social services.

Anti-oppressive advocates reject neutrality as a practice value. Gil (1998) and Domi- nelli (2002) argue that there are no politically neutral positions in the social services. Practice at all levels is intricately entwined with politics and power. "Political relations permeate all relationships because the existence of power and agency is involved in all interactions between people" (Dominelli, 2002, p. 72). Further, it is argued that not challenging inequality and oppression is a political position that implicitly supports the status quo. In fact, political practices in the social services are inescapable. Gil (1998) and Dominelli (2002) recommend that the political positions of service providers be made explicit.

> It would therefore, be more appropriate, in ethical terms, to replace unintended, covert political aspects of practice with consciously chosen overt ones, and to hold social workers accountable for their political choices and for the consequences of these choices. An appropriate political choice for radical social workers would be a commitment to social justice and human liberation. (Gil, 1998, p. 105)

Unlike conventional service providers, anti-oppressive advocates are clear in their rejection of neutral positions. They either state this position up front or demonstrate their perspectives through their approaches to practice.

Advocacy requires the use of power. Despite the fact that many service providers believe and practice as if neutral positions are superior, even conventional sources such as professional codes of ethics compel service providers to take the side of the service user and advocate on their behalf when there is a need to do so (Ontario College of Social Workers and Social Service Workers, 2008). Further, it is important to remember that neutral positions are positions that allow the status quo of inequality and injustice to continue into perpetuity. In essence, a neutral position is a political position. Fundamentally, service providers have a responsibility to use their power and take action on behalf of service users whose rights have been abused or denied.

There are many discussions in the literature focusing on power within the context of advocacy and anti-oppressive practice (Baines, 2011; Bishop, 2002; Brown & Hannis, 2008; Jansson, 2003; Kirst-Ashman & Hall, 2001; Mullaly, 2010). Bishop (2002) provides an interesting discussion of forms and uses of power in her historical account of oppression. Brown and Hannis (2008) discuss types and sources of power. Lee, Sammon, and Dumbrill (2014) provide a succinct and clear definition of power within an anti-oppressive perspective.

> Power is understood as the degree to which we are able to influence our environments—to get things done, make things happen (or not happen). It includes access to resources, free choice, and opportunity. Without power individuals cannot participate as citizens and thus become alienated. They are prevented from exercising the appropriate responsibilities and rights in shaping their lives. (p. 32)

Analyzing how power is used is an important responsibility of advocates. Power is both relational and a process (Stanbridge & Ramos, 2012). The relations of power, or the use of power between individuals and between individuals and systems, and the sources of power in each advocacy context, have a significant impact on the possible outcomes. Power is also continually contested (Baines, 2011). That is, those with power are able to do as they desire even if there is opposition, but they exercise their power with the knowledge that someone, somewhere, is trying to reclaim or reduce their power. For example, Jason Kenney, Member of Parliament, and former Minister of Defence and Minister of Multiculturalism for Canada, had a great deal of power over the legislative agenda in Canada. In another set of circumstances this type of political power would not be at all useful, as Kenney learned when he and two friends found themselves stranded on the side of a road in Ireland when none of the three young men could change a flat tire (Diebel, 2011). Power is only useful in a limited number of contexts, and in that case it lay with the Irish farmer who chose to help them.

Power is a process that is continually exercised and negotiated, depending on social relationships and context. Students in the human services may feel powerless when they are in school receiving feedback for their assignments and writing exams. However, when these students provide services in their field placements they do, in fact, have power over the service users seeking help. Students can make efforts to minimize the power differentials in field placement by using anti-oppressive practices, or they may choose or be required to use very authoritarian methods. We all experience times in our days and in our lives where we have more or less power. In these examples power may be contested by those who have less power and want more or those who have power and want even more. Workers who exercise power should expect to face resistance, and that includes advocates. Advocates need to continually analyze the relations and contexts of power to maximize their effectiveness for service users.

Sources of power abound. However, as we can plainly see, power may be transitory, unevenly distributed, and resisted. Certain types of power tend to be concentrated in the hands of very few individuals (Kirst-Ashman & Hull, 2001). Other types of power are the result of large numbers or of strong, collective beliefs. A group or individuals may have several sources of power. Regardless of the type, the critical analysis of power within the context of advocacy is an essential practice. See Table 2.1 for five common sources of power.

Table 2.1 Five Common Sources of Power in the Context of Advocacy

Sources of Power in Advocacy	Description and Examples
Money	Greater financial resources in advocacy allow the party to purchase, for example, an experienced and highly skilled specialist, professional, or expert
Information	Privileged access to off-the-record, technical, intellectual, or classified information provides a distinct power advantage
Numbers	The greater the number of service users, clients, consumers, survivors, or patients involved in a cause the greater the level of power
Status	Holding official or unofficial positions or ranks offers power advantages in advocacy. For example, a worker with a BSW (Bachelor of Social Work) has power advantages that are greater than those of a service user in many advocacy contexts
Belief or Conviction	Having a strong belief in an important cause—like social justice—or a conviction in the veracity of purpose imbues the advocate(s) with greater power

Source: Adapted from Lee, Sammon, & Dumbrill, 2014, p. 32.

The analysis of power, used within an anti-oppressive framework in advocacy, may be considered a valuable resource to be tapped. Advocates should, to the best of their abilities and whenever possible, use power *with* the service user. As Fay (2011) points out, the anti-oppressive view is "power with" rather than the conventional practice of "power over" (p. 70). This means working with the service user rather than working on their behalf. The sources of power thus come from both the service user and the advocate. Both contribute information that becomes the resource for advocacy—the service user provides a powerful account of an injustice from their perspective and the advocate brings information based on knowledge of policies, processes, and legislation.

An essential component of anti-oppressive advocacy practice is reflecting on sources of power and the privilege associated with that power. As discussed above, advocates have power of status and credentials. This power cannot be given away but it can be used to make a difference for individuals and communities. It is also important to "mitigate the power imbalances" between those who have power and those who don't (Fay, 2011, pp. 70–1). Lee (2001) sees advocacy as a way to level the differences of power. Advocates can reduce power imbalances through everyday practices. They can meet service users where they are comfortable, such as the corner where they beg for money, a drop-in centre, or their home. For instance, I worked for a social service agency that tried to meet people who were experiencing homelessness in their own environments. Rather than expecting people who are homeless to visit a social service agency during the day, the centre hired two street outreach workers who worked evenings, after most other agencies closed. The two workers met with people on street corners, under bridges, and in abandoned buildings, street locations that helped to mitigate the power imbalance. The work of examining power is an important concern for advocates whether it is in the context of working with a service user, challenging the decision of a government bureaucrat, or confronting the opposition at a public demonstration. The practice of power inevitably involves conflict. The next section will examine conflict considerations in advocacy.

Conflict is Normal

Conflict is the essential core of a free and open society. If one were to project the democratic way of life in the form of musical score, its major theme would be the harmony of dissonance.
(Alinsky, 1989, p. 62)

Conflict is a natural outcome of the unequal distribution of power, that is, some individuals and institutions have inordinate amounts of power relative to others. The conditions of "power over" and abuse of power activate resistance and conflict among those who are oppressed. Of course conflict is fraught with difficulty. As an example, many of us were raised to avoid conflict and to try to get along with everyone. Later, in our professional training, especially in the human services, we are taught to work cooperatively and are told that conflict can be avoided through rational discussion and negotiation. Service users, too, may have difficulty with conflict. Service providers and service users all have their own specific personal psychological makeups based on nature and nurture that result in particular reactions to conflict situations. Rather than think about conflict with anxiety or fear it is important to remember that conflict is natural, even ordinary. "Conflict is a fact of life—normal and often healthy" (Kirst-Ashman & Hull, 2001, p. 112). Lee (2001) sees conflict as an essential element of change or the fuel that powers transformations. Essentially, without conflict the relations of power and the distribution of resources will become increasingly more unequal. There are three considerations in regards to conflict in advocacy. These are critical self-analysis, service user considerations, and the critical analysis of conflict levels and types.

Critical Self-analysis

Critical self-analysis is necessary when it comes to conflict in advocacy. Everyone has had different experiences with conflict. It is important to make conscious our physical, intellectual, and emotional actions and reactions in conflict contexts. Our tendency may be to react impulsively or with anger when facing conflict. Some may be inclined to withdraw or acquiesce. Being prepared by being critically self-aware will help the advocate to exercise emotional control and to act deliberately. This is not to say that the advocate should be stilted or robotic; it is important to be passionate and sincere, but to learn to use these emotions strategically to the advantage of your advocacy case or cause.

Some critical self-analysis questions to ask concerning conflict may be:

- When have I experienced conflict in my life?
- What were the circumstances of the conflicts?
- What were my physical/emotional/psychological reactions?
- Were these reactions appropriate for the circumstances?
- Are these reactions appropriate for advocacy?
- Is there anything I need to change in my reaction to conflict in advocacy?

All advocates want to achieve the best possible outcomes for service users and therefore it is important to critically analyze and be aware of our personal responses to conflict situations.

Service Users' Experiences of Conflict

The second important consideration is service users' experiences of conflict. Not unlike the critical self-analysis above, it is important to help service users reflect on their personal experiences with conflict. This analysis, done with the service user, can have implications for the strategy choices in advocacy. For example, if a service user has had the experience of retreating from conflict as a victim of domestic violence, child abuse, or a residential school, they may need encouragement and support to pursue advocacy. They may also decide to initially use more low-profile strategies such as writing a letter of advocacy rather than participating in a face-to-face meeting. Different strategies may be in order for those whose previous reactions to conflict involved anger or aggression because of incarceration or street gang membership. Some service users have come to Canada from countries where challenges to authority and power are met with imprisonment, torture, and even death. Gender, race, age, class, sexual orientation, ability, and ethnic background all have an impact on conflict experiences and, in turn, on advocacy.

Past experiences of oppression may predispose service users to be passive about pursuing advocacy or, on the other end of the spectrum, some individuals, like Sam in Case Study 2.1, may be much too aggressive. Their reactions may be far in excess of what is needed in a particular context and this may have serious negative consequences.

Case Study 2.1   Analyzing Conflict Responses with Service Users

I had an experience where a service user (I will call him Sam) insisted he could do his own advocacy. Sam was profoundly illiterate and had no teeth. Due to this he was very difficult to understand. He had been seriously abused and neglected as a child and consequently had frequent angry outbursts.

One day Sam came to my office and asked me to call his worker at the welfare office (he could not dial numbers because of his illiteracy). He said he had not received his cheque and wanted to straighten things out. I called the welfare office and got his worker on the line. She had a polite phone manner. I handed the phone to Sam and he immediately started yelling and swearing, every other word was f**k. Apart from the F word little else Sam said could be understood. His tirade was completely unintelligible. This outburst went on for several minutes. Finally, Sam angrily passed the phone back to me and said the welfare worker wanted to talk to me.

Lessons Learned

Sometimes conflict can arise unexpectedly. The ferocity of Sam's attack caught me off guard. I thought Sam was going to have a short, simple, calm exchange; instead he launched into a lengthy, explicit rant. It is important to anticipate the potential for conflict and to develop a plan to contend with it while it is in process. The plan should include how to deal with the fallout from conflict.

Critical Thinking Questions

1. How did the various forms of oppression experienced by Sam contribute to his strong reaction?
2. What should the advocate do to mitigate the damage with the welfare worker?
3. What could the advocate do next time to prepare Sam for the call?
4. At what points might conflict arise in advocacy?
5. What should the advocate do when conflict occurs?
6. Is there anything the advocate could do to alleviate the adverse effects of conflict?

Critical Analysis of Conflict Levels and Types

The third consideration with reference to conflict is an analysis of the type and level of conflict. Kirst-Ashman and Hull (2001) discuss eight conflict categories as well as strategies and guidelines for conflict management. Lee (2001) explains the importance of matching the advocacy response to the type and level of conflict. It is vital for the service user and the advocate to analyze the possible conflict in each advocacy context and to develop an appropriate strategy to contest the conflict (Lee, 2001). Schneider and Lester (2001) encourage caution in certain contexts such as when there is a high level of distrust and disagreement. Advocates are encouraged to analyze the potential outcomes in such circumstances. Some basic questions should be considered. Will allies be alienated? Will the opposition become even more intransigent? Will the conflict be needlessly escalated? Ezell (2001) counsels to "do what you can to avoid taking it personally" (p. 185). The skills associated with dealing with conflict, regardless of the type or level, are part of advocacy and if "someone's getting mad, it means you're into an important change" (Ezell, 2001, p. 185).

Lee's (2001) discussion on conflict in advocacy in particular is very helpful. Advocates work with service users to analyze the type of conflict and match the advocacy response to it. Lee (2001) discusses three types of conflicts: a misunderstanding, an argument, and a contest. A misunderstanding is defined as a situation where "[o]ne side has inadequate information, or there has been some mis-communication" (Lee, 2001, p. 21). The misunderstanding level of conflict is matched with a response that includes sharing of additional information and improving communication between the two sides (Lee, 2001). For example, a service user is terminated from welfare because they missed a reporting deadline. In this case, the advocate and service user provide a doctor's note that confirms that the reporting deadline was missed because the service user was ill. The "lines of communication" are improved and the misunderstanding is cleared up (Lee, 2001, p. 21).

In the second type of conflict, an argument, the opponent is choosing not to comply because it seems difficult or different. As Lee (2001) explains, being cooperative is not a high priority for the opposition. A rational discussion is recommended as the appropriate response to an argument conflict. These rational discussions are described as consisting of three parts. One is to argue that the request is easy, the second is to argue that the request will not have any detrimental consequences, and the third is to negotiate with the opponent for something they want in exchange (Lee, 2001). An example is a service user who finds they cannot access a gym in their apartment building because it is not wheelchair accessible. The landlord is not motivated to make the changes because it costs too much and they can always find another tenant who does not require wheelchair accessibility when vacancy rates are low. The advocate, with the tenant, wants to try to convince the landlord that the renovations can be made simply and easily at a reasonable cost, perhaps with the help of city grants. In addition, the landlord needs to be convinced that accessibility will improve access to the gym for all tenants and therefore render the property more valuable and profitable. In essence the advocate and the tenant construct a rational case for the change.

In Lee (2001), the final type of conflict discussed is the contest. In a contest "one side believes it is not in its self-interest to do what the other side asks" (Lee, 2001, p. 21). The opposition is determined to avoid change. Lee recommends confrontation as the way to respond to a contest. Confrontations require the advocate and service user to do what is necessary to make the opponent "sufficiently uncomfortable," resulting in compliance with the service user's request (Lee, 2001, p. 21). Examples of contest types of conflict are regularly reported by media, for instance the National Day of Action organized by a coalition called Canadian Doctors for Refugee Care. "Join health care workers in cities across the country as we call on the federal government to once and for all reverse the 'cruel and unusual' cuts to refugee health care" (Doctors for Refugee Care, 2015, para. 2). Their poster explains that "[i]t is an opportunity to show the Federal Government that Canadians will stand up for the most vulnerable among us" (Doctors for Refugee Care, 2015, para. 3). Their website explains that citizens are going "directly to the streets" to inform Canadians of the "federal government's cuts to refugee health care" (Doctors for Refugee Care, 2015, para. 1). This is a clear contest type of conflict between Doctors for Refugee Care and the federal government.

According to Lee (2001), it is important to remember that there may be movement between the categories of conflict. The misunderstanding may become an argument and the argument may become a contest. It is also possible that the contest may be de-escalated during the advocacy. The advocate and the service users should be continually aware of the possibility of change and adjust the response to match.

In the case discussed earlier, Sam believed he was in a contest level of conflict with the worker from the welfare office. He immediately launched a very aggressive attack. Now there are good reasons why Sam might use this strategy given his personal history; however, his verbal abuse and attack was a mismatch for a conflict that was actually a simple misunderstanding. The worker had not received Sam's reporting information and therefore his monthly cheque was not issued. With my assistance, Sam provided the misplaced information and the cheque was soon issued. If an advocate is unsure about the level of the conflict, based on my experience, I would recommend that it is much more effective to initially assume that the conflict is a misunderstanding and that more information is required. If the conflict is not cleared up through this action, it is easier to escalate than to de-escalate responses. Ramping up the response from a sharing of information to a meeting or a public protest is preferable to starting too strong and then needing to back down when the opposition has become intractable.

Some important considerations when analyzing conflict with a service user include:

- What type of conflict is the service user facing?
- What is the evidence for this?
- Which response strategy is needed?
- What is needed to implement the required response?

In the context of the community and in social service agencies, conflict is wrapped up in struggles over power and small "p" and big "P" politics. While it would be convenient for political considerations, power, and conflict to fit into discrete categories and remain unchanging, this is not the case. The practice of advocacy using anti-oppressive theory requires intelligent, flexible actions in dynamic circumstances. Advocates will be challenged to do what is "right," to be on the side of social justice. The next section will discuss limitations and challenges of ethical decision making in anti-oppressive advocacy practice.

Ethical Decision Making and Anti-oppressive Theory

Some human service workers will argue that professional codes of ethics are the ultimate arbiters of right and wrong or ethical and unethical practice, that a code of ethics should dictate in the field, regardless of the nature of practice, type of theory, and service context. In social work the code of ethics supports advocacy on behalf of a case or a cause in the pursuit of social justice. For example, in the Canadian Association of Social Workers Code of Ethics (2005), under value number two "Pursuit of Social Justice," two principles speak directly to advocacy: "Social workers advocate for fair and equitable access to public services and benefits. Social workers advocate for equal treatment and protection under the law and challenge injustices, especially injustices that affect the vulnerable and disadvantaged" (Canadian Association of Social Work, 2005, p. 5). Further, a principle relating to advocacy is found in the third value "Service to Humanity": "Social workers strive to use the power and authority vested in them as professionals in responsible ways that serve the needs of clients and the promotion of social justice" (CASW, 2005, p. 6).

In effect, the code of ethics requires social workers to do advocacy when they see it needs to be done. However, it does not, nor is it intended to, provide direction in every single possible situation in the field. Advocacy in the human services and anti-oppressive practice are accomplished within a complex and changing environment. A code of ethics does generally provide a good basis to draw on; however, the practice of advocacy using anti-oppressive theory brings specific challenges to the practitioner. Some of the specific ethical challenges and considerations for decision making are highlighted in the discussion below.

Advocacy using anti-oppressive theory provides the foundation for this book but this choice does pose some additional considerations. In the social service field most advocacy happens at the personal level in the P/C/S model—in other words, doing advocacy with an individual or a family in order to obtain something they need or have a right to. Practice in this area involves analyzing oppressive circumstances together with service users and making links between their personal problems and the structural conditions involved (Baines, 2011; Mullaly, 2010). Mullaly (2010) explains that the key goals "are to counteract the personal intrapsychic damages associated with oppression and to build strengths in the individual for developing solidarity and community with others and for taking action (individual and collective) against oppression" (p. 223). In addition, the advocate, with the service user, must work through the advocacy process, which can be lengthy, complex, and emotionally charged.

Doing advocacy using anti-oppressive theory usually takes more time and energy but is, of course, the right thing to do. Anti-oppressive practice is ethical practice. In some cases it may be easier and faster to just do the advocacy and involve the service user only in a minimal way. In much of advocacy this is precisely what happens. Think of advocacy in the legal profession for example. It is hard to imagine a lawyer taking the time and resources to use anti-oppressive advocacy. In fact, those who pay for the services of a lawyer expect that the lawyer will do all of the advocacy for their case. In truth, the courts and justice system are generally structured in a way that prohibits much participation from anyone who does not have a law degree. Social workers too, may do advocacy on behalf of service users without using anti-oppressive theory. The social worker may be doing the advocacy within the context of case management, counselling, or therapy using a variety of practice models and theories. In these cases the advocacy, as has been said, is done *on behalf of* the service user not *with* the service user. In these cases work proceeds with the advocate collecting the relevant information from the service user in order to do the advocacy. In the extreme, this type of advocacy practice is much like that of a lawyer working for a client.

Ezell (2001) points out that the Canadian Association of Social Workers' code of ethics does not speak to the preferable choice of theory with regards to advocacy in the social service field. It is ethical to do advocacy without using anti-oppressive theory. However, even if the code of ethics does not stipulate the connection between advocacy and anti-oppressive theory it is important for service providers to make this connection as they advocate in the field of social services. I believe that advocates must use anti-oppressive theory if they genuinely want to contribute to change in the structures that create oppression. Anti-oppressive theory in advocacy practice is one of only a few theories that encourage the service user to partner in their own emancipation and challenge oppression at the personal, cultural, and structural levels. Baines (2011) puts this well.

> Clients are not just victims, but can and need to be active in their own liberation and that of others. Their experience is also a key starting point in the development of new theory and knowledge, as well as political strategies and resistance. Their voices must be part of every program, policy, planning effort, and evaluation. Participatory forms of helping tend to be those that offer the most dignity as well as far-reaching and lasting impact. (p. 7)

Advocacy using anti-oppressive theory may take longer and be more work but it is the way to contribute to lasting progressive change.

Ethical Dilemmas

Some ethical challenges have a greater significance in advocacy than in other forms of practice. Ezell (2001) provides a more detailed discussion of ethics and ethical dilemmas in his text on advocacy. I have highlighted three examples from Ezell (2001) in the following discussion. The first, informed consent, is an ethical challenge that may arise for advocates when service users have some form of diminished capacity that may impair their abilities to make decisions due to age, injury, or illness. Informed consent is also a challenge when the advocate is working on a case that involves many thousands of people. It is nearly impossible to ensure that all of the thousands of individuals are equally involved and agree on the advocacy undertaken on their behalf. Self-determination is another challenge. For instance, how can the best interests of the service user be ensured in the short and long term. Sometimes a service user is forced to agree to a speedy settlement (short term) because they lack the financial means or resolve to carry on with the advocacy. The consequences may result in financial hardship over the long term.

One additional ethical challenge is "one class of clients versus another" (Ezell, 2001, p. 49). These challenges arise regularly, for instance between family members (parents and children), tenants in a building, or those on a waiting list for home care. For instance, the advocate may work hard to get a senior moved to the top of the waiting list for home care but this means that everyone else on the waiting list will wait longer. The fundamental problem is a scarcity of home care services, not waiting list placement.

Ezell (2001) contends that there are no clear right or wrong answers to these advocacy ethical dilemmas. At best the advocate must try to move towards the ethical side. Ezell (2001) proposes that advocates view ethical decision making on a continuum rather than a binary of right or wrong. "There are simply too many variables, too many stakeholders in ever-changing contexts, and too many short- and long-term consequences to allow one to classify an action as absolutely ethical or unethical" (Ezell, 2001, p. 38).

Advocacy practice is a complex, changing process with competing interests and power struggles. If one were to take too much time to contemplate and analyze important opportunities will be lost—the so called "paralysis through analysis" (Ezell, 2001, p. 38). For instance, an advocacy group trying to stop police violence was prepared when news reached them of a young black man beaten while in police custody. The advocacy group was ready with a list of demands, protest signs, and a substantial number of supporters, and they converged on city hall and demanded an explanation for the injustice. The opportunity to speak out on police violence would have been lost if they had taken too much time to carefully analyze, plan, and weigh the ethical pros and cons of the demonstration. There is a small window of opportunity to attract the attention of the media and gain the support of the community to a cause, after a critical incident like an unprovoked beating of a young black man. It is probably only a few days before the media moves on to the next story.

Because action must be taken in some cases before all the research, analysis, and planning is complete, the ethical considerations, at best, should be moved towards the right (ethical) side of the continuum rather than the wrong (unethical) side. In these fast-paced, complex circumstances ethical decisions should be reviewed quickly and frequently. Also be aware that in some cases a choice must be made between several less than ideal options.

Situational Ethics

Mullaly (2010) makes a good case for the use of **situational ethics** in anti-oppressive practice (pp. 263–4). Situational ethics are defined as a "system of ethics by which acts are judged within their contexts instead of by categorical principles" (Merriam & Webster,

2015). Joseph Fletcher, an America philosopher and ordained Episcopal priest, was the founder of situational ethics. According to Fletcher, "rules are illuminators . . . not directors," "[l]ove and reason count," and laws are to be kept in a "subservient place" (Fletcher, 1966, p. 31). Mullaly (2010) explains that principles, such as those contained in professional codes of ethics, are not to be considered more important than people. "[T]he situationist respects laws and may often follow them but is free to make the right choices according to the situation" (Mullaly, 2010, p. 264).

The situational ethicist in the human services may observe a standard of social justice, equality, or fairness. This standard supersedes organizational policies and rules and codes of ethics in some practice situations. So while it is important to be knowledgeable of and adhere to professional standards and agency policies, it is more important to be compassionate and empathetic. Consider the example in Case Study 2.2.

Case Study 2.2   Situational Ethics and Anti-oppressive Advocacy

As a housing advocate I came across instances of so-called "welfare fraud" while working with service users. I found that service users collecting welfare sometimes did small jobs for cash such as babysitting, snow shovelling, grass cutting, or house cleaning to supplement their meager welfare income. Some service providers consider this unethical because additional income should be reported.

Lessons Learned

There are many nuances to ethical and unethical practice in advocacy and we need to carefully consider how our actions contribute to greater social justice.

Critical Thinking Questions

1. How does oppression at the personal, cultural, and structural levels facilitate so-called welfare fraud?
2. Is it ethical to set the welfare rates at a level of less than 50 per cent of the poverty line?
3. Is it ethical that people on welfare have to use food banks and soup kitchens?
4. Is it ethical that people who live on welfare have no choice but to rent rundown, pest-infested apartments in dangerous neighbourhoods?

Guidance for Anti-oppressive Advocacy

Advocates working with service users will be faced with difficult choices. Planning, strategies, and decision making may need to be done quickly with little time for analysis, consultation, or research. Sometimes advocates will have to make decisions contrary to their own self-interest such as advocating against a policy decision in their own agency. They may even be faced with a decision that will hurt another service user or group of service users. How should advocates make decisions when an individual is not able to provide informed consent because of a disability such as an acquired brain injury, intellectual disability, or dementia? Ethical decisions in advocacy need to be analyzed in context with the service user.

Overarching principles cannot speak to every ethical dilemma in advocacy. The following general principles, derived from advocacy literature, anti-oppressive theory, social work values, and ethical codes, provide basic good guidance for anti-oppressive advocacy.

- Analyze oppression and privilege.
- Use anti-oppressive theories and practices.
- Respect and accept service users' choices.
- Seek service users' consent on all actions taken on their behalf.
- Provide service users with as much information as possible about their options and risks.
- Only do the advocacy you are competent to do.

Advocacy using anti-oppressive theory may take more time and effort and service providers are increasingly hard pressed for time due to increased caseloads and cuts to services. Some advocates may not be supported by their agencies in their efforts to do advocacy. Social service agencies may see advocacy as unseemly or potentially damaging to the reputation of the agency (Schneider & Lester, 2001). This can result in threats from funders or even funding cuts. Service providers may worry about losing out on promotions or about damaging their reputations in the community because of their advocacy efforts. Conflicts and dilemmas will arise between what is in the best interest of an individual, the service provider, social service agencies, other service users, the community, and even society. These obstacles are legitimate, therefore advocates using anti-oppressive theory may have to make difficult choices. The choice, at times, may be between the values supporting advocacy using anti-oppressive theory and what is in your own self-interest. Alinsky (1989) recounts the following.

Each year, for a number of years, the activists in the graduating class from a major Catholic seminary near Chicago would visit me for a day just before their ordination, with questions about values, revolutionary tactics, and such. Once, at the end of such a day, one of the seminarians said, "Mr. Alinsky, before we came here we met and agreed that there was one question we particularly wanted to put to you. We're going to be ordained, and then we'll be assigned to different parishes, as assistants to—frankly—stuffy, reactionary old pastors. They will disapprove of a lot of what you and we believe in, and we will be put into a killing routine. Our question is: How do we keep our faith in true Christian values, everything we hope to do to change the system?" That was easy, I answered. When you go out that door, just make your own personal decision about whether you want to be a bishop or a priest, and everything else will follow. (Alinsky, 1989, p. 13)

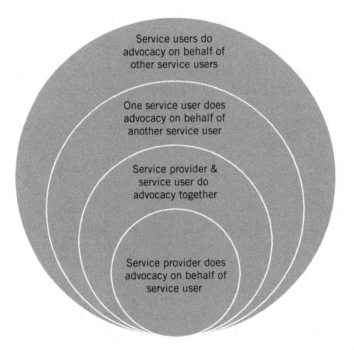

Figure 2.2   Advocacy Skill Development

To put Alinsky's advice into a human services context, advocates may need to decide whether they want to be a manager/director of an agency, or a good advocate. Being a really good advocate may not be compatible with many positions of power and authority. Contrary to what those in authority believe, advocacy may be a way to reduce the workload of the service provider. Service users can develop their own skills by working with a trained advocate and they may at some point do their own advocacy or even do advocacy with other service users. Advocacy work and anti-oppressive theory may spread like a snowball (see Figure 2.2). Eventually this will result in a reduction in the need for advocacy (Ezell, 2001).

Conclusion

This chapter began with a discussion of advocacy as a practice deep into politics and political processes. Advocacy, as a politicized practice, encompasses both small "p" politics and big "P" politics, i.e., official political systems and processes. Whether we make the conscious decision to attend to small "p" politics or not, the choices we make, even seemingly ordinary ones, are political. Anti-oppressive advocates use this political awareness to advocate in their work with service users. Connected to the discussion of political analysis is a focus on the analysis of power. Power is dependent on the situation or circumstances in which it is exercised and is continually challenged and opposed.

Anti-oppressive advocates work with service users to consider their power sources and the power sources of the opposition. This analysis of power combined with political analysis is used to develop strategy for advocacy action.

Conflict, a third key theme discussed in this chapter, is related to political and power analysis as an essential piece of strategy development. In the context of advocacy, conflict is considered necessary, even natural, when inequality and injustice exist. Both service users and service providers have personal experiences with conflict that may make them more or less likely to be helpful in an advocacy context. Careful consideration and classification of conflict types and levels help in the development of effective strategies.

The final theme considered in this chapter is ethical decision making. Professional codes of ethics provide some basic support and guidance for anti-oppressive advocates. Because of the complex, fast-paced nature of advocacy however, it is recommended that one view ethical decision making on a continuum and in context. Situational ethics offer support for anti-oppressive advocacy steeped in considerations of politics, power, and conflict. Though challenging, people must come before principles (Mullaly, 2010).

Critical Thinking Questions

1. Consider the following two phrases: "the personal is political" and "the political is personal." Explain how a political analysis based on these phrases can facilitate anti-oppressive advocacy.
2. Some managers in the social services believe advocacy practice is biased, inappropriate, and unethical. They require that front-line workers maintain a neutral stance in practice. Using advocacy skills develop an argument to persuade the manager to see that there is no such thing as a neutral stance and that power is inevitably entangled with practice.
3. List and explain your personal sources of power.
   - How do your power levels and sources change when you go to work, to school, home to your family, and out with friends?
   - What are the levels and sources of power for a victim of domestic violence, a homeless youth, or a terminally ill senior?
   - What are the implications for anti-oppressive advocacy practice?
4. Analyze your conflict response using the questions from the conflict discussion in this chapter.
   - When have I experienced conflict in my life?
   - What were the circumstances of the conflicts?
   - What were my physical/emotional/psychological reactions?
   - Were these reactions appropriate for the circumstances?
   - Are these reactions appropriate for advocacy?
   - Is there anything I need to change in my reaction to conflict in advocacy?

5. As an anti-oppressive advocate how can you help a service user who is in desperate need of advocacy but is afraid of conflict because of their experiences of childhood sexual abuse?
6. Given that anti-oppressive advocacy requires more time, energy, and resources from the advocate and the agency, explain why it is still the ethical choice.
7. Principles should not be considered more important than people. Explain what is meant by this phrase. How can situational ethics assist anti-oppressive advocates in their decision making?

Suggested Readings

Dominelli, L. (2002). *Anti-oppressive social work theory and practice.* New York: Palgrave.

Lee, B., Sammon, S., and Dumbrill, G. (2014). *A glossary of AOP terms.* Toronto: CommonAct Press.

Stanbridge, K., and Ramos, H. (2012). *Seeing politics differently.* Don Mills: Oxford University Press.

Suggested Videos and Websites

Our Country, Our Parliament: An Introduction to How Parliament Works, Process of Passing a Bill at Parliament of Canada www.parl.gc.ca/About/Parliament/Education/OurCountryOurParliament/html_booklet/process-passing-bill-e.html

Registered Political Parties and Parties Eligible for Registration at Elections Canada www.elections.ca/content.aspx?dir=par&document=index&lang=e&section=pol

An Introduction to Situational Ethics at YouTube www.bing.com/videos/search?q=situational+ethics+video&FORM=VIRE1#view=detail&mid=9AC914B01E37637AB7E59AC914B01E37637AB7E5

The Four Working Principles of Situation Ethics at YouTube www.youtube.com/watch?v=Hzs5hMTHDW4

3 Historical, Conceptual, and Contextual Developments

Chapter Objectives

After reading this chapter you should be able to:

1. Trace the origins of and influences on advocacy in the human services
2. Explain the development of anti-oppressive theory and practices
3. Assess the importance of community and social service agencies in the context of advocacy practice
4. Discuss the impact of globalization, neo-liberalism, and managerialism on advocacy in the social services

Introduction

History is boring! Why do we have to know all those old dates, names, and places? No one cares! I just want to get my credentials and find a job in the social services where I can really make a difference in people's lives.

* * *

I don't need to study theories. What really matters in the social services is practice. When I get out in the field I won't need theory. I think it is best to just be yourself when you work with service users.

* * *

Sure, I know that it can be difficult to work in the social services. The pay is poor, very few agencies have benefits, and the work is psychologically demanding, but that is the way it has always been and always will be. We can't let it affect our work with service users.

The three statements above are common student criticisms of the curricula in social service programs. This chapter will endeavour to make the case for study and dialogue about history in the social services, the importance of theory, and the significance of practice context. Knowing where we came from as a profession is a responsibility of every person who aims to practice in the social services. If we do not clearly understand the way the profession evolved, the mistakes, catastrophes, progress, and successes, we will not have a foundation to effectively move forward.

It is irresponsible to be ignorant and repeat past mistakes that have damaged service users. In the same way it is essential to understand theory. Responsible committed service providers understand and use theory to better help service users. Practice without theory is a sure way to leave your biases unchecked and to recreate oppression in practice. The final section of this chapter provides a discussion of the current context of advocacy practice in the social services. Recent global and political developments have brought changes to the social service field. An awareness of the trends in the field helps to prepare the advocate for informed practice. Grounded in history and theory, with a keen understanding of the context of advocacy, is a powerful way to begin to help others.

A Complicated History

[T]here is a political and moral imperative to enter history from the standpoints of those who are oppressed.

(Neigh, 2012, p. 13)

Some service providers make fighting for social justice part of their everyday experience while others dutifully follow the rules of the agency that employs them even if those rules are unfair and even oppressive. Schneider and Lester (2001) explain that in some circles it is assumed that social workers have always been advocates (p. 6). However, prior to 1970 the "term 'advocacy' can scarcely be found in the human service literature" (Schneider & Lester, 2001, p. 6). In fact, Schneider and Lester say they can recall when people in the field would have difficulty pronouncing the word *advocacy* (2001, p. 6). Part of the explanation is that the term *advocacy* is relatively new to the social services, while fighting for social justice and against inequality and discrimination is not new at all. So while the term is new to the field, advocacy work is not. In truth, some human service providers have been doing advocacy for a long time. Canadian advocates in the human services have a rich legacy of advocacy dating back over 100 years. Today it is quite common for human service providers to practice advocacy and use the terminology. In a survey of social workers, Ezell (2001) found that about 90 per cent said they did advocacy as part of their work (p. 10). Many service providers think of advocacy as one of the many skills they need and use in practice. They have often been exposed to advocacy in texts, courses, and programs in the human services. Forms of advocacy including anti-oppressive advocacy are now commonplace, but the road to our current state is complicated and sometimes less than complimentary to the field.

Human Service Work: A Legacy of Activism and Oppression

Human service providers taking a stand on behalf of people who are oppressed is not a new or recent development in Canada. The practice of advocacy in social service work has a long history dating back to this country's confederation in 1867. Advocacy practitioners today are the beneficiaries of that legacy. The social welfare services and programs benefitting Canadians today are the result of concerted advocacy efforts in the past by individuals and groups and social movements. Unions, civil rights groups, Aboriginal groups, and women's groups, to name a few, have made use of advocacy techniques and strategies to bring about change for people living in poverty, people with disabilities, and racialized people facing discrimination. It is important to celebrate the victories of a national health care plan, old age security and pension plans, a national child benefit, human rights legislation, and the Charter of Rights and Freedoms. It is also important for advocates in the field of human services to exercise vigilance and continue to fight for the maintenance, improvement, and development of social policy that reduces or eliminates social inequality and injustice.

Advocates in the human services should also be keenly aware of the oppressive legacy of social service practice in Canada. Students and practitioners in the human services today would be remiss if they neglected to study the profession's implicit and explicit participation in oppressive practices in, for example, residential schools, child welfare, mental health, and welfare. The '60s Scoop is one example of the profession's unequivocal participation in oppressive child welfare services. From the around the late 1950s to the mid-1980s, child welfare agencies in Canada routinely adopted and fostered Aboriginal children to non-Aboriginal families under a racist policy of assimilation (Baskin, 2011; Carniol, 2010; Chappell, 2014). Over a period of 30 years, approximately 20,000 Aboriginal children were removed from their families and communities by social workers (Chiefs of Ontario, n.d.). Generations of individuals, families, and communities have had their suffering initiated and prolonged because of the actions of human service workers. Those studying and practicing advocacy must understand and expect that service users may be hesitant, distrustful, and even hostile towards service providers and social services, due to the profession's complicity in oppressive practices. This distrust is a legacy that this book hopes to contribute towards changing.

The Anti-oppressive Approach in Advocacy: Early Developments

Prior to the 1860s human service work or charity relief in Canada was inadequate and influenced by fate and fortune. Social welfare services consisted of mostly church-based charities (Finkel, 2006). These services provided "outdoor relief" in the form of food, clothing, and advice but rarely financial assistance (Guest, 1982, p. 36). Hick (2010) describes this early help.

> Following a request for assistance, a charity visitor would be designated to visit and interview the applicant in his or her own home. Their role was to promote industry, thrift, and virtue among the poor. The visitors were volunteers, generally elite men and women from the upper classes and people from the ranks of the emerging

professional and business classes. The first task was to classify the applicants as either deserving poor or undeserving poor. People designated as deserving poor were seen as being of good moral character and only temporarily out of luck due to no fault of their own. The deserving did not ask directly for help and were clean and tidy. The undeserving was deemed to be lazy and/or morally degenerate. (p. 38)

The establishment found this system "disorganized and inefficient" (Hick, 2010, p. 38). There appeared to be too much opportunity for the poor to cheat and receive relief from more than one charity (Carniol, 2010; Mullaly, 2007).

This dilemma of how to deal with the poor and their problems motivated two distinct responses, based on dissimilar value and belief systems—the **Charity Organization Society (COS)** and the **Settlement House Movement (SHM)**, which evolved from programs and organizations previously established in England and France. The historical literature points to the development of the two services as early evidence of a divide in approaches to human service work (Chappell, 2014; Hick, 2010; Johnson, McClelland, & Austin, 2000; Mullaly, 2007). This division is still evident in the literature, theory, and practices of the human services. Table 3.1 summarizes the main characteristics of the COS and the SHM.

Table 3.1 Summary of the Main Features of the COS and the SHM

Charity Organization Society	Settlement House Movement
• Believed that poverty was caused by laziness, poor morals, and lack of discipline	• Believed that poverty was caused by social and economic conditions
• Supported a scientific charity model of service delivery	• Diverse organizations developed in response to community needs
• Thought that charity was too generous	• Provided health care, education, social services, and cultural programs
• Goal was to reduce the number of people receiving help from charitable organizations	• Middle-class volunteers and members of the "slum" community lived and worked together in the settlement house
• Services included food, clothing, and shelter but rarely financial assistance	• Received some funding from religious organizations
• Charity workers were trained to screen the deserving poor from the able bodied	• Settlement workers were expected to be non-denominational and refrain from proselytizing
• Promoted a registry for the poor and coordination of services	• Formed the origin of progressive practices in modern social services (including anti-oppressive theory and practice)
• Opposed government assistance for the poor as it was thought to create dependency	
• Mainstream social services adopted scientific charity model of practice	
• Formed the origin of conventional practices in modern social services	

Charity Organization Society

The establishment of the Charity Organization Society (COS) was a response to a perceived inefficiency and ineffectiveness in the delivery of charity, as well as what was thought to be the great potential for abuse of the charitable services (Carniol, 2010; Hick, 2010). The COS, established first in London, Ontario, in 1869, soon spread to other communities in Ontario and Quebec (Hick, 2010). These organizations made use of then current social science and business practices to bring "scientific charity" to the poor (Carniol, 2005, p. 42). The proponents of scientific charity believed the poor lacked discipline and that far too many were collecting charity when they should be working. Scientific charity was a model based on the idea that the government should be involved in a very limited way in poverty relief. The charities were managed and operated by prominent members of the business community who believed business practices were the best way to reduce costs and make the delivery of charity more efficient and effective (Carniol, 2005). The new organizations coordinated the various charities to reduce duplication and urged charities to carefully investigate each client to ensure that they were really in need (Carniol, 2005; Mullaly, 1997). From this emerged the casework method that is still used today in the social service field. Casework traditionally focused on helping the poor to adjust to social conditions rather than working for social change (Mullaly, 2007).

Within the COS there emerged a gradual transition from volunteer workers, who were recruited from the white upper class and trained by agencies, to professional social workers, who were educated in universities (Carniol, 2005; Hick, 2010). The University of Toronto was the first school in Canada to establish a program for training social workers, in 1914 (Hick, 2010). University-based training for social workers continued in the tradition established by the COS, defining poverty as the fault of the individual, and the role of social workers was to use their judgment and screening tools to separate the deserving poor from the undeserving poor (Mullaly, 1997). The deserving poor were given welfare while the undeserving poor were expected to find work and live off their wages (even when there were high rates of unemployment and wages were very low for unskilled workers).

The foremost way of working with the poor, or method of intervention, taught in the social work programs was **casework**. Social work casework is described as the process of helping individuals on a one-to-one basis by assisting them with personal or social problems. Mullaly (1997, p. 24) calls this the "reform the person" approach. Most mainstream social service agencies that provide direct services to individuals provide some form of casework (Zastrow, 1981). An early contribution to social work casework was a text by Mary Richmond called *Social Diagnosis* (1917). Richmond's casework text leaned heavily on medical and scientific approaches to explain individual and family behaviour (Chappell, 2014; Hick, 2010; Mullaly, 2007). These early phases of social work established the conventional stream of the profession that continues today in universities, colleges, and in direct practice.

Settlement House Movement

The other, more progressive, stream—and the one from which the advocacy model outlined in this book primarily evolved—is represented by the Settlement House Movement (SHM). The SHM developed about the same time in Canada as the COS and was based on European and American models. Mullaly (2007) and Hick (2010) describe SHM practices in contrast to those of the COS. The SHM arose from different assumptions about poor people and their living conditions. The SHM pursued changes in the social conditions of poor people such as improved health and housing, secure employment, and education for children rather than simply helping individuals adjust to their social conditions (James, 1998). Those involved in the SHM believed that the poor "were victims of an unjust social order that discriminated against large numbers of people so that a few might benefit" (Mullaly, 2007, p. 45). The convictions of those involved in the SHM were a distinct contrast to COS assumptions that poverty was the fault of the individual and was to be dealt with on an individual case-by-case basis. The SHM recruited young, educated, middle-class individuals to live with the urban poor (Hick, 2010). The recruits helped the poor organize and develop their communities. The workers challenged the structures and institutions that were contributing to the deplorable living conditions (Finkel, 2006). "The settlement house workers were more inclined to engage in social reform activities than those of the COS and they tended to advocate for better working conditions, housing, health, and education" (Hick 2010, p. 39).

Jane Addams established one of the most well-known **settlement houses**, Hull House, in 1889 in Chicago (Hick, 2010). Hull House (a converted mansion, which, by 1907, had expanded to a complex of 12 buildings), like other settlement houses, brought together middle class volunteers and the poor. They lived together in the same community and shared culture and knowledge with an aim to alleviate poverty. Settlement houses were flexible and diverse, developing and providing services that were specifically needed in each community (James, 1998). During the late 1800s and early 1900s settlement houses spread throughout Canada and the US (Finkel, 2006). The first in Canada, Evangelia Settlement, was established in Toronto in 1902 (James, 1998). Others followed in Montreal and Winnipeg. J.S. Woodworth, who would later become the first leader of the Cooperative Commonwealth Federation party of Canada, directed the Winnipeg settlement house, the All People's Mission (Finkel, 2006). By the time World War I broke out most Canadian cities had a settlement house (Hick, 2010). "Out of this tradition came another of social work's primary methods of intervention, a self-help model of community organization that focused on participation of the poor, community development, and social action" (Mullaly, 1997, p. 24).

The SHM focused on community-based services (James, 2001), such as basic and higher education, language classes, recreation, child care, and health care, while the COS increasingly took control of the official and more influential institutions like university education programs for social workers and professional associations like the Canadian Association of Social Workers (Mullaly, 1997). The COS perspective that poverty is the fault of the poor, and that it is the social worker's responsibility to help poor individuals change, eventually came to dominate professional educational programs and professional associations. This perspective was clearly reflected in social work's official response to public social issues such as child welfare and poverty in the early twentieth century (Guest, 1980). Guest (1980) notes that during that period a large public gathering of social workers discussed the proposed family allowance policy and a resolution against the policy was unanimously passed. At the time, the official social work reaction to important public policy debates concerning the poor ranged from silence to outspoken opposition, to obvious professional self-preservation. Some examples from the 1920s and 1930s follow.

> Mildred Kensit, a child-welfare worker, told a parliamentary committee that family allowances would encourage the increase in family size of an undesirable class of people—referring to the people in receipt of low wages—who, she said, were "frequently physically and mentally unfit." (Guest, 1980, p. 80)

> At a January 1932 meeting one of the local branches of the Canadian Association of Social Workers reported: "Social workers are paid by the capitalist group, for the most part, in order to assist the underprivileged group. Thus organized support of political issues would be very difficult if not dangerous . . . because of the danger of attempting too radical changes, since we are paid by the group who would resent such changes most." (Social Welfare 1932, cited in Carniol, 2000, p. 33)

The perspective offered by the SHM became more and more marginalized by the social work establishment as the profession developed during the first half of the twentieth century. While SHM workers were preoccupied with the poor they failed to maintain an influence in social work associations, institutions, and educational programs, which came to be increasingly dominated by the COS.

Nevertheless the critical perspective reflected in the SHM continued outside of official social work institutions, through activism and protest against social injustice in various social movements (Rice & Prince, 2000; Wharf, 1990). Certain social movements developed as a response to social conditions, especially poverty and injustice and those movements have tended to share the progressive perspectives found in services like the SHM. Over time, these social movements have helped to pressure provincial and federal governments to recognize human rights, develop social welfare policies, and provide programs. Early and continuing influences included Aboriginal groups, the Social Gospel Movement, urban reform efforts, labour reform movements, and the women's rights movement (Chappell, 2014; Finkel, 2006; Hick, 2010). Later influences would include LGBTQ movements, disability rights movements, African Canadian movements, and anti-poverty groups (Carniol, 2005; Hick, 2010; Wharf, 1990).

It is important, however, not to idealize the early progressive roots of anti-oppressive advocacy. These early advocates ignored, perhaps because they were genuinely unaware although that is questionable, the oppression of Aboriginal peoples, African Americans, and LGBTQ people. So while settlement house workers advocated on behalf of the urban poor, other groups continued to face oppression and would for many decades to come. Benjamin (2011) makes this clear:

> Populations such as First Nations Peoples faced genocide during Jane Addams' era and again with the continuation of the residential schools in the 1960s. Though the acts of resistance and the rise of a militant gay and lesbian rights movement from the 1960s onward won major gains in the last few decades, queer people were forced into the closet during both eras. And during Jane Addams' era and beyond, Blacks were being lynched with the tolerance or participation of the law. (p. 292)

Baskin (2011) adds that "when it came to the feminist, civil rights, and peace movements, Indigenous peoples were not only excluded, they were still being targeted for assimilation and cultural genocide" (p. 8). Starting in the early 1900s the links between the progressive perspectives offered by the SHM and Canadian social movements became weak and even, for a time, non-existent, as conventional approaches came to dominate the official social work institutions including the professional associations, university curricula, and services and programs in the community (Wharf, 1990). According to Wharf, "the agenda within social work calling for change has slipped away, leaving the action to social movements and other groups" (1990, p. 13). One very active social movement in Canada working outside of conventional human service work are those groups organized by Aboriginal peoples. Aboriginal social change groups are an example of sustained activism over many generations that have had, and continue to have, an enormous influence on progressive advocacy strategy and action.

Aboriginal Advocacy and Activism

The work by Aboriginal people is an example of persistent advocacy and resistance on behalf of a cause. Aboriginal social movements have, despite cruel repression, boldly persisted and made progress on self-government, land claims, treaties, and compensation for residential schools. According to Baskin (2011), an Aboriginal academic, all individuals are interconnected, interdependent, and connected to the environment. She stresses that the "community heals the individual and the individual heals the community" (Baskin, 2011, p. 113). Aboriginal values of community and respect for the environment have had an influence on community organizing in the human services.

In the human service literature Aboriginal people are often discussed as clients, as victims or the oppressed. Yet, far from victims, Aboriginal peoples and communities have been actively resistant to French and British colonial oppression since it began on this continent several hundred years ago. The strength and resiliency in Aboriginal communities today is a legacy of their advocacy and activism campaigns.

When colonizers first arrived they were ill-prepared to survive the harsh climate and rugged geography in Canada. These early colonizers depended on the knowledge and generosity of Aboriginal peoples to survive. Aboriginal people taught them how to navigate, hunt, trap, and build shelters. Later colonizers would flourish and some would become rich through the fur trade, and later farming (T. King, 2012; Mann, 2006; Saul, 2009). In the nineteenth century, colonization of Canada accelerated and stretched across the continent. Treaties were ignored as colonizers laid claim to (stole) the most fertile and productive land in the country. At the same time Aboriginal peoples were decimated by diseases carried by the colonizers for which they had no immunity and were violently pushed to the margins on remote reserves (often the least productive land available).

The deprivation in many Aboriginal communities today is directly related to government policies that systematically and intentionally stripped communities of culture, language, and land (Baskin, 2011). Despite the oppression, Aboriginal campaigns to change conditions have been sustained for many years over several generations. Initially, Aboriginal people tried diplomacy to settle disputes with an increasing number of white settlers. When diplomacy failed they turned to organized protests and physical confrontations such as the Red River Rebellion and later the North West Rebellion (H. King, 2012). The response was "heavy-handed government suppression" (H. King, 2012, para. 5). Despite the repression, Aboriginal individuals and local communities continued to resist. In an extension of these efforts, Aboriginal people organized formal political groups even when the Indian Act forbade it (until 1927), and the RCMP frequently arrested Aboriginal leaders when they were found organizing political groups to fight for social justice ("National Aboriginal," 2005). From 1919, when Aboriginal people formed the League of Indians, to the 1960s, Aboriginal people organized numerous formal and informal political groups. Today there are five core national Aboriginal organizations and numerous community- or issue-based groups advocating for change ("National Aboriginal," 2005). The large national groups are

- the Assembly of First Nations, formed in 1982, representing status Indians;
- the Métis National Council, also formed in 1982, represents Métis people;
- the Inuit Tapiriit Kanatami, established in 1971 to represent the interests of Inuit people;
- the Congress of Aboriginal People, formed in 1993 to represent mostly urban non-status and Métis people; and
- the Native Women's Association of Canada, organized in 1974 to work for the interests of Aboriginal women.

The determined advocacy of formal and informal Aboriginal groups in Canada has resulted in furthering human rights, movement towards self-government, greater control of services and programs, and recognition of and compensation for abuse and neglect. As an example, on 11 June 2008, Prime Minister Stephen Harper made an official apology in the House of Commons of Canada for the abuses suffered in residential schools. In 2008 a Truth and Reconciliation Commission was also established and completed six years later in 2015. The Commission documented the stories of the abuse suffered by Aboriginal children in residential schools in Canada. In 2007 a $1.9 million fund was established to compensate Aboriginal people who were forced to attend residential schools, where many of the children suffered physical, emotional, and sexual abuse (Truth and Reconciliation

Commission, 2015b). The Commission heard the testimony of nearly 7,000 witnesses and documented their stories. The report provides 94 "calls to action" covering the areas of health, education, justice, public inquiry, monitoring, language, funding, commemoration, and memorials (Truth and Reconciliation Commission of Canada, 2015a).

Members of the Native Women's Association were instrumental in starting Idle No More and the campaign for a national inquiry into missing and murdered Aboriginal women ("National Aboriginal," 2005). The Idle No More movement (December 2012 to the present) has successfully turned up the pressure on many outstanding issues. The Idle No More website identified the following five.

1. Repeal provisions of Bill C-45 (including changes to the Indian Act and Navigable Waters Act, which infringe on environmental protections, Aboriginal, and Treaty rights) and abandon all pending legislation which does the same.
2. Deepen democracy in Canada through practices such as proportional representation and consultation on all legislation concerning collective rights and environmental protections, and include legislation which restricts corporate interests.
3. In accordance with the United Nations Declaration on the Rights of Indigenous Peoples' principle of free, prior, and informed consent, respect the right of Indigenous peoples to say no to development on their territory.
4. Cease [the] policy of extinguishment of Aboriginal Title and recognize and affirm Aboriginal Title and Rights, as set out in section 35 of Canada's constitution, and recommended by the Royal Commission on Aboriginal Peoples.
5. Honour the spirit and intent of the historic Treaties. Officially repudiate the racist Doctrine of Discovery and the Doctrine of Terra Nullius, and abandon their use to justify the seizure of Indigenous Nations lands and wealth.
6. Actively resist violence against women and hold a national inquiry into missing and murdered Indigenous women and girls, and involve Indigenous women in the design, decision-making, process, and implementation of this inquiry, as a step toward initiating a comprehensive and coordinated national action plan. (Idle No More, 2013)

While this list is no doubt incomplete, it does provide a sense of the work that lies ahead. Activism garnering national and international attention includes Oka 1990, Ipperwash 1995, Burnt Church 1999, Grand River Land Dispute at Caledonia 2006, Day of Action 2007, and Idle No More 2012/13. Today Aboriginal people have a rich historical advocacy legacy to draw on and inspire more activism—see the profiles in Chapter 6 for the story of an activist involved in Aboriginal advocacy work. Advocates active in other progressive social movements have benefitted enormously from their inspiring successes and inventive strategies.

This has been a very brief profile of some of the organizing and advocacy work of Aboriginal groups—a list that is in no way a substitute for the already rich and growing literature on Aboriginal people in Canada by Aboriginal academics and authors. I hope it encourages students to do more research into Aboriginal social movements in Canada.

Advocacy as a Professional Responsibility

As mentioned earlier, progressive advocacy was for the most part taken up by social movements outside of conventional human service work for the better part of a century. Recently this has changed. Human service professionals now see advocacy on behalf of those they serve as part of their responsibility. As we saw in Chapter 2, advocacy on behalf of service users is listed as a professional responsibility in professional codes of ethics and standards of practice. A growing body of theoretical and practice literature has emerged to support advocacy in the human services. The theoretical and practical literature that is most compatible with advocacy—analysis of privilege and oppression and AOTP—is discussed in Chapter 1 and provides the framework for this book. The following section picks up the discussion of progressive work in the human services when it re-emerges in mainstream human service institutions in universities, colleges, and professional associations.

Anti-oppressive Perspectives: A Re-emergence in Mainstream Human Service Work

Following the two major theoretical strands that dominated the early twentieth century, there was a resurgence of anti-oppressive approaches in the mainstream social service field starting in the late 1960s and continuing to the present. Service providers became increasingly aware of the impact of oppression and discrimination on service users and communities and brought attention to the relative neglect of such issues in conventional human service work (Thompson, 2001, p. 1). As a response, anti-oppressive approaches in social service work developed during the 1960s, 1970s, and 1980s, first in Canada and then around the world. These approaches emphasized "the structural nature of social problems" (Fook, 2002, p. 5) and helped human service workers develop a strong critique of the social, economic, and political conditions that contributed to social problems like poverty, racism, and violence against women. Today anti-oppressive perspectives continue to evolve and the linkages between progressive social movements and human services are now being re-established (Carniol, 2005; Thompson, 2001).

One of the most important contributions of anti-oppressive theory is the development of a strong critique of conventional human service work, theory, and practices. Of significant importance, and a key concern, is the recognition that service providers play a key role in a system of social control over service users (Carniol, 2005; de Montigny, 1995, Dietz, 2000; Dominelli & McLeod, 1989; Healy, 2000). Razack (2002) notes that it is important for social workers who use anti-oppressive practice to understand and acknowledge that the profession has a historical basis that lies in racism and oppression.

This basis is still evident in the values that underpin much of conventional practice and theory in social work (Razack, 2002). Healy (2000) discusses three critiques of conventional social service work.

- The first point of critique, according to Healy, is that human service work focuses on the individual and individual problems as a site of intervention rather than the social structures and institutions that create the oppression.
- The second is a critique of the power imbalances between the service provider and the service user. Social workers should aim for greater equality by diminishing their own power and trying to empower the service user.
- The third critique of conventional human service work relates to authority and control awarded to service providers through their professional status. Professionalism entails a hierarchy of power and status with control over knowledge, skills, and resources. Professional knowledge should not be privileged over the lived experiences of service users (Healy, 2000, pp. 22–4).

According to Carniol (2000), social workers using anti-oppressive practice will not only change the way they do social work with individual service users, but will also become involved in broader social change through social justice movements. Carniol (2000) discusses a process to transform the current oppressive relations between social workers and service users to relations that offer liberation for both.

> This "anti-oppressive" approach challenges social work practice to "walk the talk." These new and better forms of social work are emerging alongside other practical initiatives from grass roots networks and social movements. They are calling for a restructuring of our major institutions, so that they become answerable to the public rather than being strictly controlled from the top down. Without such transformation today's social problems will be perpetuated endlessly into the future, with band-aids being busily applied by a profession that should know better. (Carniol, 2000, p. 23)

Mullaly (1997, 2002) provides one of the most extensive discussions of anti-oppressive and structural social work. According to Mullaly, much of the early development of the anti-oppressive approach originated with Maurice Moreau and his colleagues at the School of Social Work at Carleton University, the Université de Montréal, and the Université du Québec à Montréal (Mullaly, 1997, p. 105). A feature of the approach developed by Moreau is that it does not rank forms of oppression; instead he talks about these forms as "intersecting with each other at numerous points, creating a total system of oppression" (Mullaly, 1997, p. 105). The second key feature is that the service provider's efforts should be divided between helping people directly on the front line and trying to bring about a change in the structures that contribute to the suffering (Mullaly, 1997, p. 133). AOTP has continued to develop and in fact is now mainstream, as evidenced in its widespread acceptance in professional associations and academic institutions.

The progressive perspective originated in the SHM, was carried on by social movements, and re-emerged more recently as AOTP. Today mainstream human service work encompasses a range of theoretical and practice perspectives including both conventional and anti-oppressive. Some students may still contend that history and theory are not all that interesting to them (although a number of students find these studies enthralling). However, competent professionals have a responsibility to at least understand the contributions and damage done by others with a similar professional designation. The next service users coming through the door of an agency may have experienced negative or even abusive treatment because of an institutionalization, foster placement, or residential school. Their experiences with professionals in the health, education, and social service fields may have been very damaging. It would be comforting for them to know that you are different, that you are aware of their suffering and that you will not, unintentionally or otherwise, reproduce this oppression in your practice. Further, understanding the origin and development of anti-oppressive theory helps to draw the connections to advocacy and community change work today. Linking anti-oppressive theory with advocacy work in the human services is appropriate and reasonable given the way the progressive orientation was used by those involved in the SHM and social movements. Essentially, the right tool needs to be used for the job at hand; anti-oppressive theory and advocacy are the right tools to fight for equality and social justice. It is important for those new to advocacy and human service work to be grounded in history and theory but it is also important to be prepared with an understanding of the current context of practice.

Current Context of Advocacy Practice

To me the remarkable thing about poor-bashing is not that it seeps into so many aspects of daily life from so many levels, but that so many people who are poor do survive, don't commit suicide, are fierce in their dignity, and see a place for themselves helping others survive and challenge an unfair system.

(Swanson, 2001, p. 28)

Advocates in the social services need to appreciate four features of the context in which they will be practicing. The first is the recognition that advocacy is practiced in communities. It is critical to understand and value community as an integral part of human well-being and as key to successful long-lasting change. Advocacy and organizing strategy should be used to foster individual and community well-being. The second feature is that social services are a diverse environment in terms of agency size, mandate, sponsorship, and governance. Advocates are often going up against a complex, sophisticated, bureaucratic organization. Third, **managerialism** (or business management practices) has taken hold in human service organizations and is not going away any time soon. The section that follows will provide a brief description of these four significant features of the advocacy context for advocates in the social services.

Healthy Communities and Community Organizing for Change

Communities are essential both to individual and collective well-being; they play a vital role in helping us to meet a fundamental need to understand ourselves and make our environments comprehensible, predictable, and manageable.

(Brown & Hannis, 2008, p. 4)

Social service agencies are often the nexus of action in advocacy and agencies are situated in communities. Therefore, understanding the community context is pivotal to advocacy at the personal, cultural, and structural levels. Communities hold the culture, history, and geography of the people that live there. The health of individuals is dependent on the health of the community, as the health of the community is dependent on the collective health of individuals.

Baskin (2011), in her discussion of Aboriginal communities, states that "a person cannot be viewed as separate from a community" (p. 130). She explains that today Aboriginal groups are at the forefront of healing and transforming communities (Baskin, 2011). Traditionally, collectivism was central to Aboriginal peoples' view of the world. The Aboriginal community is an extension of family and all community members have the opportunity to participate in improving everyone's well-being in the community (Baskin, 2011). Interdependence and caring are important community values. The pre-colonization environment posed challenges for Aboriginal peoples, including long winter months and food scarcity. In order to survive and thrive, people gathered together in communities (Baskin, 2011)—communities that continued to offer support when faced with colonial oppression. Aboriginal academics and advocates are seldom given credit for their strong influence on community organizing and community change in mainstream practice in the social services. However, the links and influences are clear and I would be remiss if I did not acknowledge the strong influence of Aboriginal views and values of community on current advocacy practice in communities.

When communities are strong, individuals are strong and when communities are weak or damaged, so are individuals (Lee, 2011). Advocates need to be familiar with the interconnections between advocacy and community. It is of course very important for an advocate to help a service user get social housing or disability benefits; these are real and concrete improvements. But it is also important to see that the service user is part of a community and that the wellness of the community is impacting the service user's wellness, as the service user's wellness is impacting the health of the community. The tangible benefits of a disability pension and decent affordable housing will clearly improve one person's life but that person has perhaps many interconnections with the broader community, a network of family and friends and acquaintances. The community too, is improved when one person is better off because they are receiving a better income and housing. When one person's life is made more stable through improved benefits they are much better equipped to participate in contributing to their community in a positive way.

Advocates in the human services, regardless of the focus of their work (personal, cultural, or structural), should value and foster healthy communities. The Ontario Healthy Communities Coalition (OHCC) describes the qualities of a healthy community as

- Clean and safe physical environment
- Peace, equity, and social justice
- Adequate access to food, water, shelter, income, safety, work, and recreation for all
- Adequate access to health care services
- Opportunities for learning and skill development
- Strong, mutually supportive relationships and networks
- Workplaces that are supportive of individual and family well-being
- Wide participation of residents in decision-making
- Strong local cultural and spiritual heritage
- Diverse and vital economy
- Protection of the natural environment
- Responsible use of resources to ensure long-term sustainability[1] (Ontario Healthy Communities Coalition, n.d. Home page, para. 5)

Homan's (2008) discussion of healthy communities agrees with qualities in the OHCC's list above; however, he further emphasizes the importance of inclusivity and the valuing of diversity in human relationships. He explains that healthy communities find ways to include all of its members in the benefits of the community and in decision making. There is a belief in the community that everyone has something to offer (Homan, 2008). In Homan's view, diversity is celebrated and recognized as an important community resource. Positive, supportive relationships between community members are as vital to a healthy community as natural resources and community services. So, while the advocate may be challenging a single agency on behalf of one service user, they should be ever mindful of the dual purpose to successfully help the individual and improve the responsiveness of the social service agency for the entire community.

Lee (2011) emphasizes the importance of community empowerment and the value of community members developing a sense of agency to have an influence on their environment. For Lee (2011) citizen involvement is both a right and a responsibility. Healthy, empowered communities encourage citizen involvement; citizens that are empowered "have the feeling within themselves that they can act on their own behalf to be able to meet their physical, spiritual, and psychological needs" (Lee, 2011, p. 87). Empowered citizens are able to develop strong social relationships in communities and are prepared to act with others to improve the community.

According to Lee (2011), organizational development and social learning are allied with strong social relationships. Organization development is a process of bringing together people to take action on a common interest, goal, or need, creating strong community organizations that can represent marginalized people. Social learning is a key element of maintaining strong social relationships and organizations. Gaining knowledge through social learning is empowering and knowledge is an element of power; those with greater knowledge have greater power. Lee (2011) includes skill development, system knowledge, and structural analysis as important aspects of social learning.

- According to Lee (2011), skills are those things that we learn to do well through training and practice. In community organizing work, a skill may be writing a press release, chairing a meeting, or researching a topic of concern.
- System knowledge as social learning refers to the ability to understand and influence the "complex system of regulations, laws, and public organizations" (Lee, 2011, p. 93).
- Structural analysis as social learning is developing an understanding of one's personal experiences and difficulties in relation to the community and society as a whole. Structural analysis helps individuals understand how their lives are shaped by economic, social, and political factors and community organizing helps individuals to come together in order to influence these systems (Lee, 2011).

Advocates working at the personal, cultural, or structural level should be grounded in a strong, diverse social network. These relationships help to support and empower the advocate in the overall goal to improve the community for everyone, especially people who are oppressed. Healthy communities as a goal and community organizing as a strategy for advocacy action are central to the context of advocacy practice.

Social Service Agencies: A Diverse and Complex Context

Social service agencies vary in size (small to very large), mandate (what they do), sponsorship (where they get their funding), and governance (how they are managed). Agency size can be viewed from different standpoints. Size may be the number of paid employees, the number of volunteers, or the number of service users who access the agency's programs. For instance, some very small agencies consist of one paid worker and volunteers. A very large agency such as Service Canada consists of thousands of paid workers in numerous government offices across Canada.

Social service agencies are also diverse in terms of their mandates. Some agencies have a single purpose, for example, providing accommodation for service users with intellectual disabilities or counselling for alcohol addiction. Others are large multi-service agencies that provide a hot meal program, food bank, used clothing, household goods, and supportive counselling. Still others, like large provincial welfare departments, provide income support and health benefits for unemployed individuals and families.

Agencies also differ in terms of sponsorship and governance. Sponsorship is another term for funding source. Human service organizations may receive their funding from a single source such as tax payers or from many sources such as government or foundation grants, donations, or fundraising activities. Government social services like welfare or Old Age Security receive their funding from tax dollars. Not-for-profit agencies generally receive their funding from a variety of sources including grants, donations, and fundraising.

Governance also varies in the social service sector. Organizational governance refers to the formal structure of authority and accountability in an organization. Large government social services have many layers of authority forming a large pyramid structure, with numerous front-line workers serving the public, supervised by many layers of management, all falling under the minister of the department. For instance, Service Canada has front-line workers in offices all across Canada to provide benefits and assistance to individuals and families. The heads of the federal and provincial government services are democratically elected members of parliament who are then chosen by the prime minister or premier to head a government department. Government services operate according to legislation or laws passed in the House of Commons in Ottawa. Not-for-profit organizations are managed by an executive director (or some similar title) who is accountable to an elected volunteer board of directors. Not-for-profit organizations must operate according to their by-laws. Some not-for-profit organizations also have an official charitable status, which allows them to provide charitable receipts for income tax purposes to donors. Table 3.2 provides a summary of the key features of not-for-profit and government social services.

Table 3.2 Summary of Organizational Features in the Not-for-profit and Government Social Service Sectors

	Not-for-profit	Government
Size	Very small to medium (1 or 2 staff to several hundred)	Very large (thousands of staff)
Mandate	Diverse (provides food, clothing, shelter, or counselling, but not financial benefits)	Less diverse (financial benefits and some health benefits)
Sponsorship	Fundraising, donations, and grants from government and foundations	Tax dollars
Governance	Volunteer board of directors; executive director; by-laws; charitable status	Federal or provincial government; a government minister; legislation
Bureaucratic	Relatively flat pyramid organizational structure with a few layers	Very steep pyramid organization structure with many layers

Dealing with Bureaucracy

It is my strong belief that all service providers can do advocacy irrespective of where they are employed. The different organizational contexts require different strategies and actions but it is always possible to bring about positive change that contributes to greater social justice. One of the most common forms of advocacy is fighting for a service user's benefits or rights and this frequently takes place in the context of a bureaucratic organization. Bureaucracy is one of the most difficult contexts for advocacy and is most often associated with large government programs. Bureaucracies pose particular challenges for advocates, and therefore it is especially important to have an intimate understanding of how they are structured and how they function.

All Canadian families and individuals access services and benefits through large government organizations or bureaucracies. As an example the federal and provincial governments provide financial benefits for people who are unemployed, families with children, seniors, and people with disabilities. Some service users face barriers to access because bureaucratic organizations use technical language, automated communication systems, and complicated application procedures that require computer skills and access to the internet. Also common is less than friendly customer service. All of these hinder access for even the average citizen, and even more so for people with disabilities, those who are new to the country, and those with poor literacy skills.

Lee (2001) describes the advocacy context in Canada as bureaucratically rigid and increasingly complex. In a bureaucracy, power is concentrated at the top in executive and management positions while workers on the front line have very little discretion or decision-making power (Kirst-Ashman & Hull, 2001, p. 151). The policies and procedures framing service delivery are rigid and stable. "The [e]mphasis is on structure and the status quo" (Kirst-Ashman & Hull, 2001, p. 152). For service users and advocates this means dogged persistence in the face of complicated appeal procedures with strict deadlines along with the need for substantial credible documentation. Advocates must also follow the procedure and protocol instituted by the bureaucracy. If deadlines are missed or forms are incomplete or inaccurate, the rules of the bureaucracy apply and the loser is the service user. Advocates need to know that bureaucracy and complexity are an important part of the current context of advocacy work.

This discussion provides a brief overview of the diversity in the social service network. Advocates would be remiss if they do not have a clear understanding of the social service organizations in the community in which they work. Case Study 3.1 illustrates two, nearly opposite, organizational contexts for doing advocacy.

Advocates cannot always choose the circumstances in which they work. Jobs can be scarce and everyone needs money to provide for themselves and their families. Therefore, advocates in all social service organizations must develop a clear understanding of the advocacy possibilities within each setting. Context knowledge can be used to further social justice goals and advocate even in the most restrictive organizational environments.

Case Study 3.1 The Tale of Two Advocates

Advocate 1

Yana is a front-line counsellor for a large government social service. She and the 20 other counsellors in her office take applications and assess eligibility for financial and health care benefits. Yana knows the benefits are insufficient. The families and individuals coming to her for help live in very poor-quality housing and must go to the food bank every month when groceries run out. Yana spoke to her supervisor about the inadequacy of the benefits and she was told to follow the regulations in the legislation or she would be disciplined or terminated. Yana really needs her job and cannot risk getting fired, so she does what she can to make life easier for the people coming to her for help. She treats all service users with kindness and respect. She uses her position to make sure that each person coming to her for help receives as much as the legislation will allow. Whenever possible she uses her discretionary power to approve additional benefits. She has to build a strong case to make sure the service users receive the additional benefits, which takes a lot of time and effort but she feels this is the least she can do to ease suffering. Outside of work she is very involved in anti-poverty advocacy groups and has participated in many campaigns including No One Is Illegal, Raising the Roof, Make Poverty History, and the Occupy Movement.

Advocate 2

Tarek works as an advocate for a small not-for-profit social service. He and six other front-line workers do housing and income maintenance advocacy. Fifty per cent of their time is spent doing case advocacy on behalf of service users who may have received an illegal eviction or been cut off welfare. The other half of their time is spent participating in and leading campaigns to end the circumstances that lead to poverty and homelessness. Tarek and his co-workers have organized petitions to end homelessness, they have held demonstrations in front of the Parliament Buildings in Ottawa to demand action on climate change, and they braved tear gas and police batons during a global trade summit. The job description for this small not-for-profit agency is to advocate at the personal, cultural, and structural levels.

Lessons Learned

The organizational context of advocacy is a prime determinant of the type of advocacy possible. Yet advocacy is possible in all organizational contexts, even the most bureaucratic.

Critical Thinking Questions

1. What organizational factors affect a service provider's ability do advocacy?
2. Is there any way to change the organizational features impeding advocacy practices?
3. How might community organizing efforts be used to improve social service agencies?

In order to accomplish this, advocates need to have a detailed knowledge of the social service network in the community. They need to understand that they will be confronting injustices in their own agencies or other social service organizations on behalf of service users. The social service agency type, size, mandate, and governance will impact the advocacy planning, strategy, and action. The social service organization is a principal point of action and is therefore of prime importance to all advocacy.

Understanding the complex structure of the social service network and bureaucracy is key to successful advocacy. However, recent global and national developments have imposed an additional layer of challenge for advocates in the social services: Managerialism is an expression of the **globalization** and **neo-liberalism** trends that have permeated every aspect of work in the social services, including advocacy. The implications for advocates are discussed in the following section.

Managerialism: Business Management Practices in the Social Services

Human service work has undergone, and continues to experience, considerable change. Changes have impacted the social service network, service provider practices, and most importantly the relationships between service providers and service users. Advocates at the front line need to be prepared for conditions created by neo-liberalism, globalization, and managerialism. Working within and against the changing conditions is a responsibility of anti-oppressive advocates. The first step is to understand how global and national conditions have changed the nature of human service work. The second step is to try to advocate for families and individuals to get the services they need and have a right to in order to relieve their suffering. The third step is to use the knowledge of the impact on service users of neo-liberalism, globalization, and managerialism to fight for structural change. This section will define these three forces and provide a description of the impact on human service work and advocacy.

Neo-liberalism, globalization, and managerialism have had a profound effect on the context in which service users and advocates find themselves on a day-to-day basis. Neo-liberalism is a perspective that promotes a free market system without regulation by governments. It favours minimal government, resulting in inadequate funding for social services and programs. The effect is "a growth in poverty, decrease in democracy, and increased social and environmental devastation" (Baines, 2011, p. 30). *Globalization* is the term for a progressively more integrated capitalist market economy around the globe. Under globalization the negative effects of neo-liberalism noted above are experienced worldwide. In addition, cultures around the world are imperialized by the cultures with economic power such as Canada, the US, and Western Europe.

Neo-liberalism and globalization have had an impact on the social, political, and economic conditions in every country in the world (Chappell, 2006; Dominelli, 1996, 2002, 2007; Fook, 2002; Healy, 2001; Healy & Leonard, 2000; Hick, 2014; Rice & Prince, 2000). As Baines (2007a) argues, "globalization has increased poverty, environmental degradation, and economic and political insecurity for many, while amassing wealth and privilege for corporations, their executives, and investors" (p. 10). The sweeping changes at both the global and national levels have many implications for advocates in Canada. Rice and Prince (2000) explain that some of the transformations in the social service field are due to the changing needs in the service user population in Canada. Forced and voluntary migration and immigration have resulted in many new-comers in nearly every community. In addition, the depth, duration, and breadth of poverty have increased, as has the complexity of service user needs (Hick, 2014). Advo-cates in the social services have had to adjust to changes in the needs of service users, while at the same time they have had many changes imposed on them in their own employment contexts due to managerialism.

Managerialism as discussed by Baines (2011), Dominelli (2002), Fook (2002), and Healy and Leonard (2000) is a common feature in democratic, capitalistic countries in-cluding Canada. Managerialism entails the restructuring and downsizing of the social service sector to a model consistent with the private sector. Under managerialism, social services, like the private sector, have had to adjust to the free market obsession of global capitalism (Dominelli, 2002; Fook, 2002; Healy & Leonard, 2000). Govern-ments, once a provider and funder of social services, have become purchasers through contracts with private and not-for-profit organizations (Chappell, 2014; Dominelli, 1996; Fook, 2002). Globalization and the neo-liberal agenda in Canada has reduced the ser-vices provided directly by the government and increased the size and number of private and not-for-profit services. So the government social service sector is shrinking while the not-for-profit sector is growing. These changes allow the central government to reduce the costs of social services while claiming to maintain control through standards and requirements (Chappell, 2014; Dominelli, 2002; Fook 2002). Not-for-profit social services have been forced to adopt business principles and practices.[2]

According to Dominelli (1996, 2002), the move to managerialism has deeply altered service provider and service user interactions, including a requirement to provide services to only the "most deserving poor" (Dominelli, 2002, p. 141)—a goal reminiscent of the ideology of the COS discussed earlier in this chapter. It is a perspective that was then, and is still, degrading and oppressive to service users and that provides no long-term solutions. The cumulative effects of managerialism on the social service sector are "stan-dardization, fragmentation, deskilling, and increased stress" in the workplace (Baines, 2007a, p. 12). Standardization is breaking down service provider practices into smaller and smaller components. The result is a loss in the breadth and depth of practice skills (Baines, 2011). Work volume and pace can be increased and assigned to workers with less skill. Over time, skilled workers will be replaced with less skilled, part-time, and con-tract workers and in some circumstances volunteers and field placement students (Baines, 2011). Fragmentation causes isolation and the individualization of social problems like poverty, homelessness, and addiction. Services are restrictive, limited, separated, and seg-regated. The outcome is that service users receive partial and insufficient assistance. For the service provider standardization and fragmentation result in deskilling and a general loss of practice knowledge and skill over time.

Under managerialism the salaries of service providers and numbers of service users become commodities. Essentially service users and service providers are reduced to items on a spreadsheet, to be controlled and manipulated according to market forces (Healy & Leonard, 2000). Service users are considered consumers who may be "exploited for profit" (Dominelli, 2002). Agencies use the number of service users they help (their statistics) to compete with other agencies for grants. Organizations that provide grants—governments, foundations, and organizations like the United Way—hold competitive processes called CFP (Call For Proposals) or RFP (Request For Proposals). When a CFP is announced, social service agencies use their program ideas and the number of service users they help to compete for funding. The caring, helping relationships between service providers and service users are not easily commodified and are therefore not an important element in a competitive funding environment. Relationships are the bedrock of human service work but are difficult to turn into numbers for a CFP.

Prior to managerialism the caring, helping relationship between a service provider and service user was the key to service provision. "Positive changes for clients were thought to occur through the establishment of respectful and caring relationships" (Baines, 2007a, p. 12). The importance of establishing a caring, helping relationship has become much less important in the delivery of service under managerialism. Service providers are regulated so that they provide standard care. The difference between before and after managerialism is akin to home cooking versus a fast-food restaurant. The home cooking type of service providers used caring and respect and tailored services to the needs of service users. Fast-food service providers, on the other hand, are rushed by high volume and quickly provide the same services and products over and over again in exactly the same way irrespective of service users' needs. Service providers under managerialism are regulated through volume (number of service users they serve), time (how long they spend with each service user), and formal policies and procedures. They are expected to treat each service user the same. They must complete the same forms and documents, in a specified period of time, day in and day out. Those advocating for the rights of racialized people or those in the LGBTQ communities fought hard for equal treatment by human service providers, but managerialism was probably not what they had in mind.

Increasingly, organizations in the human service sector are required to use "pro-market, business-like management solutions, rather than non-market initiatives stressing social connection, equality, and public service ethos" (Baines, 2011, p. 32). Caring, respect, and decision making have been removed from the purview of service providers and re-placed with regulation and structure. Further, under managerialism there is a tendency to break the service provision into smaller and smaller elements. A service provider's work is divided into many component parts such as intake, assessment, service delivery, and follow up. Instead of doing all of the component parts a worker will be expected to do only one, for example assessment or follow up. Other service providers will complete the other compo-nent parts. The result is a routine, industrial-like approach (Dominelli, 1996, 2002; Fook, 2002). A euphemism in the field for this process is "best practices" (Baines, 2011, p. 34). When best practices become the standard, service providers are more readily replaced with part-time, contract, and lower paid workers and volunteers who can be more easily managed (Baines, 2011). In the past, practice was "constantly evolving in creative and innovative ways to address the unique aspects of each case"; as managerialism gains ground, Baines argues, inventive practices will become less and less possible (2007a, p. 13).

Managerialism evolved from "private sector models used in retail and sales work" (Baines, 2007a, p. 14). Profit is increased and costs are decreased by limiting the time spent with each customer (service users). Also, a feature of the private retail sector that has now become a mainstay in the social service sector is flexible work or employment (Dominelli, 2002). The permanent, full-time position with a union, pension, and benefits is becoming less and less of a prospect for service providers in the field. Instead social service workers can expect part-time, contract, or casual work options. This shift to agencies structured like private sector business models results in more insecurity and lower wages in the social service field.

Clearly advocates in the human services are impacted by the changes brought about by globalization, neo-liberalism, and managerialism. Lee (2001) makes a good point that there is a greater need for advocates in the new managerialized human service sector but there is less funding for advocacy services. As a result a greater number of service providers will need to do more advocacy to compensate for the lack of services. This responsibility falls on service providers already under stress due to the effects of managerialism. Service providers taking up advocacy will need to work hard to maintain caring, helping relationships with service users and also advocate to reverse the regressive changes in social service work and the social service sector.

Conclusion

It is important for advocates in the social services to be aware of both the historical and current contexts in which they do their work. The human service field has a past that includes both oppressive and anti-oppressive work. Hopefully the discussion in this chapter has inspired some thoughtful reflection about work in the social services past and present. In addition, it is important to be aware of the development of AOTP and the key players responsible for that development. Part of the aim of this section was to show the compatibility of anti-oppressive theory and advocacy practice in the human services.

This chapter also introduces healthy communities as an important concern for advocates and service users. The literature on community, especially by Aboriginal scholars, points to the interdependency and interconnections between individuals and communities. The latter part of the chapter is a discussion of the deleterious effects of neo-liberalism, globalization, managerialism, and other regressive trends impacting advocacy work in the social services. These challenges mean that advocates must have courage and look to creative and critical thinking in planning, strategy development, and action (see Chapters 4 and 5). Despite these daunting trends, anti-oppressive advocates will need to continue to struggle against, and resist, unjust practices and policies in their organizational settings. The biggest mistake is to bury your head and try to ignore what is happening. Over time those that ignore the regressive structural changes begin to shame and blame themselves, their co-workers, and service users. The result is frustration, distress, guilt, and regret over your perceived inadequacies, when in fact it is the system that is inadequate not the individual advocate or service provider. Knowing what is happening and joining with others to contribute to positive changes is one of the best ways to avoid burnout and to work towards equality and social justice.

Critical Thinking Questions

1. Many of the values and practices from the past are still with us today in modern social service organizations. Reflect on the service provided by an agency that you have used, or where you have been a volunteer, placement student, or staff. How does the service provided compare or contrast to the Settlement House Movement and the Charity Organization Society?
2. Advocacy can be practiced even in the most oppressive circumstances such as large bureaucratic human service organizations. Provide three examples of how advocacy may be practiced in an oppressive organizational context.
3. This chapter details the evolution of AOTP from the early beginnings in Canada to more recent periods. Explain why it is important to examine and analyze the historical context of anti-oppressive theory.
4. Healthy communities and community organizing are important to anti-oppression advocates. Use the qualities of a healthy community to assess the health of your community. When you are finished consider the advocacy and community organizing that will be needed to bring improvements to your community.
5. Neo-liberalism and globalization have had significant and ongoing impacts on the social service sector. One of the concepts used to explain the impact is managerialism. Examine a social service organization with which you are familiar and find three examples of managerialism in the agency.
6. This chapter explained that worker burnout is the result of ignoring the structural changes taking place in the human services. Think of at least three ways to avoid burnout due to the effects of managerialism.

Suggested Readings

Baines, D. (2011). An overview of anti-oppressive social work practice: Neoliberalism, inequality, and change. In D. Baines (Ed.), *Doing anti-oppressive practice: Social justice social work* (pp. 1–24). Winnipeg: Fernwood Publishing.

Baskin, C. (2011). *Strong helpers' teachings.* Toronto: Canadian Scholars' Press.

Carniol, B. (2005). *Case critical.* Toronto: Between the Lines Press.

Finkel, A. (2006). *Social policy and practice in Canada: A history.* Waterloo, ON: Wilfrid Laurier University Press.

Lee, B. (2011). *Pragmatics of community organization.* Toronto: CommonAct Press.

Suggested Videos and Websites

Journey to Justice. Roger McTair, 2000, National Film Board Canada www.nfb.ca/film/journey_to_justice

The Gift of Diabetes. John Paskievich and O. Brian Whitford, 2005, National Film Board Canada www.nfb.ca/film/gift_of_diabetes

Notes

1. The "qualities of a healthy community" principles on the Ontario Healthy Community Coalition website were adapted from a report for the Senate Subcommittee on Population Health in March 2009. The report was authored by Dr Hancock (2009) called *Act Locally: Community-based Population Health Promotion.*

2. The global financial crisis of 2008, the worst financial crisis since the Depression of the 1930s, left many questioning the efficacy of business practices. Business practices contributed to the near collapse of financial institutions, with the resultant drop in the stock market, collapse of housing prices, evictions, foreclosures, homelessness, and prolonged unemployment. These types of results bring into question the credibility of business principles and practices and their applicability to non-market government and social services.

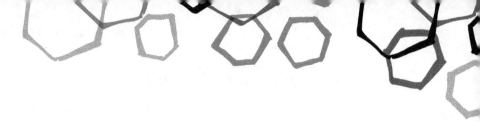

4 An Anti-oppressive Advocacy Development Model: Structure, Process, and Strategy Considerations

Chapter Objectives

After reading this chapter you should be able to:

1. Develop an effective advocacy plan on behalf of an individual, group, or community
2. Work with service users to identify advocacy problems and goals
3. Recognize the value of background research in advocacy
4. Generate and implement strategy options at the personal, cultural, and structural levels
5. Effectively evaluate and monitor advocacy

Introduction

> [P]rogressive change is won by activists and their constituencies. . . . Those who believe in social change must fully accept their own leadership role in the process and recognize that neither politicians nor political parties are the prime movers of progressive change.
>
> (Shaw, 2001, p. 278)

This chapter provides a framework for understanding the advocacy process with helpful insights from case examples, experience, and the literature. (Chapter 5 completes the overarching picture of advocacy work by examining the action stage.) Advocates new to the field will find the advocacy development model a useful guide for practice. More experienced advocates may find new insights because of the blend of advocacy and AOTP. This chapter begins with an overview of the anti-oppressive advocacy development model (AOADM). A more detailed discussion of each element of the model follows: defining the problem, background research, planning, **strategy**, evaluating and monitoring. The planning section features an outline advocacy plan followed by a completed plan and case example. Advocates new to the field may find the outline helpful in planning their initial cases. Experienced advocates may also find the outline useful when clarity is fading and options become elusive. The AOADM will help advocates navigate the complex context of work in the human services.

Anti-oppressive Advocacy Development Model

The AOADM presented in this chapter incorporates context, background, theory, and practice discussions from previous chapters with a more detailed description of advocacy from the initial meeting with an individual, group, or community, to the final reflection/evaluation meeting. In the model (see Figure 4.1), service users and advocates begin by defining the problem and then follow the steps of the process.

While the model is depicted as a logical process where an element follows from the previous one, it is important to recognize that research and strategy elements are frequently revisited throughout the advocacy process. That is, research informs the problem, planning, strategy, and evaluation and monitoring, and strategy is influenced by changes in the definition of the problem, research, and planning. In the field, the advocacy process may move back and forth between the elements in the model, but overall the aim is to move towards successfully completing the advocacy. The advocacy process is generally finished after evaluation.

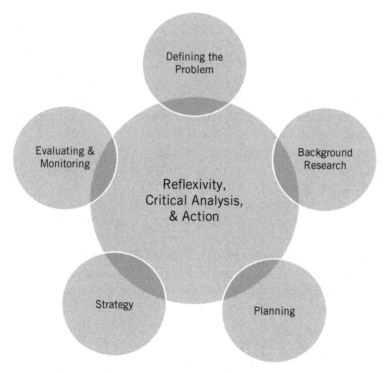

Figure 4.1 Anti-oppressive Advocacy Development Model

The exception is when the advocacy requires ongoing monitoring. For example, ongoing monitoring is required after a community successfully advocates to have a local manufacturing site install a scrubber (a pollution control device) as a first step to reducing the particulates and gasses that fall over a low-income neighbourhood. In this example the community will need to monitor the air quality to ensure that the industrial polluter is using the scrubber appropriately and that it is having the desired effect, improved air quality.

If the advocacy is less than successful, or a clear loss, then evaluation can be used to inform a new advocacy problem and a new way to go at the issue. In these circumstances, when the advocacy is not entirely successful, the advocacy process continues with new information, analysis, and action. The model presented below also includes three concepts previously identified in Chapter 1 as key to anti-oppressive advocacy: reflexivity, critical analysis, and action. These concepts will be woven into the detailed discussion of each element in the model.

Defining the Problem

What is the problem? Initially defining the problem may appear to be straightforward and uncomplicated. However, even problems that at first appear clear and simple may unexpectedly turn into difficult, complex situations. In these circumstances a clear definition of the problem is imperative. In the field the majority of advocacy is done with and on behalf of a single service user with a single difficulty such as an appeal for disability benefits. The P/C/S analysis helps to connect problems at the personal level to those at the cultural and structural levels. Most service users, however, will not have the time or resources to fight problems at the cultural and structural levels. They are generally consumed with trying to survive day to day on an extremely low income, often 50 to 60 per cent below the low income cut-off (LICO).[1] Even if the service user is unable to pursue advocacy at the cultural or structural level, an advocate should help to make the connections. Doing an analysis with the service user helps to relieve their isolation and personal feelings of failure and links them to the cultural and structural problems that contribute to their circumstances. For instance, at the personal level a service user is denied a disability pension, at the cultural level discriminatory attitudes and beliefs prevent people who are poor or disabled from finding employment, and at the structural level the problem is defined as the welfare legislation that condemns many thousands of people to a marginalized and deprived existence every day in Canada. Analyzing this problem contributes background information, context, and conditions that will help in the planning and the selection of strategy and **tactics**.

Schneider and Lester (2001) offer an important reminder that the issue or problem is not understood in the same way by everyone concerned. Whether it is an advocate working with a single service user or a large group, it is important to remember that there are numerous and sometimes changing definitions of any given problem. Case Study 4.1 illustrates two perspectives, a service user's and the advocate's, on a problem.

Case Study 4.1   Using Advocacy to Fight a Housing Eviction

Eric expresses that, following an eviction notice, he needs to find different housing as quickly as possible because he does not want to become homeless. After exploring some discussion, Sandro, the advocate, feels there is a good chance of fighting the eviction if they act quickly. Eric defines the problem as needing housing, and Sandro sees the problem as fighting an eviction and helping Eric to maintain his current housing. After further discussion, though, it becomes clear that Eric may not see the issue the way Sandro does; he feels he has been a bad tenant and does not necessarily want to maintain his current housing.

Eric is in his mid-forties and a quadriplegic. He spends most of his day in a wheelchair and has some limited use of his arms. Homecare aides come to his apartment twice a day to provide assistance. He needs help with cooking, cleaning, and personal grooming. After discussing the situation further Sandro gains insight into why Eric thinks he is being evicted. He is, in fact, a very poor tenant. Few of us would want to live next to such a tenant in a crowded, airless, high-rise primarily accommodating seniors in the city core. Eric has very little contact with his family and has very few friends. In fact the friends he does have generally come around once a month when they know Eric has received his disability pension cheque. That is when Eric buys liquor, cannabis, and other street drugs and invites his "friends" over for a party. His friends are a "rough crowd"; many are involved in prostitution and the drug trade. Eric loses control of his parties, which go on all night and sometimes for days while drug and alcohol supplies last. In addition, some of his guests stay with Eric in his bachelor apartment for weeks at a time because of their own precarious housing situations. It is all too much for the seniors living in the building and they have registered numerous complaints over several months because of the noise and the fear they feel about Eric's guests.

Eric's definition of the problem arises from his feeling of guilt and regret about his behaviour as a tenant and his lack of knowledge about the tenancy legislation and advocacy. Sandro's perspective of the problem comes from his advocacy experience and understanding of the relevant legislation.

Lessons Learned

The lesson to consider from this case study is how important it is to do a deeper analysis of the service user's definition of the problem. Sandro fights Eric's eviction and wins but Eric still wants to move. Eric knows he does not belong in a seniors' building. Fighting the eviction buys time for Eric and Sandro to look into other housing options. Eventually Sandro helps Eric find an apartment in a subsidized housing complex that is specifically designed for younger people in wheelchairs.

continued

Critical Thinking Questions

1. What information is Eric using to define the problem?
2. What information informs Sandro's definition of the problem?
3. What can be done to help the people that only come to see Eric when he has drugs and alcohol?
4. Eric is decades younger than the seniors in his building; why is he living there?
5. How does the advocacy problem connect to cultural and structural level concerns?

In Case Study 4.1, Eric's initial definition of the problem changed from finding a new place to live to fighting an eviction. Later he decided to find a new apartment because he felt ashamed of the impact his behaviour had on his neighbours. It is important for the advocate to respect the choices of the service user without judgment (even if you think otherwise). Spindel explains, it is "the 'client' who will always live with the results of an advocacy effort—for better or worse" (2000, p. 5). Using anti-oppressive advocacy means the power and control is in the hands of the service user. The problem is defined by the service user. They are the expert on their own life and situation and this "expertise" must be respected. The service user's skills and personal experiences of oppression, combined with the advocate's critical analysis skills, are key to coming to a clear definition of the problem. Baines (2011) makes this point clearly when she says, "Clients are not just victims, but can and need to be active in their own liberation and that of others" (p. 7). Therefore, defining the problem is clearly a cooperative effort between the service user and the advocate, with the advocate making every effort to see the problem from the perspective of the service user. So Sandro learned that even though he had successfully saved Eric's tenancy, Eric still wanted to move to spare the seniors in his building any more grief because of his partying.

To identify the problem facing the service user Spindel (2000) recommends a process of "root cause questioning to ensure that the underlying systemic issues are identified" (p. 12). **Root-cause questioning** necessitates asking *why* type questions until there are no more answers. Having done this with students in class on a regular basis, I know that root-cause questioning will, at first, substantially broaden the focus. In doing so students will acquire a big picture view that helps to highlight all types of relevant issues, such as sources of power, conflict, small "p" and big "P" political factors, and relevant policy and legislation. A good example of this comes from my work with Jerry (not his real name). Jerry had a psychiatric disability and had spent much of his adult life in an institution run by the Ontario government. Like many other jurisdictions in North America in the 1970s and 1980s, Ontario initiated a process of deinstitutionalization as a response to widespread reporting of abuse and neglect in mental health facilities. Erving Goffman (1961) was one of many academics who studied the problems in the institutions and advocated for a process of deinstitutionalization and community care. As a result thousands of survivors, as they have come to be known, now live in the community. Some live independently but many need community support and supervision. Numerous small and medium-sized residential businesses sprang up to take advantage of the demand for housing. The accommodations go under various names across Canada such as group homes, residential care facilities, lodging homes, and room and board accommodations. Jerry came to me for help because he wanted to move from his current residential care facility to another facility where a friend lived. Jerry said he was told that he was not allowed to move. I told Jerry this was not true, that he was free to move after he gave sufficient notice to his landlord. He said the facility owner told him he had been placed there by social services, and that social services paid for his rent and meals and they would not approve his move. For a while Jerry believed the landlord because of his previous experience in a mental health institution. In the institution he was not allowed to come and go as he pleased. His life had been strictly managed according to specific routines. He had to ask for permission from staff for nearly everything he did. In due course, I helped Jerry write an official legal notice to the landlord that Jerry said he would deliver the following day. Late in the afternoon the next day, a large, 40ish man dressed in an expensive black suit arrived at my office and demanded to see me. He did not sit down, he physically towered over me and did a lot of finger pointing and speaking in a loud, angry voice. He told me to stay out of his business and that he knew what was best for Jerry and the other guys in the residential care facility.

Before I had a chance to say much he stormed out of my office and drove away in his expensive car. I have to admit I was shaken. I called an advocate friend for some support and to discuss the case further. While I do not remember exactly what we discussed, it is important to seek out support and advice from other advocates or mentors when you feel threatened, unsure, or disheartened. My advocate friend and I may have used some root-cause questioning to clarify the issues on this case as recommended by Spindel (2000). Root-cause questioning can be used to help define the problem with colleagues but the process is particularly helpful when working with service users.

Root-cause Questioning

Why has Jerry been told that he cannot move when according to the tenant protection legislation he can move with proper notice?

- Because the landlord needs Jerry and other tenants to stay so he can maximize profit.
- Vacancies mean a potential loss of income/profit.

Why does the landlord want to maximize profit?

- He wants to make as much money as possible to live in comfort and luxury or to use the profit to invest elsewhere.
- Or he may be accountable to shareholders or business partners and must increase profits and make the business a success.

Why does he need to increase profits and make the business a success?

- Because in a capitalist market system successful businesses earn more profits and can compete better. (Adapted from Spindel, 2000)

This analysis helped to develop some perspective on the problems faced by landlords in the business of housing people with psychiatric disabilities. These landlords need to keep their facilities at full capacity and ensure the rent is paid regularly as vacancies result in losses to the business. I still wondered at the over-the-top aggressiveness of this landlord but his behaviour did give me insight into why Jerry worried about giving notice and moving. After the landlord's visit to my office I felt a new urgency to help Jerry move, and the sooner the better. I continued to support Jerry through his move and his intimidating landlord backed off. Perhaps the landlord did not want to attract any investigative attention from social services to his businesses. On the other hand, he may have educated himself about the legislation and become aware of the fact that he did not own the people who lived in his facilities. Jerry and the other tenants had rights and choices, and there were people in the community willing to advocate for and support them in their choices.

Advocates need to define, or participate in defining, the problem depending on the context. As was previously discussed, the most common forms of advocacy are at the personal level on behalf of/with a service user. However, advocates in the social services will also work with families, groups, and communities. The process of exploring the problem and root-cause questioning may also be done in these contexts, though the number of viewpoints increases with the number of people involved. In these circumstances, the definition of the problem and finding a focus for the advocacy may take longer and at times involve disagreements between participants. Respectful disagreements are part of a healthy process. If the advocate is facilitating this discussion it can be challenging but it is important to maintain civility at all times. People can be entrenched in their views, especially when the stakes are high. In some circumstances if a large number of people are affected by the problem and involved in the advocacy, finding a common definition of the problem may be a constantly moving mark. Mediation, negotiation, and facilitation skills are essential for the advocate. The important thing to remember is that effort and compromise are essential.

The careful analysis of advocacy problems with service users is essential, as the advocacy goal or goals will derive directly from the process. According to Schneider and Lester (2001), without goals "it is difficult to promote clarity of purpose, identify next steps, find resources, organize people to help, and create strategies and symbols for change" (p. 120). The advocacy goal is the difference between where you are now and where you want to be. Work to develop a single, short statement that outlines the goal, that is, where the service users want to be at the end of the advocacy process. Some examples of goals may be: (1) the reinstatement of social welfare benefits for a service user; (2) opening a community service program to fight discrimination and racism; (3) establishing a national child care program in Canada. These examples also fit into the three levels of the P/C/S analysis model. Some of the literature recommends establishing short-, medium-, and long-term goals that are tied to specific strategic successes or timelines. These are good suggestions that apply to some but not all advocacy work. Be pragmatic and make use of ideas that work for the specific advocacy context in which you are engaged. It is also suggested that goals should be measurable, observable, realistic, flexible, positive, and attainable. The above are all good recommendations but the idea here is to not get too formalistic. Instead strive for practical, understandable goals that reflect the service users' intentions. In summary, goals state what is to be accomplished before we take action.

Some of the key points in this section are in Box 4.1. The next section will discuss the importance of research in anti-oppressive advocacy.

Box 4.1 Key Points: Defining the Problem

- Use privilege and P/C/S analysis to bring background and context to the problem definition.
- Respect service users' decisions as they are the experts on their own lives and ulti-mately have to live with the decision.
- Use your support networks when you are feeling discouraged, uncertain, or intimidated (your network will understand).
- Be as inclusive as possible—include all family members, all group members, and as much of the community as possible in defining the problem.
- Make sure goals are consistent with, and follow from, the analysis of the problem.

Background Research

According to Schneider and Lester (2001), few things can undermine an advocacy action faster than having incomplete or incorrect information. The legitimacy of the advocacy and the reputation of the advocate are compromised if the advocacy is poorly supported by facts. Failing to do background research or to understand the historical context may result in losing a case. Baines (2011) encourages anti-oppressive practitioners to under-stand the problem in relation to its historical context. Lee (2001) stresses the impor-tance of constructing a "clear idea of the situation and events that led to the need for the intervention of an advocate" (p. 23). Moreover, Schneider and Lester (2001) explain that advocates need to be ready for the demands of questioning by those in authority. They encourage advocates to focus on facts, not "guesswork, hunches, and anecdote" (Schneider & Lester, 2001, p. 121)—however, I would not entirely discount or disregard them either. Advocacy is complicated and dynamic; therefore, guesswork, hunches, and anecdotes used with discretion and reason by an experienced advocate can contribute to unique and creative strategies and solutions. For instance, it is important to attend to a rumour that an authority figure has personal circumstances that may make them predisposed to a positive decision for a service user. Or, you would want to take note of off-the-record information that a high-level politician has a child with autism spectrum disorder (ASD) if you are looking for allies among decision makers for your advocacy to develop comprehensive early interventions for children with ASD.

Some of the advocacy literature makes use of the **generalist** or **problem-solving approach** in social work (Hoefer, 2012; Kirst-Ashman & Hull, 2006). The model is one human service professionals will be familiar with, which requires the service provider to gather information and do research relating to the problem during all initial stages of work. The research and background information is incorporated into the work of understanding the problem, issue, or need or as part of the assessment stage (Kirst-Ashman & Hull, 2006). Regardless of the labels, the intent is similar to the one described above in that significant information is gathered pertaining to the service user's need for advocacy. While much of the literature outlines distinct stages where specific work is undertaken by the advocate, it is important to remember that research and information gathering are essential ongoing elements of advocacy work at every stage. Even though advocacy is often thought of as action focused, research and information gathering is a necessary practice to adequately ground the advocacy action.

While much of the collection of background information is done during the initial stages of contact, it is important to be in the habit of continuous current inquiry. The use of smartphones provides almost instantaneous access to current legislation and policy. (Although the internet is an excellent source of information, it is important to be critical of what you read as there is also a lot of misleading and incorrect material.) Excellent sources of information are the municipal, provincial, and federal levels of government in Canada. Most have posted complete copies of legislation, regulations, and policies. Instructions on filing appeals, complaints, and requests for information are readily available. The public library can also be a tremendous resource. Access to professional and academic journals as well as newspapers and news magazines helps the advocate research the social and political conditions associated with the problem. Spindel (2000) recommends developing working relationships with a wide range of experts. Of particular help may be lawyers, nurses, doctors, academics, government bureaucrats, and policy analysts. For instance, one important source of information for advocates are those I call "good bureaucrats"—high-level bureaucrats in health and social service institutions with whom advocates might cultivate lines of communication. These "good bureaucrats" will be able to provide pertinent information (not illegal or confidential) for advocacy. The information can help advocates to be prepared and preemptive when regressive changes are proposed, rather than always reacting once changes are made. The identity of these good bureaucrats should be protected so that they do not face reprisals in their workplace, such as the denial of promotions or demotions. Good bureaucrats are strongly motivated to try to stop regressive policy changes that may have a detrimental impact on thousands of people, but are not able to take on the issue themselves. Other specialists may also be helpful depending on the particular advocacy problem. An environmental scientist may be a very useful source of expert advice for an advocacy group fighting to stop an oil pipeline in their community, or a pediatric specialist for advocacy on behalf of children. In the two cases discussed above, Eric facing an eviction and Jerry being misinformed by his landlord about his ability to give notice, it was important for the advocate involved to have a clear understanding of the legislation that provides protection for tenants. Each province and territory in Canada has legislation governing landlords and tenants. If an advocate is going to do advocacy in a particular policy area, it is important to become an expert on the laws, policies, and procedures governing that policy area.

Box 4.2 Key Points: Background Research

- Remember that an advocate's reputation depends to a large degree on the quality of their research.
- Focus research on legitimate, quality sources.
- Assess carefully but also attend to guesswork, hunches, and anecdote. I would add rumours, gossip, intuition, and other subjective sources as important contributions to advocacy.
- Understand that gathering information is good practice and part of every stage of advocacy work.
- Use critical analysis skills in research to find valid sources as there are many pranksters and charlatans on the internet.
- Turn to other professionals as important sources of information and supportive allies in advocacy work.
- Know the legislation in the area of advocacy in which you are working.

Planning

Without a clear understanding of what you want to accomplish, it is unlikely that you will achieve what you thought you wanted.

(Hoefer, 2012, p. 85)

Advocacy planning is a process of determining where you are now, where you want to end up (or your goal), and how or what you want to do to get there. Spindel offers an advocacy planning model called "Six Steps to Success" (2000, p. 12). Her model includes identifying the problem, doing research, identifying decision makers, reviewing alternatives, ensuring informed consent, and executing the strategies as requested by the client. While Ezell (2001) does not specifically discuss advocacy planning, he contributes a decision-mapping plan that requires the advocate to consider a series of questions.

The first question asks, "[w]hat tasks need to occur to change the advocacy target, when, and by whom" (Ezell, 2001, p. 148)? The second and third questions ask, what is needed to complete the tasks and when should decision makers be contacted? The fourth question asks, who are the key decision makers? Finally, a determination needs to be made as to the "sources of resistance or opposition" (Ezell, 2001, p. 149). Kirst-Ashman and Hull (2006) recommend a plan that, first of all, considers the advocacy assessment and then reviews the "resources, strategies, and tactics" (p. 473). Hoefer (2012) offers a comprehensive discussion of advocacy planning, providing a definition and a helpful discussion of the purpose and useful tables and examples. While more experienced advocates may fold the planning process into assessment, research, or strategy, I think it is important to make it a distinct step especially when advocacy is a relatively new action for the service provider or the service user.

The advocacy plan recommended here will draw on the approaches discussed above, as well as power, politics, conflict, the analysis of privilege, and the P/C/S model of oppression from Chapters 1 and 2. As was noted above, the approach discussed here is most appropriate for service providers and service users relatively new to advocacy. However, planning is important in advocacy even for the experienced advocate because the consequences are borne not only by the advocate but also by the individual, community, or group the advocate is trying to help. If planning is done well it will provide the advocate and the service users with confidence and power. The strength and comprehensiveness of the plan provides an anchor for strategy choices and a form against which to integrate the analysis of the problem, goals, context, and the background research. The plan is a concretization of the ongoing analysis. While analysis takes place throughout the advocacy process, at this stage the advocate and the service user(s) should commit the plan to paper in a clear, structured format. Strategy choices and actions should relate to the plan.

Hoefer (2012) explains that many advocacy actions have failed because of a lack of planning. Likewise, as we touched on in Chapter 2, too much planning without action can result in "paralysis through analysis" (Ezell, 2001, p. 38). That is, too much planning without action can result in missing important opportunities to bring about change. A balance must be struck, based on the context of the advocacy, between the time spent doing analysis and action. Box 4.3 provides an advocacy plan outline. This is followed by another outline (Box 4.4) using an example from my experiences as a college professor. As with all case studies in this book, it is inspired by real experiences but does not describe a specific person or circumstance. I use a personal experience here to illustrate that the need to do advocacy or to support someone in their advocacy efforts can arise at any time and in many different circumstances. It might surprise students to learn that professors would be involved in advocacy of this type; they may only be accustomed to seeing professors as authority figures who hold power over students and in many cases are the opposition in advocacy, for example with respect to academic appeals. Students do not often seek to ally with their professors when they face personal difficulties. (Although it is my sincere hope that more professors will be encouraged to use their considerable positions of status and power to improve the lives of others including their students.)

Box 4.3 Advocacy Plan Outline

Date:

Advocacy Problem
As defined by the service user, group, or community (may be facilitated by the advocate).

Advocacy Goal
Comes from a shared analysis of the problem and is defined by the service user, group, or community (may be facilitated by the advocate).

Background Research & Current Context
Describe the background and current situation in relation to the advocacy goal.

Consider all factors important to the service user(s) including the following:

- historical circumstance of the advocacy problem
- relations of power and privilege (key decision makers)—Who has the power to make a decision? What are the service users' sources of power? Is there anyone who can be called upon who has sources of power (weath, status, numbers, information, belief, or conviction) to help the service user(s) reach their goal?
- political considerations, small "p" and big "P"
- relevant policy and legislation

Strategy Options: P/C/S
For a more detailed discussion of strategy see the next section in this chapter and review the P/C/S model in Chapter 1.

- Is the strategy aimed at the personal level of oppression and changing the way others think, feel, and act?
- Is the strategy intended for a cultural level of oppression or at community "values, norms, and shared patterns of seeing, thinking, and acting" (Mullaly, 2002, p. 49)?
- Is the strategy meant for the structural level of oppression or the social, economic, and political institutions and organizations (legitimized, legalized, and institutionalized through laws, regulations, and legislation)?

Execute the Plan
Be specific about what has been selected as an overall strategy and what will be the tactics used to achieve it. See Chapter 5 for a more detailed discussion of action.

Box 4.4 Sample Advocacy Plan: Abby—Social Service Work Student in Conflict with the Law

Date: April 20, 2017

Advocacy Problem

Abby, a full-time student who will soon graduate from the Social Service Work Program at a community college, has come to her professor with a problem. She was out with her friend, Tory, a few weeks ago having a night out before final exams. Abby and Tory were sitting in Tory's parked car before going to a club to meet some friends. Tory suggested that they first smoke a joint (cannabis). They were smoking the joint when a police officer appeared at the window of the car. Subsequently they were both given an Appearance Notice, which included a court and fingerprint date.

Advocacy Goal

Abby's goal is to avoid a conviction for possession of cannabis.

Current Context

In Canada a possession of cannabis (under 30 grams) charge could result in a $1,000 fine and/or six months in jail in addition to a criminal record. However, because the charge is minor and this is a first offence, the judge may decide on an unconditional or conditional discharge. A discharge means the person is found guilty but because of their history and character they will not have a criminal record. A conditional discharge means the person charged is on probation and must carry out the conditions of the probation for a specified period of time, after which the person is treated as if they have not been convicted of a crime (Canadian Bar Association, 2014).

The political situation in Canada with regards to possession for small amounts of cannabis is evolving. While the official charge remains in the Criminal Code, the actual practice on the front lines in the courts and with law enforcement officers is varied. Minor occurrences of cannabis smoking are often ignored by front-line police officers or in some instances the officer simply confiscates the cannabis and does not issue an Appearance Notice.

In some jurisdictions minor offences such as Abby's may be flagged for diversion even before they are sent to court. In these circumstances a meeting is scheduled with a diversion worker and the accused is required to pay a fine, or perform community service work. The charges are put on hold until the accused completes the community work or pays the fine and then the charge is withdrawn.

It is unlikely that Abby will receive a jail sentence but she is very concerned about the possibility of having a criminal record. She has been offered a position at the agency where she is doing her field placement, working with youth who are homeless. The agency expects their workers to have a clean criminal record check.

Many social service agencies require their volunteers, placement students, and staff to have a criminal record check. Policies vary from agency to agency. Some agencies require staff to have no criminal record while other agencies will hire staff with a criminal record depending on the number of charges, the type of charge, and the length of time since the conviction. A criminal record may also limit someone's ability to join professional regulation bodies such as the Ontario College of Social Workers and Social Service Workers. In addition, a criminal record may limit travel outside of the country and the ability to obtain certain types of insurance. Therefore, people with a criminal record wanting to work in the social service field are at a distinct disadvantage. Employers have little difficulty finding new staff with a clear record because of the competitiveness of the employment market in this sector.

Abby is at the end of her two-year diploma program so her personal finances are exhausted. She is a low-income student and lives with her parents and two younger siblings. Everyone in her family works to try to make ends meet; even her two younger siblings have part-time jobs in addition to attending school. Abby's parents are very proud of her because neither of them had the opportunity to attend college. Her two younger siblings look up to her and now are thinking about pursuing higher education too. Abby feels deeply guilty and ashamed about the charge and has not yet told anyone in her family. Further, because of her financial situation Abby does not have money to hire a lawyer or to pay a fine. She had to muster all of the courage she had just to come to speak to me, her professor.

It is because of these circumstances that Abby is really motivated to do whatever it takes to avoid a criminal record for this charge.

Strategy Options: P/C/S

Abby's advocacy will focus on the personal level of oppression. She is focused on convincing the Crown attorney to send her file to a diversion worker because of the serious consequences a criminal record would have for her career as a social service worker. Abby clearly wants to keep her strategy options low key and confidential.

Although she feels intimidated, she thought she would try to organize a meeting with the Crown attorney to explain her situation further. Abby's plan is to convince the Crown attorney to withdraw the charges. Abby and I discussed whether it would be better for her to go alone or to bring someone to the meeting. After some consideration it was decided that Abby would go to the meeting on her own to present her case. If she is not successful she will try to make another appointment and bring along someone who could support her advocacy.

I gave Abby the contact information for the Students' Association (SA) at the college. Through the SA, Abby will have access to free legal advice provided by a lawyer. The lawyer will not represent her but it is a good idea to know your legal rights in these circumstances.

We discussed the kinds of information and documentation she should bring with her to the meeting with Crown attorney. We came up with the following:

- a copy of her field placement evaluation with an excellent rating
- a copy of her academic transcripts (75-80 per cent grade average)
- a letter from me, her professor, advocating to have the charges dropped and attesting to Abby's good character. I also offered to call the Crown attorney and/or to attend a meeting if it was needed.
- a letter from her part-time work employer and her field placement would have also been useful but Abby wanted to keep the situation confidential.

continued

The advocacy in this example did not target oppression at the cultural or structural levels. However, the oppression experienced at the personal level is interconnected with the cultural and structural levels of oppression. An example of a strategy at the cultural level in this case is to organize a public education campaign to dispel the myths concerning the harmful effects of casual cannabis smoking. An example of a strategy at the structural level of oppression is to try to advocate for the legalization of cannabis—to have the charges removed from the Criminal Code of Canada.

Execute the Plan

In summary the advocacy plan had Abby as the primary advocate and the professor acting as a consultant and support.

Her overall strategy is to quietly convince the Crown attorney that she is deeply sorry about smoking cannabis and that she would not participate in this behaviour again. She is a serious and committed student and soon will be a social service worker. She is a hardworking, goal-oriented person and this charge is clearly an exception. Her career in the field of social service work may be in jeopardy because of this charge.

Abby will gather information about her rights from her meeting with the SA lawyer. She will assemble the relevant supporting documents listed above. Then she will make an appointment to meet with the Crown attorney to try to have the charges sent to a diversion worker.

As a contingency tactic if she is not successful, Abby will schedule a second meeting with the Crown attorney and bring someone to support her advocacy efforts.

An additional contingency tactic is to try to find a lawyer who will agree to represent her pro bono or on a payment plan. The lawyer may have more success pleading her case with the Crown attorney or the judge in court.

A third contingency tactic is to explain the charge and the circumstances honestly and clearly to her potential employer in the social service agency and advocate for an exception to their need for a clear criminal record check.

Finally, if Abby is convicted and receives a criminal record, she will apply for a pardon so she will not be held back in future employment opportunities. Currently she would have to wait five years before she would be eligible to apply for a pardon for a summary conviction. During those five years Abby should be law abiding and not receive any additional criminal charges. If her application for a pardon is successful, a subsequent criminal record check would not show any charges or that she was given a pardon.

Advocacy planning is an important part of working with service users to bring about change. Whenever conceivably possible, the service user should lead the advocacy, be an active participant, or at the least be keenly involved. In the example above, Abby took the lead in the advocacy planning and used the professor as a consultant. In some circumstance this may not be possible when the service user has a disability or other personal circumstances that prevent full participation. Small children and service users with dementia, acquired brain injuries, or active psychosis may be temporarily or permanently limited in their ability to participate in advocacy planning and action. Under these circumstances, the advocate may work with family members or close friends of the service user.

When advocacy planning moves beyond the personal level to the cultural or structural levels, one or more individuals may be planning advocacy on behalf of small or large groups of people. For instance, in the advocacy plan above, Abby's strategy at the cultural level may be to initiate a community education campaign to inform the public on the detrimental effects of criminal records due to the criminalization of cannabis. Those involved in this type of strategy will be advocating on behalf of a large number of people who may not even be aware of the advocacy. In 2011 alone, over 28,000 people were charged with possession of cannabis in Canada (McKnight, 2011). Equally, if Abby becomes involved in a structural level advocacy strategy to have possession of cannabis removed from the Canadian Criminal Code, she would be advocating for thousands of people who are not involved and not even aware of her advocacy campaign.

Advocacy plans need to be flexible and should be revised when resources, commitment, and other circumstances change. In fact, the plan may be rewritten several times when a particular strategy or tactic is unsuccessful. Some students in a course I teach on community change found this out during their efforts to complete a social action assignment. The five students planned to run a community education campaign and raise money for a local social service agency. The initial advocacy plan they constructed had to be revised several times when unforeseen circumstances came up. One group member became ill and was hospitalized, the group was not able to secure permission from the college to set up a public information booth, and they were not able to sell tickets for a raffle to raise money for their cause because it required a lottery licence from the municipality. Advocacy plans should to be living documents that are revised as circumstances evolve.

Advocates may need to establish contingency plans as was done in the case study above. Abby and the professor worked on immediate, intermediate, and long-range plans. The plans projecting into the future provide a path for service users who may be discouraged or even distraught about the current situation. The plan can bring hope and inspire initiative when service users encounter a setback. Abby could see that if she was not successful in convincing the Crown attorney to divert and withdraw the possession charges, she already had alternative plans to pursue her goal. It is important not to underestimate the power of hope, optimism, and confidence in any advocacy. Planning with the service user can help them to feel empowered and confident about continuing to fight the oppression they are experiencing.

According to Hoefer, advocacy planning should be both strategic and tactical (2012, p. 97). The further the advocacy plan stretches into the future, the more relevant the strategy. I would add that strategy is also fundamental when the advocacy moves to the cultural or structural levels or when greater numbers of people are involved. As the advocacy plan unwinds successfully, or not, tactics are developed to carry the overall strategy.

Advocates may also want to consider the focus and order of the strategies and tactics in the advocacy plan. In Abby's advocacy plan it was pretty clear that the initial and central focus would be on trying to convince the Crown attorney to withdraw the charges (or ask for a diversion). The service user and the advocate will need to decide which strategy will be carried out first, second, and so on. Perhaps some strategies will need to be carried out simultaneously. Further decisions will need to be made about which tactics will be used within the chosen strategy area and in what ways they will be completed. In some contexts, strategies and the associated tactics should be readied in advance for if or when opportunities or circumstances permit: A press release is written and ready to be released by Abby's group when the government tables the new legislation to legalize cannabis possession. The next section will focus more specifically on strategy decisions and types as discussed in the literature.

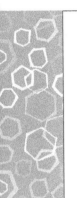

Box 4.5 Key Points: Planning

- A good, clear advocacy plan provides confidence and power to service users and advocates.
- Planning is a comprehensive practice that draws on the advocate's experience, knowledge, and understanding of theory, process, and policy.
- It is preferable that service users lead the advocacy and the advocate acts as a consultant and support.
- Advocacy plans should be flexible and pragmatic to accommodate inevitable changes in circumstances.

Strategy

Identifying and selecting strategy options are vital parts of the advocacy planning process. Elizabeth G., an Aboriginal woman active in advocacy and community change work, advised that strategy is the most important consideration of advocacy. (For more of Elizabeth's personal story and advocacy work see Chapter 6.) Selecting a strategy is a mutual process between the advocate and individuals, groups, or communities. This section will differentiate between strategies and tactics, review consent and risk factors, and discuss the importance of assessing the opposition. It finishes with a discussion of five broad advocacy strategy approaches.

Differentiating Strategy and Tactics

In the literature the terms *strategy* and *tactic* are sometimes used interchangeably (Ezell, 2001). Others use either *tactic* or *strategy* (Lee, 2001), while Schneider and Lester (2001) note that there is a difference between the two. I am not a disciplinarian for precise terminology, although I believe it is important for service users and advocates to have a common interpretation of frequently used terms in order to move the process along efficiently. For the purposes of the discussion about advocacy in this book, *strategy* will be used to discuss the general, more abstract, approach to an advocacy effort. The term *tactic* will "represent the specifics" of the plan (Kirst-Ashman & Hull, 2006, p. 473). That is, tactics are the smaller, specific steps that are consistent with the overall strategy. For instance, a strategy for a group of people with physical disabilities trying to improve accessibility in the community might be a public education campaign. The first tactic associated with such a strategy involves meeting with city officials to educate them about the importance of accessibility planning in public transportation and curb cuts. The second tactic is to develop a pamphlet to educate the general public about the barriers faced by people in wheelchairs and to leaflet a neighbourhood, perhaps one with a higher number of accessibility problems. (To "leaflet" means to put the pamphlet in mailboxes and hand copies out on the street to people passing by.) A third tactic is to plan a public forum for the community, inviting presenters from organizations that speak out on behalf of people with disabilities such as DAWN-RAFH (Disabled Women's Network-Réseau d'Action des Femmes Handicapées), the Council of Canadians with Disabilities, or NEADS (National Association of Disabled Students). The strategy and tactics are represented in Figure 4.2.

The same type of model could be developed for an overall strategy choice that involves changes in legislation, legal advocacy, or administrative advocacy (to be discussed

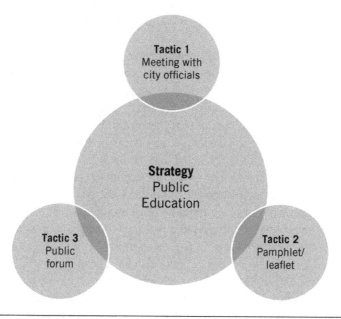

Figure 4.2   Strategy and Tactic Options

further below). Each strategy choice will include several tactics that will need further refining, by asking questions like:

- Will the tactics be carried out in a specific order or will two or more be carried out simultaneously?
- Are any tactics dependent on the success or failure of another tactic?
- Are any of the tactics dependent on specific external timelines?

Examining Consent, Capacity, and Risk

Spindel (2000) stresses the importance of respecting service users' strategy choices. She makes a good point when she says that "no advocacy initiative is entirely risk free" (p. 12). A full range of strategy and tactic options should be discussed with service users, including the potential risks and benefits of each. Some service users feel that strong public advocacy is not something they want to become involved in and only consent to participation in advocacy approaches that remain behind the scenes and out of the public eye. A service user I once worked with had been the victim of severe abuse at the hands of her husband, a police officer. She was afraid that any open or public advocacy on her behalf would result in further abuse and perhaps even death. She felt we could only use quiet and private advocacy strategy and tactics. Fear can influence a service user's capacity to consent to and participate in certain strategies and tactics in other circumstances as well. For instance, a service user may have arrived from a country where advocacy actions are severely punished with physical brutality, imprisonment, or even death. Open public advocacy strategy may be curtailed by these and other considerations. A former colleague of mine worked as a social worker in a family doctor's office. Her primary role was counselling; however, she also found it necessary to do advocacy on behalf of some of the service users. She was nearly always successful when the service users allowed her to do advocacy on their behalf. For example, she helped one woman receive additional time away from her work while recovering from the ravages of surgery and treatment for cancer. Initially, her physician had recommended that she return to work almost immediately after treatment. Unfortunately many service users she saw would not agree to advocacy because they were afraid of challenging their doctor or of appearing ungrateful. Even if the advocate believes strongly that a certain strategy is the best choice for success, the decisions of the individual, group, or community must be respected.

Spindel (2000) highlights the importance of examining each strategy and tactic option with the service user in order to consider if they have the capacity to follow through. For instance, low-income, busy, working parents may not have the time, energy, or financial resources to take on a long, multi-layered advocacy strategy over several years to battle a local school board intent on closing the community school their children attend. In addition, the likely possibility of success must also be carefully considered. The advocate should research whether similar battles to fight school closures have been successful all the time, sometimes, or never. The advocate should research what strategies were successfully used in other similar efforts. Participants need as much information as possible in order to assess their capacity to contribute and follow through on the advocacy strategies. Spindel (2000) categorizes strategy choices into low-, medium-, and high-profile depending on the degree to which the strategy has the potential to receive broader public exposure. The intent of low-profile strategies is to keep the advocacy efforts out of the media. A low-profile strategy may be to write a letter of complaint about a service provider in a Service Canada office because of the offensive and racist treatment of a recipient of CPPD (Canada Pension Plan Disability). The letter of complaint may have the intended result, such as a change in the behaviour. However, it is important to consider, too, that every advocacy strategy has the potential to become public regardless of the precautions taken. Electronic communications, while immensely convenient, also open up the prospect that private correspondence, part of a low-profile strategy, may be inappropriately shared and spread through various online networks. Individuals, groups, and communities need to be aware of the potential risks and benefits of strategy and tactic choices. It is also recommended that the service user and advocate sign an agreement once the plan is finalized giving the advocate permission to access relevant confidential information and to carry out the advocacy plan. An example of an advocacy agreement form is provided in Appendix 1.

Assessing the Opposition

It may seem obvious that service users and advocates must assess the opposition. In fact, it is a very natural thing to do when individuals and institutions stand in the way of rights or progressive social change. In advocacy the opposition is sometimes clear, such as a front-line service provider treating service users rudely and denying them legitimate benefits. Or the opposition can be as broad as public opinion or community values—some members of the community believe that people are poor because they are lazy or that people with addiction problems are weak-willed. Different forms of opposition require different strategies. This section will discuss the importance of assessing the opposition in order to be more successful and to make the best use of time and resources.

Schneider and Lester recommend analyzing "the people, issues, and environment in order to determine the nature of the opposition" (2001, p. 124). The analysis should consider the strength of the opposition in terms of personal power and influence, financial resources, strategic or confidential information, and number of supporters. In Chapter 2 we examined power from the perspective of those doing advocacy. The same type of analysis applies to the opposition and what resources they will employ to stop you from achieving your advocacy goals. The targets of most advocacy action can be found in the upper levels of government and business. For example, if the minister of social services is against an increase in welfare rates, advocates know they will be up against someone with considerable power and resources. Working together, the advocate and the service users should review the capacity of the individual or group and that of the opposition to determine if they have the resources to proceed with the advocacy action.

Another consideration is whether the target of the advocacy is a single person or a group, community, or the general public. The target, for example, may be a single person such as the executive director of a group home for people with acquired brain injury, or the president or CEO of a nursing home chain. Spindel calls these individuals "key decision makers" (2000, p. 9). She recommends that advocates and service users not waste their time working their way up from the front-line workers. Instead, advocates should find out who in the organization has the ability to make a decision about the service user's concern. Working through the official lines of authority is time-consuming and unnecessary.

If time and circumstance permit, try to find out as much as possible about the advocacy target. Google their name and organization, and/or contact people who know the key decision maker. Small details about the individual may help to frame the advocacy. For example, if the executive director of the group home has a close relative with an acquired brain injury (ABI), this information may be helpful if the advocacy action is aimed at helping a service user with ABI who is experiencing abuse.

Lee (2011) cautions against a simplistic analysis of the opposition as "those for us, and those against us" (p. 213). In advocacy strong polar divisions are rare and therefore the analysis of the opposition requires time and considerable deliberation. Schneider and Lester (2001) offer a categorization of the opposition into three levels: those who may need additional knowledge; those who are uninterested; and those who are undoubtedly unsupportive. Strategy decisions follow from the analysis of how the opposition in each category should be managed. Those who are expected to be supportive if they receive additional information may be provided with a brief, outlining, for example, the benefits and costs of a skate park and basketball court in an underserviced low-income neighbourhood. For those who are uninterested, the advocacy strategy may be organizing an event or engaging the mainstream or electronic media through video or print. Imagine a YouTube video featuring youth skateboarding on the streets because they do not have a safe place to go. Do not dismiss the unsupportive category as hopeless in terms of changing their mind. It is wise to listen to their concerns and understand why they oppose the advocacy. Perhaps a compromise can be reached through mediation. However, it is important not to waste too much precious time and resources on this unsupportive group unless it has the capacity to turn the other two groups discussed against your advocacy. If the advocacy focuses on those who need more information and those who are indifferent, it will be more successful and the youth in a low-income neighbourhood may have a new skate park, basketball court, or playground. Figure 4.3 is a model adapted from the discussion in Schneider and Lester (2001, p. 125).

Broad Strategy Fields

There are several broad strategy areas discussed in the advocacy literature. Some of the literature focuses on cause or systemic advocacy (Ezell, 2000; Kirst-Ashman & Hull, 2001). Most outline a range of strategy options for advocacy with individuals, groups, and communities. The most common strategies include legal, legislative, administrative, public education, and community organizing options. In the literature, these strategy categories are discussed as discreet processes; however, in reality the strategies are often used together to further the goal of the advocacy. For instance, public education and community organizing strategies are often used with legal, legislative, and administrative strategies. These broad strategy fields should be considered using the analysis of privilege, P/C/S analysis, and AOTP. That is, the five areas of legislative, legal, administrative, public education, and community organizing strategy may be utilized when fighting oppression at the personal, cultural, or structural levels. This section describes each strategy area and provides examples of the strategy in action.

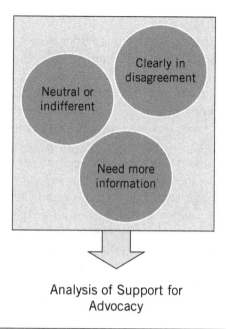

Analysis of Support for
Advocacy

Figure 4.3   Assessing Advocacy Support

Figure 4.4   Broad Strategy Fields

Legislative Advocacy Strategy

Legislative advocacy strategy is referred to as *policy advocacy* in some of the literature. The broad intent of the advocacy is to champion, change, or defeat legislation at the municipal, provincial/territorial, or federal level of government. This type of advocacy requires that the advocate has a deep understanding of political processes and a commitment to long and sustained advocacy action. One author explained that a decade is a reasonable estimate of the time it takes to bring about a change in legislation (Schneider & Lester, 2001). It is also important to understand that legislative advocacy is an ongoing process. Even after legislation is successfully passed, such as unemployment insurance, old age security, social assistance, or health care, the advocacy to maintain or change the legislation continues. The legislation may not be as comprehensive as was advocated for or measures may have been omitted or included that limit eligibility, and so the work goes on. Subsequent elected officials with different political ideologies may attempt to narrow the scope of coverage or dismantle the legislation entirely. Changes to the Employment Insurance Act that redefine "suitable" work are an example of the reduction in coverage. Unemployed Canadians under the new legislation will be required to accept positions that are up to an hour commute from their home and for as little as 70 per cent of their previous wage ("Employment Insurance," 2013). This is a policy that hits low-wage earners particularly hard. Advocates concerned about the rights and benefits for unemployed workers in Canada will try to make sure the legislation is improved and made fair and reasonable. Another example of legislative strategy is the efforts of environmental advocates. Greenpeace and other environmental activists want the Canadian government to set a cap (that cannot be traded away) on the emissions of big industrial polluters (Greenpeace, n.d.). At the 2015 United Nations Conference on Climate Change, environmental activists pushed to strengthen the Paris Agreement with an aim to pressure the Canadian and other governments to legislate a drastic reduction in greenhouse gas emissions in order to slow global warming. Common tactics for legislative advocates include one-to-one lobbying, writing briefs, working on political campaigns, petitions, letter writing campaigns, and participating in demonstrations. In addition, all legislative advocacy strategy includes the use of social media to develop webpages, video, and information sharing capacity. A webpage provides a central online location to share information, host discussion forums, blog, post links and videos, raise money, build membership, facilitate e-petitions or email writing campaigns, and post information about events and demonstrations.

Legal Advocacy Strategy

Legal advocacy strategy in the literature is sometimes discussed under the umbrella of legislative advocacy; however, there is an important distinction between the two, and the advocacy strategies and the tactics that flow from each. Legal advocacy strategy uses existing statutory conventions and institutions such as the criminal or civil legal systems to fight for the rights of individuals, groups, and communities. This type of advocacy practice requires specialized skills and knowledge of the legal and regulatory systems. Courts, tribunals, and hearings are formal, often intimidating settings for the general public.

Advocates comfortable with formal procedures and atmosphere can be exceedingly help-ful to apprehensive service users. An inspiring example of legal advocacy is the fight for equality by Aboriginal women in Canada. Prior to 1985 Aboriginal women lost their status under the Indian Act if they married a non-Aboriginal man. In addition the chil-dren of the couple were not allowed to be status Indians. On the other hand, an Aborig-inal man did not lose his status for marrying a non-Aboriginal woman. In fact, through marriage she acquired Indian status and so did their children. Jeannette Corbiere Lavell was the first to bring action in 1971; she was followed by Yvonne Bédard and later Sandra Lovelace. While Lavell and Bédard won their cases on appeal, the Canadian Government did not take action by making the appropriate changes to the Indian Act. Lovelace lost in Canadian courts, so she took her case to the United Nations Human Rights Committee. In 1981 the UN "found Canada in breach of the International Covenant on Civil and Political Rights" (Indigenous Foundations, University of British Columbia, 2009). In 1985, embar-rassed nationally and internationally, the Canadian government finally made changes to the Indian Act and removed the gender discrimination from Bill C-31.

Legal advocacy can be exceedingly helpful in gaining important rights and re-sources for individuals, groups, and communities. Legal advocates may be employed in a community legal clinic filing appeals to a landlord–tenant board to stave off evic-tions or to a welfare tribunal for disability benefits. Tactics frequently associated with legal advocacy are filing appeals, complaints, reviews, and, in some circumstances, lawsuits. The use of the internet has helped to expedite some of the processes and many official government sites offer printable forms or applications. Often correspon-dence between the advocate and the official government department is through email contact. Processes and notices about meetings, hearings, and deadlines are posted on government websites. But it is important to carefully understand the specific require-ments for each legal process. Even if a substantial portion of the correspondence and filing is electronically based, most legal processes will require official, original copies of evidence such as medical records.

Administrative Advocacy Strategy

The need for specialized skill sets, financial resources, and long-term commitment re-quired for legal and legislative advocacy may sometimes seem to be beyond the reach of new advocates. The point here is not to be discouraged but to be realistic. **Administra-tive advocacy strategy**, on the other hand, is a strategy that often comes naturally to human service workers, especially those new to the field. I have many students, in their first field placement in a community social service agency, confiding their frustration and concern with regards to the treatment of vulnerable service users. The students are burning with the desire to change agency rules, regulations, policies, and practices to improve the lives of service users. One student was very effective at pointing out the inconsistencies (biases) in service delivery in a food bank program where she was doing her first field placement. She noticed that the all-white food bank staff consistently gave the white families with children little treats like chocolate bars or candies in addition to the food package. The racialized families only received the food package, no treats. The student was upset but afraid to bring her concerns to her supervisor at the agency. Together we discussed a tactic where the student would ask "innocent" questions such as "Why do some families receive treats and others don't?" and "When I am working in the food bank how do I know which families to give the treats to?" There is a fairly short period of time that this tactic can work in administrative advocacy, as you have to be new to an agency and plausibly unaware of agency policy and processes. The tactic was effective; after the student brought her concern to her supervisor, the agency developed a policy that *all* families with children would receive treats, when they were available and while they lasted, in addition to the food package. The student was successful in her administrative advocacy and she managed to do it safely so she was not punished for speaking out. Most administrative advocacy involves an element of risk but those with more tenure, power, and authority are in good positions to help develop social agencies into fair, accessible services. Administrative advocacy is a strategy that targets agency policies that are "inefficient, ineffective, or discriminatory" (Kirst-Ashman, 2010, p. 107). Administrative advocacy can be carried out by those who work in an agency; that is, a worker or several workers advocate for changes that need to be made to a social service. Service providers may also advocate for changes in other agencies or for changes in the social service system as a whole, such as the need for new mental health programs for children and youth. Service providers can be involved in administrative advocacy when they start their first job (or even their first field placement) and they can have a significant impact on the progressive change process. Some examples of tactics in administrative advocacy practice include recommending changes to agency policies; attending and organizing meetings to improve services; filing complaints, grievances, or appeals; organizing a union; whistle-blowing; writing letters; petitions; and even participating in or organizing demonstrations when necessary. (For an example of administrative advocacy see Meaghan's story in Chapter 6.) As with legislative and legal advocacy, administrative advocacy can be facilitated by using the internet to research organizational policies and processes. Access to some processes such as filing a complaint may be done online. Connecting with other workers in the agency you work for, or networking with workers in other agencies, is fast and simple with email or texts. Those advocates taking on more risky administrative advocacy such as whistle-blowing or organizing a union should make use of electronic communication with a great deal of caution. Texts and emails can be easily shared and/or hacked. Often administrative advocacy will remain low-key and in-house so the need for webpages, YouTube videos, and Twitter accounts is not necessary. Only when a campaign moves outside of an agency or involves workers from several agencies is it important to make greater use of social media.

Public Education Strategy

Helping the general public to understand an advocacy cause is referred to as **public education advocacy**. The primary goal is to "alter the attitudes and beliefs that support particular policies and practices" (Ezell, 2001, p. 121). One group that has been consistently effective in this category is MADD Canada (Mothers Against Drunk Driving). In the past 30 years the public perception of drinking and driving has shifted from finding it naughty but inevitable to deviant and unacceptable. This change is largely due to the efforts of MADD. According to the group's website, the Canadian chapter of MADD estimates they have saved over 36,000 lives since 1982 (Solomon & Pitel, 2013). Most of the broad strategy fields discussed here, legal, legislative, administrative, and social action would also use public education strategy to further their advocacy cause. Common tactics of public education strategy include using the media to publicize the advocacy message through news stories, editorials, personal testimonials, interviews, advertising, posters, press releases, and press conferences. In addition, advocates make use of newsletters, reports, presentations, conferences, workshops, and even door-to-door appeals. Social media tactics play an important role in public education strategy. Once again a webpage is essential as a hub for information and communication. It can publicize face-to-face community events such as workshops and speakers. Advocates might also use webinars, or a YouTube video, to reach online followers. Today the popular English-language social media sites are Twitter, Vine, YouTube, Flicker, Pinterest, Instagram, Bebo, Google, Habbo, Tagged, LinkedIn, and Tumblr. (By the time you read this book this list may well have changed as new platforms emerge and older ones drop in popularity.) Public education advocacy strategy is ubiquitous with social media and therefore essential to do well whatever the cause.

Community Organizing Strategy
Community organizing strategy is an important part of advocacy at the cultural and structural levels. The strategy brings individuals, with common interests or concerns, together in organizations. Lee (2011) defines the community organizing process as, "the ability of oppressed or disadvantaged people to take action and influence their environments. . . . The aim is to develop power and so they are able to act: to acquire resources; change inadequate institutions and laws; or build new ones, more responsive to their needs and those of all human beings" (Lee, Sammon, & Dumbrill, 2011, p. 8). Schneider and Lester (2001) and Ezell (2001) discuss the importance of bringing people together in coalitions to broaden the base of support for a cause—greater numbers are a source of power (see Chapter 2).

Community organizing is an advocacy strategy that works well when advocates and groups of people are faced with complex problems involving a number of people. The group of people may share a specific geographic location, such as a neighbourhood, reserve, ward, or constituency. They may have a common interest such as concerns about climate change and the environment. Or the people concerned may share a specific attribute such as race, gender, or disability. One advocate used community organizing strategy when she worked with the community on a reserve to try to stop a sudden increase in youth suicides. The community shared race and geographic location, a remote reserve in northern Canada. Their problems were complex and included poverty; overcrowding; lack of adequate sanitation and drinking water; poor quality, rundown housing; lack of indoor plumbing; alcoholism and drug addiction; and mental illness.

Community organizing strategy is often combined with legal, legislative, and public education strategies, and these work well together to take on advocacy at the cultural and structural levels. An example is the Indian Day School class action suit. Here legal action is combined with community organization to sue for compensation for physical and sexual abuse, and the loss of language and culture. Essentially community organizing strategy should be used when the advocacy problem is complex, when the problem is impacting a number of people, and when there is a need for the power that greater numbers will bring.

Community organizing strategy is sometimes portrayed as risky to service users and advocates. It is criticized as being unprofessional and beyond the scope and mandate of ethical practice. The rationale of critics is that community organization may involve breaking rules, regulations, laws, and even risking arrest with detrimental consequences for service users, service providers, and the professions they represent. Yet most community organizing tactics are not controversial or confrontational, such as petitions or letters to the editor. Other tactics are designed simply to garner attention such as street theatre or flash mobs. A few tactics have the potential to evolve into violence or property damage but for the most part the demonstrations, sit-ins, blockades, and occupations are well organized and controlled. When problems arise it is often due to aggressive policing, bystander provocateurs, and undercover agitators, not legitimate protesters.

Community organizing tactics, like all strategy options, must be carefully assessed as to the potential risks and benefits. It should not be ruled out as unethical, unprofessional, or too perilous without careful consideration for the potential gains. Community organizing is an effective and legitimate advocacy that is closely aligned with social justice. This point has been made before, but as a reminder, the important social programs in Canada today—health care, education, and social services—exist because Canadian citizens organized social movements and used social action tactics to fight for the programs, not because benevolent politicians saw a need.

These five broad strategy areas should be considered by the individual, group, or community and the advocate. Together, service users and advocates will use the analysis of privilege and the P/C/S model to consider the level of oppression and the choice of strategies and tactics. Decisions should be carefully documented in an advocacy plan and executed in the agreed upon order. Work may finish when the advocacy is a win, a partial win, or a loss. The advocacy may also conclude without a resolution because the resources of the service users run out or their will to carry on is weakened or lost. Any outcome that is not a complete win is an opportunity to do more advocacy.

Box 4.6 Key Points: Identifying Strategies

- Help the service user assess their capacity for low-, medium-, and high-profile advocacy strategies.
- Carefully analyze the opposition and develop strategies to contend with different types or levels of support.
- Consider the efficacy of the five broad strategy fields for advocacy with individuals, groups, and communities.

The next section will discuss the importance of reflection and evaluation and monitoring in producing important learning opportunities and considering next steps.

Evaluating and Monitoring

Evaluating advocacy work is presented here as a distinct phase in the advocacy process and plan; however, reflecting, reviewing, questioning, and analyzing should be ongoing. Lee (2011) explains that "evaluation is most helpful and most possible if it is built into the organizing process at the onset" (p. 259). In anti-oppressive advocacy the individual, group, or community is made aware of the evaluation process from the start. They must know why it is being done and how it will be used. A good evaluation process is built into the ongoing work of advocacy but understandably, sometimes the advocacy action moves so quickly that there is little time for reflection and documentation. Try to schedule regular reflection after each significant action into the ongoing process, and document this reflective work as it will contribute to the overall evaluation process. Lee (2011) makes a good point when he says that a well-designed evaluation process will result in very few surprises. That is, the evaluation process is designed to be inclusive, with service users participating in design, implementation, and recording. No one should be caught off guard by the results.

The culminating evaluation begins when the advocacy is complete. At that point, the service users and advocate should try to meet and examine the entire advocacy effort. The evaluation should be as inclusive as possible including as many of the advocacy participants as possible. Clearly the larger the number of people involved in the advocacy the more effort it takes to be inclusive, while advocacy evaluations with individuals, families, or small groups may be accomplished by organizing a gathering in an agency meeting room. A meeting or two in a community centre or hall may be a way to evaluate advocacy with a community or group. It is important to focus both on those who attend, and those who do not. There is a variety of reasons why some people do not attend and sometimes the most important information comes from those not attending the large meeting. For example, they may have felt silenced, excluded, or marginalized by the large group. When and where the meeting is held and whether or not day care, interpreters, or food are provided can also have a significant impact on attendance. This is very important information for the advocate and the remainder of the group as it means that more effort should be made to be inclusive. The nature of the exclusion should also be clarified. Was the exclusion based on race, class, gender, religion, sexual orientation, age, or ability? The advocate may need to meet with members individually or in small groups to understand why they felt excluded. In addition the advocate may distribute a survey to the respondents and ensure them that their feedback will remain anonymous. The advocate should try to create an inclusive, relaxed atmosphere for advocacy evaluation, where individuals do not feel excluded or judged.

Setting the context for a constructive advocacy evaluation is primary, but also important is the framework of the evaluation. Service users need to be aware if an evaluation is part of the advocacy process. They should be included in the evaluation process from the start, helping in framing the questions and critically examining the process. Ideally, service users should also decide who will have access to the evaluation document. However, the ideal process is not always reality. Most advocates are employed by not-for-profit human service agencies that need to provide evaluations of their work in order to receive government or foundation funding. These agencies are accountable to a board of directors and community members who expect the work of the agency to be evaluated. If the advocate needs to produce evaluation documents for the agency this needs to be made clear to the community from the start. The community should be encouraged to participate fully in the agency evaluation, and the advocate should also help them meet their evaluation needs by assisting in the design of a community-directed evaluation process. Some of the questions in Box 4.7 may help advocates and communities develop an evaluation.

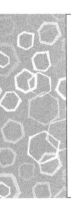

Box 4.7 Sample Advocacy Evaluation Questions

- Did the advocacy work meet the goals set out in the advocacy plan?
- Did the advocacy meet any unintended goals?
- Which strategies and tactics were successful, which were not?
- What did the advocate do well and what could they have done differently?
- Was the service user/community included as an active participant in the process?
- What was learned from the advocacy process?
- Is there unfinished advocacy work to be done?

The final sample question in Box 4.7 leads to the work of monitoring the advocacy. Most advocacy work will have a logical conclusion. That is, the service user's advocacy goal is met as their social assistance is reinstated, or the eviction order has been overturned, or the Employment Insurance appeal is successful. However, a great deal of advocacy requires ongoing monitoring. For instance, through advocacy a landlord has been obliged to make needed repairs to a central heating system. The tenants in the building have been successful in their advocacy efforts. However, the work on the heating system will need to be monitored by the tenants to ensure that it is done in a timely way, that the heating system is working, and that ongoing maintenance and repairs are scheduled and completed. A second example: Community members may be successful, during an election campaign, in getting the environment minister to agree to invest in clean energy and to discourage the use of carbon-based energy sources. However, the community group must continue to monitor the minister's work after the election to ensure that promises made while campaigning are kept. The community will need to make sure the minister is working towards the legislation, regulations, and programs consistent with clean energy that should follow. Sometimes individuals and community groups come to be known as watchdogs, those who identify and document progress and may initiate another advocacy action. A series of advocacy actions may result to ensure all concerns are addressed.

Box 4.8 Key Points: Evaluating and Monitoring

- Schedule reflection and evaluation into the advocacy from the start.
- Though challenging with larger groups and communities, plan an inclusive evaluation process.
- Involve service users in every aspect of the evaluation.
- Build monitoring functions into advocacy when needed.

Conclusion

The five elements of an AOADM explored in this chapter are key to supporting service users and advocates in their advocacy efforts. Woven into the discussion are the principles of P/C/S and privilege analysis as essential supports to advocates working with individuals, groups, or communities. Together, service users and advocates analyze the locus of oppression relating to the advocacy problem and the interconnections between personal, cultural, and structural levels of oppression. Together they define the problem, research, plan, strategize, and evaluate and monitor the advocacy work. Anti-oppressive advocacy connotes full active participation of service users in the entire advocacy process.

Critical Thinking Questions

1. Service users are the experts on their own lives and ultimately must live with the results of the advocacy. Explain why this is an important principle to remember when defining the problem.
2. Discuss why the advocate's professional reputation depends on background research.
3. From your personal or professional experience think of an advocacy problem, then complete the advocacy plan provided in this chapter using your example.
4. This chapter warns against a simplistic assessment of the opposition as the "the bad guys." Find an advocacy problem in the media and apply the spectrum of support and opposition model discussed in this chapter.
5. Five general strategy areas were discussed in this chapter. Find examples online of how these strategies have been used by individuals, groups, or communities to advocate for their cause.
6. It is often not enough to win an advocacy case. Explain why monitoring is an important part of advocacy.

Suggested Readings

Ezell. M. (2001). *Advocacy in the human services.* Toronto: Brooks/Cole Thomson Learning.

Hoefer, R. (2012). *Advocacy practice for social justice.* Chicago: Lyceum Books.

Lee, B. (2001). *Case advocacy.* Scarborough: Nu-Spin Publishing.

Schneider, R., & Lester, L. (2001). *Social work advocacy: A new framework for action.* Toronto: Brooks/Cole Thomson Learning.

Spindel, P. (2000). *Advocacy an empowerment strategy: Confronting systemic injustice.* Scarborough: Nu-Spin Publishing.

Suggested Videos and Websites

World Health Organization (WHO). Stop the Global Epidemic of Chronic Disease: A Practical Guide to Effective Advocacy www.who.int/chp/advocacy/chp.manual.EN-webfinal.pdf

Canadian CED Network and Habitat for Humanity. The Art of Advocacy a Handbook for Non-Profit Organizations www.habitat.ca/files/4752180162832249.pdf

Canadian Federation of University Women. Advocacy Handbook: A Quick Guide to Successful and Fun Advocacy www.cfuw.org/Portals/0/ADVOCACY_HANDBOOK_2011.pdf

National Student Campaign against Hunger and Homelessness. Student Advocacy Handbook www.virtualcap.org/downloads/WCEH/NSCAHH_Advocacy_Manual.pdf

Association for Progressive Communication (APC) www.apc.org/en/home

Note

1.   Low income cut-off, or LICO, is Canada's unofficial poverty line.

5 Taking Action in Anti-oppressive Advocacy

Chapter Objectives

After reading this chapter you should be able to:

1. Carry out anti-oppressive advocacy action based on the strategy and tactics in an advocacy plan
2. Recognize the complexity of the advocacy context and select appropriate strategies and tactics to take action
3. Assess the intersections of the personal, cultural, and structural levels of oppression and anti-oppressive advocacy action
4. Appreciate that advocacy action can have unexpected and negative consequences for the advocate—mutual support is essential

Introduction

> The basic requirement for the understanding of the politics of change is to recognize the world as it is. We must work with it on its terms if we are to change it to the kind of world we would like it to be.
>
> (Alinsky, 1989, p. 12)

Nearly everyone who thinks about advocacy pictures the action—the advocate confronting the unscrupulous government bureaucrat, corrupt cop, or deadbeat landlord. This image is usually inspired by portrayals in the popular media. We observe one or more victims facing off against a nasty, arrogant opposition across a highly polished table in a court or boardroom. Sometimes the advocacy action is more public, such as a demonstration with signs and speeches in front of the Parliament Buildings in Ottawa or thousands of people occupying public spaces in major cities in Canada and around the world. Since the public generally is exposed to the action stage of advocacy, it is sometimes thought that these uprisings are spontaneous reactions to oppression. However, advocacy is rarely entirely unplanned or accidental. In reality, most of the advocacy action we see on the internet or in traditional media has been carefully planned and analyzed for months or even years; and I hope at this point, as discussed in the previous four chapters, that I have made a clear argument for the need to spend time and energy on research, analysis, and planning in advocacy. And while the media's portrayal is correct to a certain extent, that advocacy action may involve loud, confrontational demonstrations, advocacy action is also a creative, nuanced, and introspective process often involving a great deal of planning behind the scenes.

Chapters 4 and 5 work together to complete the advocacy process. Chapter 4 focused more on advocacy planning and Chapter 5 digs deep into the action stage. In this chapter advocacy action is discussed somewhat discretely at the personal, cultural, and structural levels, though in the complex contexts of work in the real world there is rarely such a clear division between levels (personal, cultural, structural). It is more common that advocates and their individual, group, or community partners tackle oppression at more than one level and use one, two, or many strategies. Figure 5.1 depicts the three levels of oppression and strategy options.

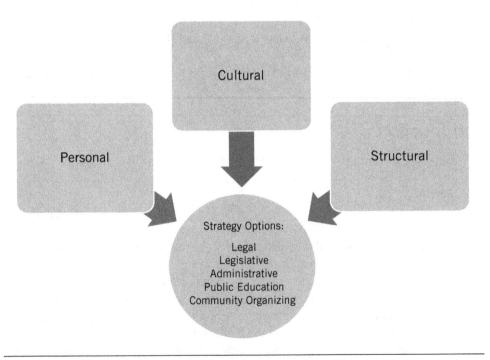

Figure 5.1   Three Levels of Oppression and Strategy Options

How This Chapter Is Organized

The following three sections discuss anti-oppressive advocacy action using representative examples from practice in the field. The first case study focuses on personal level oppression and anti-oppressive advocacy action as Veata, an advocate, tries to help Nada when her welfare is cut off. Confronting oppression at the personal level is how advocates will spend much of their time and attention. Advocacy at the personal level involves advocating for, and with, an individual or family to get something they need or have a right to, or to prevent something from happening that will adversely affect them. Frequently advocacy action at the personal level takes place within the context of social service agencies and government institutions.

The second case study in this chapter describes strategies and tactics used by advocates and service users to target oppression at the cultural level. Power and control of culture by dominant groups over subordinate groups is produced and reproduced through various means including prejudice, discrimination, intolerance, bigotry, and stereotyping. In this section, cultural level oppression is challenged by a network of advocates using pragmatic strategies and tactics, working to change community attitudes towards men who are homeless, specifically those using shelters and how they are impacted by rules there.

Advocacy at the structural level is addressed in the third case study, which looks at a group advocating for more social housing for people with low incomes. The group's efforts are directed to changing institutions, regulations, and legislation that protect privilege and maintain oppression (Mullaly, 2010).

The strategies used in the three case studies are shown in Table 5.1. However, it is important to note that advocates may be confronting injustice at one, two, or all three levels simultaneously and using a single strategy. In other circumstances they may be taking on oppression at one level but using several different strategies. The case studies in this chapter focus on one or two strategy areas as represented in Table 5.1.

Table 5.1 Summary of Case Study Strategy Options

	Reinstating welfare payments— Nada's case (personal level oppression)	End the Seven-day Rule in Shelters Network case (cultural level oppression)	Coalition for Social Housing case (structural level oppression)
Legal Strategy	X	X	X
Legislative Strategy	X	X	✓
Administrative Strategy	✓	X	X
Public Education Strategy	X	✓	X
Community Organizing Strategy	X	✓	✓

In all three case studies the focus is on class oppression, or more specifically oppression aimed at people who are poor. The intent with these examples is to illustrate anti-oppressive advocacy action where it is most commonly employed by advocates. However, it important to point out that service users and advocates also face oppression because of many other factors, among them gender identity and expression, disability, race, sex and sexual orientation, age, religion, ethnic origin, family and marital status, and record of offences. Advocates may work with service users, groups, and communities who are facing oppression in any and all of these areas at the personal, cultural, and or structural levels, and using one or more strategies.

Service providers may find that the majority of their advocacy practice is focused on personal level oppressions. This is also generally the level at which most paid employment is found. However, anti-oppressive work means the use of critical analysis, and the linking of personal problems to cultural and structural issues. Advocates, with service users, will analyze the personal experiences of poverty such as homelessness or food insecurity by making the linkages to cultural level discrimination against people who are poor and oppressive legislation at the structural level. Even if front-line workers are not paid to do advocacy at the cultural and structural levels, it is still important to do the analysis and help the service user to be aware of the linkages. When service users understand that their personal problems are linked to cultural and structural level problems, they may be relieved of self-blame for their circumstances. Advocates also benefit from this analysis even if they do not practice advocacy at the cultural and structural level—working on too many cases, day after day, year after year, and lacking the sense of perspective and context that is gained from this analysis, can result in professional burnout. Occasionally employers will allow front-line workers paid time to be involved in advocacy action at the cultural or structural levels, but most advocates will need to pursue this type of advocacy outside their places of employment.

Personal Level Advocacy Action

This section will discuss advocacy and action at the personal level of oppression. This advocacy is action aimed at the thoughts, behaviours, and beliefs of an individual (Mullaly, 2010; Thompson, 2001). The advocacy action (see Figure 5.2) is preceded by a, typically, standard process (discussed in Chapter 4)—in most social service settings the service users and the advocates meet to define the problem and consider the historical and current contexts. Examples of problems include a young, unemployed woman denied social assistance or a middle-aged man with a disability turned down for independent living in not-for-profit housing. After the discussion, the service users, in consultation with the advocates, arrive at a goal for the advocacy. From this analysis the service users and advocates decide on strategy and tactics. Generally the strategy will fall into one of the categories discussed in Chapter 4: legal, legislative, administrative, public education, or community organizing. The execution of the action is shaped by the strategy and tactics but also the unpredictable circumstances that arise during the action, so even the most carefully developed plans must contend with the unexpected.

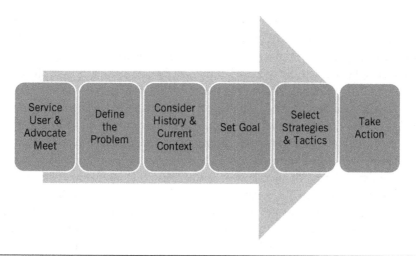

Figure 5.2 Advocacy Planning and Action

Figure 5.2 above is a summary of the advocacy planning process discussed in Chapter 4. To highlight the final stage of the process—taking action—I will provide a fairly typical example from the field.[1]

Case Study 5.1: Reinstating Welfare Payments—Nada's Case

Nada, a welfare recipient, has an appointment with Veata, an advocate at a community and legal advocacy centre. Nada did not receive her welfare cheque at the end of October and she cannot pay her rent or buy groceries. She is a single parent of two children, an eight-year-old boy and a ten-year-old girl. Nada desperately needs to have her welfare reinstated as she has no other means of support. Since Nada's children are in school during the day, the welfare department expects her to be participating in activities that will lead to full-time employment or **workfare**. When Nada first applied for welfare she signed an agreement that required her to attend classes to improve her English. The teachers at the English as a Second Language (ESL) classes are required to take attendance and report absentees to the welfare department. During her first three months on welfare Nada went to the ESL classes regularly. However, in September Nada suddenly stopped attending classes because her son came down with the flu and five days later her daughter contracted the same illness. For nearly three weeks Nada was very worried about her children's health and was distracted taking care of their needs, which included several visits to the doctor and the pharmacy. Finally, towards the end of September, her children were well enough to return to school and Nada returned to her ESL classes. Her money from welfare arrived on time at the end of September and Nada paid the rent and purchased groceries for the family.

In October Nada received two letters from the welfare agency but she is not able to read English very well and put the correspondence aside. She was busy trying to catch up on what she had missed in her ESL class and helping her children get settled into school again after their long absence. At the end of October Nada tried to buy groceries, but found that she had insufficient funds in her account. She was very embarrassed and confused; this had never happened before and she quickly left the store without the groceries she desperately needed to feed her children. In a panic she called her ESL teacher and quickly explained the situation. The ESL teacher referred Nada to a community and legal advocacy centre.

Nada arrives for her appointment with Veata, an advocate at the centre and briefly explains that she had come to Canada from Iraq in 2009 with her two small children. She was happy with her life in Iraq until the war started. Her husband worked for the American military during the war and he, along with four American soldiers, was killed in a roadside bomb blast in 2008. After his death, life became very difficult for Nada and the children. They were very poor as her husband's salary had been their only means of support. Safety was also an issue, as it was well known that families of Iraqis who worked for the Americans were threatened and sometimes killed by opposition forces.

The Advocacy Action Proposal

After getting the background on Nada's situation, Veata completes an advocacy plan with the goal of having Nada's welfare returned as soon as possible. They settle on administrative strategy for the advocacy action. Administrative advocacy strategy targets agency policies and processes. The advocacy action (summarized in Box 5.1) begins with one initial tactic associated with the administrative advocacy strategy—contact the welfare department and persuade them to reinstate Nada's benefits. In Nada's case, and in most advocacy cases, there is no need to use the additional tactics or strategies as the first tactic is often successful. As a reminder, the advocacy tactics are outlined in Box 5.1 to demonstrate what may be done in a specific case within a certain context; the list is not a formula, as contexts are complex and each case must be carefully analyzed and planned. As was noted above welfare is a provincial/territorial responsibility and advocacy practices must contend with different administrative contexts, and therefore plan carefully based on the precise circumstance of practice. The advocacy action proposal summarized below imagines what might be developed for a service user such as Nada.

Box 5.1 Advocacy Action Proposal—Personal Level

Develop advocacy action proposal and use administrative advocacy strategy →

Tactic #1   call the welfare department and advocate for the reinstatement of Nada's welfare →

Tactic #2   write a formal letter to the welfare supervisor/manager and ask for an internal review of Nada's case →

Tactic #3   file a formal appeal and carefully prepare for the hearing →

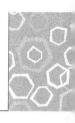

Tactic #4   file a formal complaint

If the administrative advocacy strategy is not successful, the following strategies may be pursued: legislative, legal, public education, and community organizing strategies and tactics to develop changes at the cultural and systemic levels.

Inside and Outside Advocates

I want to take a slight departure to discuss an important consideration for service users and advocates using administrative strategy—**inside** and **outside advocates**. When administrative advocacy is pursued by service providers who want to advocate for change within the agency where they work, they are called inside advocates. Outside advocates, in contrast, advocate for change in other agencies. Veata, in the example above, is an outside advocate. Both inside and outside advocates can effectively bring about change and indeed the two may work together in some circumstances (Ezell, 2001; Schneider & Lester, 2001). Inside advocates, however, must pursue advocacy within their own agency with caution, because pushing too hard may result in being ostracized, marginalized, or even terminated. They should carefully assess their personal circumstances and the seriousness of the cause before they commence any advocacy action and they must also clearly inform the service user of the limitations to their advocacy work as an inside advocate and be willing to make referrals to outside advocates. Outside advocates are free of many of the pressures faced by inside advocates; however, no worker is without organizational constraints. Even outside advocates (like our example, Veata) are accountable to supervisors, managers, and boards of directors for their advocacy work. Agencies that employ advocates set limits to the advocacy work done in their organizational regulations, policies, procedures, and practices. Table 5.2 outlines some of the benefits and limitations of inside and outside advocates.

In Nada's case the inside advocate may be someone who works for the welfare department and is sympathetic and willing to advocate within that agency. Service users may be well-informed and deliberately seek out either an inside or outside advocate depending on their cases. However, in most circumstances the decision making is less calculated. Generally, service users first attempt to resolve the issue themselves. If this is not successful they turn to, or may even be referred to, an outside advocate. In some jurisdictions service providers in welfare departments are expected to refer service users who need advocacy to agencies in the community that provide outside advocates. It is my view that referrals to independent community advocacy services should be compulsory in all Canadian welfare programs and codified in policies and regulations.

Determining the Tactics

Veata and Nada meet to discuss the problem fully and carefully and consider the level of conflict anticipated in the advocacy action. Advocacy action connotes an interplay of power and conflict (Lee, 2001). In Chapter 2 it was noted that advocacy action should

Table 5.2 Inside and Outside Advocates

Inside Advocate	Outside Advocate
Benefits:	Benefits:
• expert knowledge of the agency regulations, policies, procedures, and practices • influential relationships with key decision makers • professional respect and personal relationships • knowledge of organizational culture and terminology • understanding of formal and informal power structures in the agency	• has a more objective view from which to access and exploit agency regulations, policies, procedures, and practices • is backed and supported by their own employing agency's policies • has respect and status in the community as a successful advocate • is free of conflict of interest with regards to salary, promotions, and relationships
Limitations:	Limitations:
• reliance on the agency for personal well-being, salary increases, and promotions (conflict of interest) • risk to professional and personal relationships in the agency • professional role boundaries may be challenged • personal emotional connections to other agency personnel • allegiance to agency structure and policies	• may not have an up-to-date or expert understanding of agency regulations, policies, procedures, and practices • may have acrimonious relationships with agency staff due to past advocacy activities • lacks intimate knowledge of agency culture and informal power structure

*Inside advocates and outside advocates can develop powerful alliances with one another that can minimize or eliminate the limitations in each column for the benefit of the service user.

match the type of conflict. In all likelihood this is a rather straightforward "misunderstanding" type of conflict (Lee, 2001, pp. 21–2). If the level of the conflict is miscalculated and the advocacy response does not match the level of conflict, the result may be that the opposition becomes more entrenched. For example, if Veata were to miscalculate and use advocacy action that is way too aggressive for the level of conflict, such as a letter to the editor or a petition, the result might be that the welfare agency will more aggressively oppose reinstating Nada's welfare. It is important to remember that it is easier to increase the pressure if a confidential advocacy action—such as an email or phone call—is not successful. It is more difficult to back down from more aggressive public actions—like protests—when the opposition's position is fixed. Given that Nada's case appears to be a misunderstanding, the advocacy action is to call the worker responsible for Nada's case to see if her benefits can be reinstated by providing additional information and an explanation. Nada asks Veata to make the call on her behalf as Nada lacks confidence in speaking to someone in authority and is new to the English language and knows she is difficult to understand over the phone. Box 5.2 provides Veata's side of a phone conversation with a caseworker from the welfare department. The advocate's tone during the call should be respectful, serious, and calm.

Box 5.2 Veata Calls the Welfare Department

Veata calls the worker at the social service department and succinctly provides the following information:

Hello my name is Veata Pang and I am an advocate for the Centre for Community and Legal Advocacy.

I am representing Nada Azizi today.

I have sent you an email with a scanned copy of a form, signed and dated by Nada, authorizing me to speak to you on her behalf.

Nada came to see me because her welfare cheque was not deposited in her bank account in October and is seeking my assistance to have her benefits reinstated.

Nada brought a letter to our meeting from your department stating that her benefits are suspended because she missed three weeks of ESL classes in September.

The letter from your department was in English and, although Nada is enrolled in English classes, her language of proficiency is Arabic so she was not able to read the letter.

I reviewed the letter with Nada and she now understands that she should have contacted your department immediately when her children became sick and she could not attend ESL classes.

She has only been in receipt of welfare for three months and is unfamiliar with her responsibilities with regards to welfare.

Nada and I have talked about her situation at length and I would like to take a few minutes to explain the reason why she was unable to attend ESL classes.

Nada's children, ages eight and ten, were both sick with the flu in September. The children were not able to attend school. Nada's eight-year-old son was sick from September 4 to 10 and her ten-year-old daughter was sick from September 9 to 16. I have scanned and sent the doctor's notes to you by email to confirm the diagnoses and dates of confinement.

Because Nada is a single parent without supports it was necessary for her to temporarily suspend her participation in ESL classes to care for her children.

According to welfare policy, recipients are able to apply for the temporary suspension of their responsibilities in order to care for sick family members. Nada should have contacted your office to inform you of her situation and she is sorry for this neglect, but she is new to the requirements and the language barriers contributed to the misunderstanding.

continued

Nada is a dedicated parent and is committed to working hard to improve her English and to finding paid work. She has assured me that in the future she will contact your department if she is unable to meet her commitments. At this point Nada can complete any forms or documentation you require.

I am asking you, on Nada's behalf, to reinstate her welfare immediately as she is behind in her rent and unable to buy food for her children.

Do you need any additional information to make your decision? (*Very likely the welfare department will ask you to follow the conversation up with an email or letter reiterating what you have said in the conversation.*) (*They may also ask that the original doctor's note be sent by courier.*)

When can Nada expect a decision on her welfare?

In summary, when making a call on behalf of a service user:

1. Identify yourself, state your position at the agency, and the name of the agency where you work.
2. Identify who you are representing and that you have written consent to speak on their behalf.
3. State the purpose of your call and the desired outcome.
4. Explain the misunderstanding/mistake that led to the problem and if responsibility lies with the service user this should be acknowledged with an apology.
5. Briefly describe the circumstances/events relating to the misunderstanding/mistake and provide evidence such as doctor notes, records, and references.
6. Say something positive about the service user and their commitment (or steps taken) to ensure it will not happen again.
7. Ask if there is any additional information required to make the decision and when the decision may be expected.

It is likely that Veata, through making the phone call and providing documentation, will be successful in having Nada's welfare reinstated. However, if she is not then the tactics may need to be escalated. The next step may be to follow up the phone conversation with a letter to a supervisor or manager in the welfare department. That person should be the key decision maker, "someone who can implement a client's wish, or reverse a decision which affects a client negatively" (Spindel, 2000, p. 9). It is important to address the letter to a specific person, using their name and title. The letter, even if it is sent by email, should be formal. An example of a letter of advocacy can be found in the Appendix 2. It is very important to use all formal means available in welfare policy to fight Nada's case. Every welfare system in Canada must have an appeals process; in most provinces all decisions can be appealed. Generally the first step is to ask for an internal review. This may involve filling out a specific form or simply sending a letter or email. Typically there is a limited period of time to ask for an internal review, often within 30 or 60 days. If the internal review is not successful the service user may file an appeal. Again there is a limited amount of time to file an appeal. It is important for the service user and the advocate to pay close attention to any deadlines as it would be very unfortunate to lose a case for filing too late. An appeal may involve considerable preparation and there may be specific rules for presenting evidence. Generally it is a good idea for the service user to be represented by an experienced advocate. See Box 5.3 for points to remember when working on an appeal, grievance, or complaint.

Box 5.3 Appeals: The Basics

An appeal presents a good argument and evidence as to why a request should be granted, along with suggested outcomes or resolutions. Advocates should consider the following points when filing appeals, grievances, or complaints.

- Appeals are time-sensitive. Pay close attention to deadlines for filing forms and supporting evidence.
- Be aware that all appeals follow specific procedures or rules on how forms are to be completed, how evidence should be presented, and how meetings are conducted.
- Most appeals require the service user to complete and sign specific forms. The forms must be completed accurately and completely.
- The evidence documents must be discussed in the appeal and attached in the order they are discussed.
- The appeal should present a good argument as to why the request should be granted along with the suggested outcomes or resolutions.

Presenting the Case

Veata does not file an appeal for Nada in this case, but if she had she may have needed to prepare for a formal presentation of the case in front of decision makers at the welfare department. In some ways the formal presentation of a case is similar in format to a phone call or letter, with a few exceptions. Use an approach that conveys self-confidence and respect for those attending the meeting. Spindel (2000) recommends making eye contact with the listeners (especially key decision makers) and maintaining an appropriate volume and pace when speaking. How you appear and even what you wear is important in face-to-face presentations. Schneider and Lester suggest dressing "slightly more formally than the group you are addressing"; the idea is to be remembered for what you said not what you wore (so leave the AC/DC t-shirt at home that day) (2001, p. 105). Hoefer (2012) explains that advocates should also attend to their posture and gestures, as slouching and fidgeting communicate nervousness. Involving the audience in the presentation is also a good idea. This can be accomplished by asking questions, providing visuals, distributing copies of the evidence, and addressing people by their names. The audience is also more involved if the advocate can stimulate their compassion for the service user's position. Try to use a storytelling approach to involve the audience emotionally with the plight of the service user. It is a good idea to write an outline of the presentation, but do not read it. Practice the presentation ahead of time and only refer to your notes for specific facts or quotations. Support the points with evidence and provide copies to those attending the meeting. If there is a time limit to the meeting, stick to it; if not, be reasonable about your timing as most people have an attention span of about twenty minutes (Fisher, 2014). At the end of your presentation restate the request and explain what will happen if the appeal is not successful. Remember to thank those in attendance and ask if they have any questions.

Continuing the Advocacy

In the example used here, it is very likely that Nada's case will be resolved by clearing up the misunderstanding and she will not have to file an appeal. This is a good time to evaluate the advocacy with Nada and consider if there is a need for any ongoing monitoring. Once the evaluation is complete it may be important, in some circumstances, to continue the advocacy even after a successful outcome. In Nada's case the welfare worker is professional and administers the policy appropriately. However, sometimes, because of lack of training, experience, or personal biases, an agency worker may be standing in the way of resolving the misunderstanding. Or a policy may actually be the problem. In these circumstances the service user may want to pursue strategies and tactics to ensure justice for others. Administrative tactics, then, may involve taking action to change policies or practices. For instance, a tactic might be to start a letter writing campaign or file an official complaint to improve training for front-line caseworkers if they were found to make inaccurate, inconsistent, or discriminatory decisions. An advocacy tactic such as a petition may be used to ensure a worker receives anti-racist or anti-oppressive training. If a violation is serious enough the advocacy action may focus on having the worker terminated. Other strategies may also be employed if the advocacy needs to focus on legislative changes or legal issues. These broad strategy areas may be used in combination with public education and community organizing strategies. Broadening the advocacy action further brings the issues to the realm of cultural and structural levels of oppression, which will be discussed more fully in the following sections.

The Intersection of P/C/S

It is clear that welfare legislation contributes to oppression at the cultural and personal levels for Nada and her children. As discussed earlier this case focuses on a single level of oppression and one strategy option. However, let us review again how the levels of oppression intersect to preserve oppression and how advocacy aimed at oppression attempts to roll it back. Veata and Nada's work has a positive impact at the personal level for Nada and her children. It might also be that Veata and Nada's advocacy has resulted in more understanding at the welfare department of the barriers faced by newcomers to Canada— thus impacting the cultural level. If their advocacy had continued using additional administrative tactics and strategy options they may have had an impact at the structural level of oppression on welfare legislation. The next case study focuses on advocacy to fight cultural level oppression.

Cultural Level Advocacy Action

"Cultural meanings are not only 'in the head.' They organize and regulate social practices, influence our conduct, and consequently have real, practical effects" (Hall, 1997, p. 3). Thompson (2001) and Mullaly (2010) emphasise the need for advocates to attend to the cultural level of oppression. Oppression at the cultural level supports racism, sexism, classism, ageism, ableism, homophobia, and other forms of discrimination, all of which profoundly impact the people who come to advocates for assistance. These oppressions are created and recreated in everyday interactions at the personal level and reinforced through language and the media at the cultural level. Advocacy action at the cultural level targets the "values and patterns of behaviour" shaped by dominant groups in society in order to maintain the status quo of inequality and oppression (Thompson, 2001, p. 22). Giroux (2006) and Freire (1998) use the term **cultural workers** to describe those who commit to being culturally conscious and working towards social change and social justice. Cultural workers are politically engaged and work to deconstruct the meaning and motives behind representations of culture that preserve and grow inequality. Cultural workers use social action to help raise awareness, develop alternative culture, and work for greater social justice for oppressed groups. Like advocates, cultural workers use critical analysis, are politically engaged, and action-oriented.

In the human services a common form of oppression for service users is social class, more specifically the effects of poverty and income inequality. Poverty in Canada is intersected by race, gender, age, ability, and sexual preference. That is, you are more likely to fall into poverty if you are a woman, if you are a racialized person, if you are old or young (child or youth), if you have a disability, or if you are a member of the LGBTQ community. The incidence of low income in Canada hovers around 10 per cent of the Canadian population or 3.2 million people (Statistics Canada, 2013). Even though poverty in Canada is a clearly documented fact with a visible presence in our communities (food banks, soup kitchens, homelessness), inaccurate cultural beliefs about the poor persist. Swanson (2001) calls this oppression **poor bashing**. She defines poor bashing as "when people who are poor are humiliated, stereotyped, discriminated against, shunned, despised, pitied, patronized, ignored, blamed, and falsely accused of being lazy, drunk, stupid, uneducated, having large families, and not looking for work" (Swanson, 2001, p. 2). According to Carniol (2005), evidence of poor bashing today can be found, among other widespread instances, in communications from conservative special interest groups that promote neo-liberal policies and take a moralistic view on social issues. These organizations have an excessive amount of influence over policy making in Canada. "Their message is further amplified by a repeated chorus of editorials from media outlets, almost all of them managed and owned by wealthy individuals and corporations" (Carniol, 2005, p. 18).

Case Study 5.2: Changing the Seven-day Rule at Emergency Shelters

The type of work advocates do to fight cultural level oppression is discussed in this section. This example describes how a small network of community advocates works together to change the viewpoints of community service providers and municipal policy makers. It shows how community-based advocates systematically pursue a public education campaign strategy supported by community organizing strategy to change strongly held beliefs about men who are homeless and poor. The result is improved emergency shelter services.

Housing advocates in a medium-sized Canadian city work long, frustrating hours trying to find shelter for a steady stream of poor, unemployed men. Many of the men coming to the housing service for help suffer from mental illness, addictions, or both. Poor physical health is also common, as many of the men live in rundown rooming houses, emergency shelters, or on the streets when it is not too cold. Part of the frustration for housing workers is that there are only three emergency shelters for men in the city, each operated by a different not-for-profit organization and funded by charitable donations and city grants. The three shelters share a common policy that limits a man's stay to seven consecutive days, after which they are required to leave the shelter. For men who are homeless, moving from shelter to shelter is bad enough, but knowing that after three weeks there is no shelter to turn to is frightening, especially when the weather turns colder in the fall. Advocates in the city are very much aware of this problem and speak out publically against the so called seven-day rule at every opportunity. But nothing seems to change. The three shelters have been using the same policy for many years and feel that it is working.

Box 5.4 Homelessness in Canada: The Basics

At a minimum 200,000 Canadians are homeless each year. At least 30,000 people are homeless on any given night. Of these, as of 2013,

- 2,880 are unsheltered,
- 14,480 are staying in emergency shelters,
- 7,350 are staying in violence against women shelters, and
- 4,464 are temporarily in institutional accommodation.

Source: Gaetz, Donaldson, Richter, & Gulliver, (2013), *The state of homelessness in Canada*, p. 5.

Still, though it is difficult for advocates to find the time to discuss the problems created by the seven-day rule because they are too busy working with many service users day after day, informal discussions between them and those affected persist. Advocates meet, too, at community events and social gatherings and the seven-day rule often comes up as a priority issue. The problem is that the many shelter administrators hold outdated and stereotypical views about men who use emergency shelters. They believe that people who are homeless spend the small amount of welfare they receive on alcohol, cigarettes, and illegal drugs—essentially that these men are wholly responsible for their circumstances because they lack motivation and willpower. It is thought that some basic chastisement—in the form of the seven-day rule—discourages dependence and encourages discipline, forcing men to clean up their lifestyles, get jobs, and stop living off the welfare and charity systems. Many front-line shelter workers disagree with the harsh treatment and the seven-day rule, as they have a more realistic perspective based on working with men who are homeless on a daily basis. They see that many men are seriously mentally ill, and that many also have physical illnesses or disabilities. Certainly some use drugs and alcohol to help deal with their circumstances but few have the means to support an addiction. Many of the shelter workers have tried to explain the situation to their managers but to no avail, the seven-day rule remains. Shelter workers are forced to follow the rules set out by their managers, and few are willing to risk their position to try to advocate for change.

The Advocacy Action Proposal

A network of housing advocates and some service users hold a meeting to consider the options and form the End the Seven-day Rule Network. Networks are comprised of "like-minded people in touch with each other so they can share resources and further common interests" (Homan, 2004, p. 385). After several meetings and sessions to do collective critical analysis the members decide that shelter managers will not change the rule until their stereotypical and outdated views about men who use the shelter system are challenged. The rule change, then, depends on challenging and dismantling the views held by those in control of the shelter bed policy. The small network of advocates, shelter workers, and service users, after significant research and analysis, develop an advocacy plan (see Chapter 4). They decide that public education strategy is the best way to target oppression at the cultural level and the public education advocacy action proposal they draw up focuses on providing information based on legitimate research and personal accounts. The Network's tactics start off as low-profile and move to medium-profile. If necessary they commit to going high-profile with extensive use of online and traditional media. The advocacy action proposal summarized in Box 5.5 imagines what a group like the Network might develop.

Box 5.5 Advocacy Action Proposal—Cultural Level

Develop advocacy action proposal and select public education strategy →

Tactic #1   research and write a report based on evidence about men who are homeless →

Tactic #2   write a position paper based on the research, to be distributed at meetings and workshops →

continued

Tactic #3   write one-page articles based on interviews with men who are homeless →

Tactic #4   organize a meeting with shelter managers and present the report and stories →

Tactic #5   organize a one-day workshop for front-line service providers and managers →

Tactic #6   develop a webinar (a live interactive seminar online) for people who could not attend the face-to-face workshop and for the broader public →

Tactic #7   develop a webpage to share information and engage the public (post the report, position paper, stories, photos, videos, interviews, workshop proceedings, and upcoming events) →

Tactic #8   start an online newsletter to keep the public up to date and share information →

Tactic #9   create a short video featuring men who are homeless, to be posted on the End the Seven-day Rule website, YouTube, and Facebook

Legal and administrative strategies may be used in combination with the strategy and tactics above.

In addition to selecting a viable strategy and developing tactics, the Network is using community organizing strategy to build their group. The Network starts off, as is typical in community organizing, with a small number of people concerned about a specific issue. Homan (2004) explains that issues are those things that cause "your blood to boil," or cause you to "shake your head in disgust" (2004, p. 359). The initial small group of front-line workers and people who are homeless knows that it is important to recruit additional members who offer unique perspectives, skills, and resources. Members approach people they know as well as people in the community who are perceived to be sympathetic to their cause. They set out to recruit key people to ensure their organization is representative of the diversity in the community and who they know are the decision makers in the community. According to Lee (2011), key members are needed

- because they possess particular skills;
- because they have credibility within the community;
- because they represent a diverse perspective; and/or
- because of the credibility they have within the opposing group or institution or with media. (Lee, 2011, p. 188)

The Network's efforts to develop and maintain a strong, active community organization contribute to positive, effective strategy and action.

As the organization grows it is clear that more formal leadership is required. Fatima, a front-line worker for a social service agency working with people who are homeless, emerges as a natural leader early in the organizational development and is elected unanimously to represent the End the Seven-day Rule Network. Fatima knows that effective organizations need to keep people busy and involved, so everyone leaves meetings with something to do. The Network uses several meetings to analyze the portrayal of men who are homeless in common cultural institutions—online news, entertainment, social media, mainstream news, and political, cultural, and religious organizations. The Network members discover that men who are homeless are typically portrayed in several stereotypical—and often contradictory—ways: humorous, dangerous, pathetic, drunken, as bums or hobos. The serious news media almost completely ignores the issue of homelessness. When the subject is covered, it is usually in connection to a serious crime, and men who are homeless are identified as having "no fixed address."

After the analysis of the cultural portrayal of men who are homeless, the Network recruits a volunteer professor and graduate student to help with the research and report (Tactic #1 and #2). The 20-page report features evidence, analysis, and recommendations based on data, statistics, scholarly articles, in-depth studies, current stories in newspapers and news magazines, and research papers from other jurisdictions, all pertaining to men who are homeless and use emergency shelters. Jansson (2003), Ezell (2001), and Schneider and Lester (2001) all stress the importance of fact gathering and research to support advocacy. While the report is excellent, the Network knows that busy decision makers, like the managers of shelters, have little time to read and review lengthy documents, so they write a brief two-page position paper based on the research and evidence (see Box 5.6). Ezell describes a position paper as a "well-documented analysis of the presenting problem," and suggests that advocates "propose a solution (at a reasonable price) that has demonstrated effectiveness" (2001, p. 82). The research and position paper should provide support for the advocacy, and it is important to remember that inaccurate, incorrect, or mistaken, information can derail an advocacy campaign. Advocates and their cause are discredited or supported by the quality of their research.

Box 5.6 Position Paper Outline

- **Introduction**: briefly states the purpose of the position paper and identifies the main issues
- **Background/history of the problem/issue**: outlines how the issue evolved to the current context, includes any actions taken to try to solve the problem and analyzes how well these worked
- **Proposed solution**: uses the evidence gathered to develop a well-supported solution to the problem or issue, includes a discussion of why the position (solution) is better than what has been done previously, and explains the implementation plan, viability of the proposed solution, and the expected results
- **Conclusion**: provides a brief summary of the main points and ideas and provides the highlights of the proposed solution

The position paper presents information in a clear and concise manner, with the result that stereotypes on homelessness that result in misguided policies like the seven-day shelter stay rule are skilfully dismantled with ample and credible evidence. The Network makes use of respected sources such as the report *The State of Homelessness in Canada*. That report noted that "causes of homelessness reflect an intricate interplay between structural factors, systems failures, and individual circumstances. Homelessness is usually the result of the cumulative impact of a number of factors, rather than a single cause" (Gaetz et al., 2013, p. 13). In fact, people are generally homeless through no fault of their own. According to Gaetz (2013), structural factors such as unemployment, lack of affordable housing, compromised access to health care, and discrimination are key contributors to homelessness. Other factors noted in the Gaetz report include system failures such as inadequate transition planning for those leaving the child welfare system, hospitals, and other institutions. A third set of contributing factors includes personal crisis, poor mental or physical health, and relational problems. With the facts soundly documented, the Network pursues the remainder of the tactics. They are careful to take time to reflect and evaluate when they complete a tactic. When shelter managers finally agree to change the seven-day rule, the Network continues to monitor the policy change, to ensure managers actually implement the changes.

The Outcome

The seven-day rule is eventually removed by all three shelters in the city. The public education strategy helps shelter managers understand that men who are homeless are a diverse group of people who came to be homeless through circumstances mostly beyond their control. They need to be cared for, encouraged, and above all treated with respect and dignity. Following the advocacy, shelter managers use a consultative approach, including front-line workers, funders, and men who are homeless, to develop a new shelter stay and service policy that reflects their new understanding of homelessness. Shelter stays are extended to six weeks. In addition, case managers are hired to work closely with men to help them find permanent housing, connect them with health and community services, and look for employment. Not only is the new service more compassionate, it is also found to be less expensive as the men, helped by the case managers, no longer need costly shelter beds. The average monthly cost of a shelter bed is high—$1,932 in 2013. This is well above the cost of food and rent for a single person in most cities in Canada (Gaetz et al., 2013, p. 32). Fortunately the public education and community organizing strategies are successful; if however the shelter managers had remained unmoved by the campaign, advocates may decide to examine and pursue other strategies.

The Intersection of P/C/S

Chapter 1 discussed the connections between oppression at the individual, cultural, and structural levels. In this example advocates had tried to fight oppression at the individual level with men who were homeless, but their efforts were frustrated because cultural level oppression blocked the door to policy changes. The cultural level of oppression (stereotypes about homelessness) shapes the oppression experienced at the individual level (by men who are homeless). Conversely, the experiences of oppression at the individual level lead to a public education campaign that challenges the oppression at the cultural level (stereotypical views about men who are homeless). Likewise, cultural level oppression and stereotypes are supported and secured by institutions at the structural level. The next case study will discuss a collective effort to reverse regressive policy changes at the structural level.

Structural Level Advocacy Action

Advocates need intelligence, unshakable ethics, a commitment to social justice, good strategy sense, excellent verbal and written communication skills, a high degree of critical thinking ability, creativity, the ability to motivate and influence others, a lot of sheer grit, and determination.

(Spindel, 2000, p. 1)

According to Thompson (2001), structural level oppression is evidenced in "the network of social divisions and the power relations that are so closely associated with them; it also relates to the ways which oppression and discrimination are institutionalized and thus 'sewn in' to the fabric of society" (p. 22). Structural oppression is conveyed through public institutions, legislation, regulations, and policy. Anti-oppressive advocacy at the structural level engages in actions that take on the social, economic, and political systems in Canada. The goal is transformation of these systems rather than reform. Advocating for reforms to the welfare system in Canada does not eliminate poverty, just like building more emergency shelters or opening more food banks and soup kitchens does not bring an end to homelessness or hunger. Mullaly makes a good point when he says structural oppression is a form of "social terrorism" used by dominant groups to exploit and oppress marginalized groups in Canada and around the world (2010, p. 127). Reform in this context is seen not as an end goal but as a step towards transformation. Sadly, in Canada over the past 40 years, simply maintaining basic social benefits, rather than transformation, has become a significant advocacy priority. One example of the steady erosion of benefits to Canadians is the cuts to employment insurance (EI). It is estimated that the percentage of people able to collect EI benefits fell from 74 per cent in 1990 to 35 per cent in 2014 (Wood, 2014). Advocates have also fought to reverse regressive changes to health care, education, and social services. And while reversing the changes is the goal, in many circumstances, unfortunately, they have often had to fight just to protect the eroded inadequate benefits from further cuts. These efforts frequently derail advocacy aimed at reform and transformation.

Case Study 5.3: The Coalition for Social Housing

This section will highlight the reform type of structural level advocacy action rather than advocacy aimed at transformation. There are however some very hopeful exceptions in

Canada and around the world that show that transformation advocacy work is alive and well. These include the Idle No More, Black Lives Matter, No One Is Illegal, and Occupy movements in Canada and around the world. These efforts seek to transform social and economic inequality at the structural level. While I strongly encourage advocates to become actively involved and supportive of transformative advocacy actions, it is more likely that they will be drawn into local or provincial efforts aimed at improving and maintaining existing services, programs, and benefits that are threatened by cuts. The example of this type of advocacy, which we will be looking at next, is of a coalition to increase the stock of social housing for tenants with a low income. This section will first place this advocacy work in context and then discuss the advocacy action undertaken to improve the lives of low-income tenants by increasing the number of social housing units.

Setting the Context

Advocates across Canada will be familiar with the difficult spending choices made by families and individuals with a low income each month. As of 2011 about 3.2 million people, or about 10 per cent of the population, live on a low income in Canada (Conference Board of Canada, 2011). They struggle with restricted budgets that result in difficult choices such as whether to pay the rent, or the heating, or the electricity bill. Will there be enough money left over for food, transportation, medicine, and other necessities? Every month about 850,000 Canadians are helped by food banks; about 34.6 per cent of these are children and youth (Food Banks Canada, 2015). Housing is the most significant fixed cost for Canadians with a low income and there is a shortage of decent affordable rental accommodation. About 1.5 million Canadians, or 13 per cent of the population, are in core housing need (Canadian Housing and Renewal Association, 2011). Core housing need means these Canadians cannot find housing that costs less than 30 per cent of their income, has an appropriate number of bedrooms for the family size, and requires no major repairs (Canadian Housing and Renewal Association, 2011). Every month advocates work with tenants across Canada to help prevent homelessness by negotiating with landlords, overturning eviction orders, finding alternative housing, or securing loans from a rent bank. When advocates are successful tenants are temporarily secure, but with the high and rising cost of rent and low and dropping vacancy rates, tenants with a low income remain in precarious circumstances.

A more permanent solution to a precarious housing situation is to secure social housing. Generally social housing provides adequate, suitable, and affordable rental units to tenants with a low income (Canada Mortgage and Housing Corporation, 2014). Adequate is defined as housing that does not require major repairs such as structural, plumbing, or electrical. Suitable housing is that which provides enough bedrooms for the size and makeup of the household. Affordable housing for renters is defined as costing 30 per cent or less of before tax household income for rent, electricity, water, and heating. Social housing is owned and managed by provincial and municipal governments and numerous not-for-profit organizations. Tenants of social housing pay no more than

30 per cent of their household income for rent regardless of the household or the accommodation size. Needless to say, advocates and tenants with a low income see social housing as a highly desirable option. Unfortunately, there is an inadequate supply of this type of housing. Large urban centres have long waiting lists. For instance, in April 2016, Toronto, Canada's largest city, had over 177,502 people on the waiting list for social housing (Housing Connections, 2016). Other large and medium-sized cities also have extensive waiting lists and applicants can wait years for a unit. So while advocates work hard to help tenants with low incomes get into social housing, they know the supply is limited and the wait is long.

The Organizing Efforts Begin

Three service providers in a mid-sized Canadian city become increasingly exasperated with the local housing situation. They are experienced advocates and have spent years helping tenants, one at a time, day after day. The work is feeling increasingly futile. Some social service providers in these circumstances burn out or quit in frustration, but advocates in this community take a different path. They decide to try to bring about a change to the structural level housing problems that contribute to so many tenants waiting for social housing.

The organization starts with three friends, Francis, Adele, and Yann, all housing advocates, meeting for coffee after work. Their conversation turns, as it always does, to the dire housing needs of the individuals and families they are trying to help, like a family of five living on the minimum wage earnings of one parent. They are concerned that the family will soon be homeless and split up between a men's shelter and a shelter for women and children. The advocates really want to keep the family together but there are no apartments available except rundown, pest-infested buildings in noisy, crime-ridden neighbourhoods. The family applied for social housing several years ago after the birth of their first child but they have not yet received an offer of accommodation. The waiting list for three-bedroom units is monumental and the provincial government has just cancelled the social housing program, which means no new construction. The advocates express their mutual anger over the government's decision. They decide that they will use their frustration, anger, and tears to develop an organization aimed at reinstating the social housing program and increasing the supply of social housing—essentially using two of the broad strategy areas discussed in Chapter 4, legislative and community organizing strategy.

The next time the three advocates meet for coffee they plan a public meeting, where they hope to develop a broad-based coalition to pressure the provincial government to build more social housing. The coalition will be comprised of advocates representing a number of social services, tenants with low incomes, and people who are homeless. "Coalitions are temporary associations created to consolidate power in support of a specific issue, such as a piece of legislation" (Jansson, 2003, p. 368). Ezell recommends "that coalitions remain issue-specific, short-lived, and informal" (2001, p. 94). The advantages of coalitions are outlined briefly in Box 5.7.

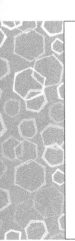

Box 5.7 Advantages of Coalitions

- The work can be shared by coalition members and their organizations.
- Resources can be pooled among coalition agencies, as not-for-profit agencies may have some difficulty launching a campaign on their own because of the financial cost.
- They bring in diverse expertise, such as professionals and people with lived experience.
- They unite power and influence, because individual voices can be easily silenced.
- They allow different levels of access to the decision makers. Some coalition members have cultivated close ties to those in power and can use it to influence on the inside, while those with less access to formal power can critique strongly from the outside.

The Coalition for Social Housing Is Shaped

Francis, Adele, and Yann carefully plan the meeting as they want the coalition to get off to a good start. Their goal for the first meeting is to present the problem and build the membership. Lee (2011) offers recommendations to ensure good attendance at meetings.

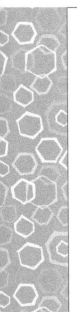

Box 5.8 Things to Remember When Organizing Meetings

- Your organization should be diverse and inclusive.
- When choosing the time, date, and location, appreciate that community members are hardworking people with personal lives that involve caring for children, elderly, or disabled family members.
- Choose a location for the meeting that is central and safe. The space must be accessible for people with physical disabilities and easy to access by public transportation, walking, or car. Be careful not to meet in a location that will exclude people because of the negative reputation of the facility (e.g., some churches and schools are negatively associated with residential schools for Aboriginal people).
- The room should be well heated/air conditioned with good lighting.
- Stipulate how long the meeting will be.
- Ensure that equipment is available and working (e.g., projectors, internet access, laptops).
- Choose someone to chair the meeting and someone to take notes.
- Develop a clear, short agenda and leave lots of time for discussion. The agenda should provide information about what items will be covered, who will be speaking about each item, and how long each item will take.

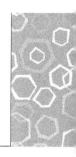

- Someone should provide a short presentation of the problem (here, the need for more social housing).
- Send out the invitation for the meeting well in advance. Include information about the purpose of the meeting. Consider using email, tweets, texts, and public service announcements in traditional media, radio, television, and newspapers. Also, use posters, community newsletters, and face-to-face communication.
- Send out a second reminder of the meeting.

There is a good turnout at the inaugural meeting and a lot is accomplished. By the end of the meeting they have an advocacy goal and have chosen a name—Coalition for Social Housing (CSH). They form a small delegation to represent the group publically and several subcommittees are struck. CSH members write and sign a participation agreement that clearly outlines the advocacy plan, proposed actions, and basic expectations of involvement. Participation rules for this kind of organization should cover the following: designated speakers and negotiators, method of decision making (consensus, majority, or other), communication methods and requirements between meetings, how often the coalition meets and attendance requirements, and conflict of interest and how to deal with it (Ezell, 2001). The neglect of these organizational details can lead to disagreement and conflict among coalition members and openings for internal sabotage.

The Advocacy Action Proposal

In addition to organizing strategy, that is, developing and maintaining the coalition itself, the group's overarching goal to increase the supply of social housing is a form of legislative strategy (see Chapter 4). The aim of legislative advocacy is to have an impact on legislation at the municipal, provincial/territorial, or federal level of government. As was noted in Chapter 4, legislative advocacy requires a full understanding of political processes and a tenacious dedication to the cause over long periods of time. In legislative advocacy, timelines are often not driven by the advocate but instead by the political process. Key events in the political process offer opportunities for advocates pursuing a legislative strategy. These include budgets and budget hearings, legislative committee hearings, consultant reports, and of course elections. For instance, if an advocate is not ready to take action in the few months before an election, then important opportunities for advocacy may be lost. The advocacy may have to wait another four years for a federal election and up to five years for a provincial level election. Municipal terms of office vary across Canada between two and four years, although many have recently changed to a four-year term (Union of British Columbia Municipalities, 2010).

CSH organizes several meetings to do background research and to develop an advocacy plan (see Chapter 4). The advocacy action proposal summarized in Box 5.9 imagines what a group like CSH might develop.

Box 5.9 Advocacy Action Proposal—Structural Level

Develop an advocacy plan and select community organizing and legislative strategy →

Tactic #1   organize and maintain broad coalition →

Tactic #2   collect background information and do research on social housing →

Tactic #3   write a report outlining the need for social housing →

Tactic #4   write a position paper based on the report and research →

Tactic #5   organize a public forum to present the report to the community →

Tactic #6   write op-eds for traditional and online media →

Tactic #7   lobby local members of the legislative assembly[2] (MLAs) and key decision makers →

Tactic #8   write a letter of cause advocacy to the provincial minister responsible for housing and organize a letter writing campaign →

Tactic #9   develop a petition to distribute through social media →

Tactic #10   organize an information picket →

Tactic #11   campaign for MLAs that support building more social housing

(CSH may also consider developing a Public Education Strategy to try to involve the broader community in the campaign to increase the supply of social housing.)

CSH Takes Action

CSH gathers relevant information, research, and statistics in order to write a report on the need for social housing (Tactics 2 and 3). The report uses a standard outline (see Box 5.10) and aims to be about 15 to 20 pages in length, including graphs, tables, and pictures to encourage interest. Chapin recommends that policy analysis reports should follow a logical framework using a principle of inclusion (2014, p. 56). Basically a policy or program is evaluated on how well or how poorly it includes people. The ideal is programs that are as accessible as possible. CSH uses Chapin's (2014) advice and does their best to develop a clear, logical report, supported by evidence and based on inclusion. They choose a logical framework used by well-respected social policy researchers at the Caledon Institute for Social Policy (2015).

Box 5.10 Policy Analysis Outline

- **Problem statement**: briefly, in one to two paragraphs, explain the major concerns with the policy
- **Policy objective**: concisely, in about one paragraph, describe the problem the policy is designed to address
- **Current status**: provide a detailed critical discussion of the current policy. Some points may include eligibility, benefits and services, and delivery systems.
- **Drivers of change**: discusses the forces influencing change in the policy area (political, economic, social)
- **Recommendations**: clear, concise, well-supported, specific recommendations for policy change
- **Conclusion**: a strongly worded half to one-page summary of the report
- **References**

CSH members make use of a well-developed body of research evidencing the benefits of social housing, they also include the experiences of social housing tenants and those families and individuals on the waiting list, and their own experiences as advocates. They know that policy makers are more likely to be influenced by certain types of arguments, including statistics and data, logic, benefit/cost, emotional appeals, and moral responsibilities, and try to include all of these in the analysis. CSH uses their policy analysis to write a report and to develop presentations for various audiences. They plan to present the report to the public at a community forum and use it as a basis for an op-ed, a letter of cause advocacy and letter writing campaign, and a two-page position paper (see Box 5.6, page 115) to hand to politicians, bureaucrats, and community members at meetings. CSH anticipates that there will be media interest in the campaign and so they prepare a press package that includes copies of their report, position paper, recent press releases, and a brief biography of the group including contact information to distribute at the community forum. They also make posters and write media releases for the forum (see sections 8 and 6 of the Appendix). "The mass media can often help policy advocates reach a broad audience that will, in turn, place pressure on politicians to take action" (Jansson, 2003, p. 354). CSH decides that the forum will be about two hours long. The first hour will consist of a 20-minute presentation of the report by two members. This will be followed by a panel discussion of representatives from social housing providers, people living in social housing, people on the waiting list for social housing, and representatives from the municipal and provincial government. The remainder of the session would be a question and answer period facilitated by two CSH members.

The forum goes well and membership in CSH grows to 25 organizations and individuals. There is a lot of momentum coming out of the forum and the new members are keen to pursue the remainder of the tactics outlined in the Advocacy Action Proposal. Francis, Adele, and Yann are really excited about all the enthusiasm and eagerly participate. Adele joins a subcommittee to write an op-ed piece for online and traditional media and to start a letter writing campaign. Francis works with another subcommittee to lobby politicians and key decision makers. Yann joins the picket/petition subcommittee. Interest in their work is so great and momentum so positive that instead of carrying out the tactics outlined in their plan consecutively, they are able to develop several subcommittees and combine tactics and work on them concurrently. It seems like a good idea to get everything going at once, to really create some buzz about the issue and garner a lot of public attention. They do not take time to reflect and evaluate tactics as a subcommittee or as a coalition because everything is moving along so quickly. The media is very interested in the social housing issue—the op-ed piece goes viral online and this triggers thousands of people to sign the online petition and to participate in the email letter writing campaign. At about this time Francis and her subcommittee meet with politicians to lobby for social housing. The MLAs and other key decision makers know about the campaign and the opposition MLAs are elated with CSH's success because it is a criticism of the party in power. Meanwhile, MLAs who are members of the government in power are hostile to the criticism and ask Francis and her colleagues intimidating questions about where they receive their funding and if the board members and managers in their organization are aware of their lobbying activities. This should have been a warning but because the campaign is moving along so quickly, and for the most part successfully, the lobbying subcommittee carries on undaunted.

Unfortunately, behind the scenes in the provincial government offices, unhappy with having their policy decisions questioned, senior bureaucrats are instructed to question the lobbying activities of the CSH, specifically their sources of funding.

CSH meanwhile has attracted attention from allies in the union movement and a large provincial union offers free office and meeting space and a small amount of funding for website development, printing, and transportation. The extra support is timely because Yann's subcommittee is organizing a demonstration in front of the constituency office of the minister responsible for housing, and Yann uses some of the money from the union to rent school buses to transport about 150 protesters.

The day before the protest, Yann is called into his supervisor's office at work and told he can no longer use agency time to participate in CSH. Francis, Adele, and other CSH members are also told to dissociate themselves from the work of the coalition. Francis, Adele, and Yann meet over coffee to discuss these new negative developments. They are dismayed that their organizations are withdrawing support for CSH but understood that the agencies cannot operate without provincial funding. They all decide that people who are homeless and people on the waiting list for social housing deserve better and that they will continue with CSH outside of their work hours.

Francis, Adele, and Yann join about a 150 others on the buses heading to the protest. They know a lot of the people attending, but they also see a lot of new faces, which makes them excited about the possibility of more people joining CSH. Once arrived at the

MLA's constituency office, Yann notices that about 25 people from one of the other buses are now carrying signs with anti-immigration messages. Yann immediately approaches the group and politely asks them to join the CSH protest and to please put their anti-immigration signs away. They refuse and soon there is a loud argument between several CSH supporters and the anti-immigration contingent. The media has arrived to cover the protest and the argument draws their attention. Soon they are focused on filming the heated argument and not the protest for social housing. CSH has a quick meeting and decides to continue with the protest even if the uninvited anti-immigration people insist on protesting. CSH protesters walk in a circle in front of the constituency office, holding up their signs and chanting. Everything is going according to the plan they had made when suddenly and unexpectedly the anti-immigration protesters block the road in front of the MLA's constituency office and refuse to move. Cars are honking loudly and angry drivers yell and gesture. The media's attention is soon focused on the anti-immigration protesters blocking the intersection. The police arrive and promptly clear the protesters from the road, but also put an end to the CSH protest, threatening tickets and arrests.

In the days that follow, the online and traditional media coverage is squarely focused on the anti-immigration protest. The only mention of CSH is that they had provided transportation for the anti-immigration protesters and that there had been an argument over something. The heated exchange between CSH and the anti-immigration protesters is also featured in a video taken by a passerby and uploaded to YouTube. The video makes the CSH members look like bullies and Yann is at the centre of the dispute. Someone sends the video to Yann's supervisor the next day and Yann is subsequently terminated from his job. Yann is told that he is being fired for cause, as his behaviour has seriously damaged the reputation of the agency.

CSH calls a general meeting a few days later to assess the damage done by the protest. After a lengthy discussion the members decide it is time to evaluate the actions taken so far and focus on community organizing strategy. The group realizes that they had come together quickly and aggressively pursued legislative change without working hard to strengthen and develop their organization. They also acknowledge that they need to evaluate the tactics that were successful and unsuccessful, in order to ensure greater success in the future and that they need to, whenever possible, make time to reflect and evaluate after each action in the future.

The Backlash and Outcomes

Unfortunately the negative fallout from the protest is not over. The MLA responsible for housing is very angry about the protest. CSH is uncertain about what occurred in the private offices at the provincial legislature, however it seems almost certain that the minister responsible for housing shared his anger about the protest and lobbying with other MLAs, including those responsible for funding to various CSH member agencies. The backlash comes soon after. Several agencies receive calls from their provincial government funders about their involvement in CSH and the protest. These agencies swiftly resign from CSH, fearing that funding will be cut if they continue their support. One CSH member with lived experience is investigated by his welfare worker. The welfare department says that if he can participate in advocacy he shouldn't be receiving welfare. Some member organizations reprimand the individuals they sent to participate in CSH; they need a scapegoat in order to show their provincial funders they are distancing themselves. Francis, Adele, and Yann are singled out by some of the media as radical ring leaders that let things get out of control. Yann has some difficulty finding another job but eventually receives an offer from an organization that advocates for a cleaner environment—they like his so-called radicalism. Francis and Adele continue to work at their organizations but find as time goes on that they are passed over for promotions and salary increases, likely because of their participation in CSH. Francis, Adele, and Yann stay in touch and in their time outside of work continue to participate in advocacy aimed at structural oppression. When the next provincial election is called all three of them work on the campaign of the opposition party with a platform that includes building more social housing. The sitting government is defeated and the new government follows through with their promise to build social housing. Soon social housing projects are being built again across the province.

Bishop (2002) cautions that those who speak out against injustice can expect a counterattack. Reprisals are likely to be indirect such as isolation, a tarnished reputation, and being "branded troublemakers" (Bishop, 2002, p. 54). Spindel (2000) stresses that advocates need the ability to withstand criticism from opponents if they want to achieve their goals.

The Intersection of P/C/S

The CSH advocacy at the structural level is a qualified success. More social housing is being built but the backlash has dampened CSH's structural level advocacy and organizing efforts. Individuals are afraid of losing their jobs and agencies are afraid of losing their funding. It would be nice if we could say that the work of CSH contributed to the election results and therefore the increase in the supply of social housing, however, the links are not that clear. It likely takes the cumulative work of many individuals, advocates, and organizations to influence social policy legislation and elections. Advocates for structural change need to celebrate when change goes their way but realize that usually legislative changes achieve less than what was advocated despite many years and prolonged efforts. If CSH stays together they may continue to monitor the building of social housing to ensure that the government meets their obligations. However, transformative structural change such as the elimination of homelessness is beyond the means of CSH.

A large, broad-based, provincial or national coalition using various strategies, legal, legislative, public education, and community organizing is needed to advocate for transformative structural level change. Still any structural level change (like social housing policy) will have an impact on the personal and the cultural levels. Because of changes to social housing policy, some families and individuals on the waiting list now have homes. The cultural level too, is challenged and changed as more social housing improves communities, reduces crime, and improves health and education outcomes. The three levels of oppression intersect and impact one another. Conflict and apathy at any of the three levels will have an impact on the other levels. This is why it is important to find every opportunity to challenge oppression as an individual in your personal networks, as your efforts will have an influence on the cultural and structural levels of oppression. Also, seize opportunities to join with others, as the CSH members did, to challenge oppression at the personal, cultural, and structural levels.

Conclusion

The emphasis of this chapter is on advocacy action. New advocates often spring to action in advocacy to more, or less, successful outcomes. "Change efforts that are planned, organized, and sustained will produce more than those that are random and sporadic" (Homan, 2008, p. 41).

The importance of planning in advocacy was discussed in Chapter 4; this chapter emphasized analysis and strategy and tactic development as the basis from which to carry out action. The three case studies highlighted in this chapter illustrate the analysis and planning involved in advocacy at the personal, cultural, and structural levels and are representative of the types of advocacy work that goes on in Canadian communities every day. In each case study the advocates used strategy and tactics to push for positive, progressive outcomes. Advocacy in the first two case studies was a positive and rewarding experience for those involved. The third case study revealed both destructive and constructive outcomes of advocacy—advocates felt satisfaction at having contributed to social housing policy changes and they learned from their tactical mistakes. They also suffered several personal setbacks as a result of their work. All advocates should anticipate conflict, opposition, and backlash. It is important to take care of yourself and those who you are working with to ensure that you will be strong and healthy to advocate again. There is really no such thing as an advocacy failure—not being successful in advocacy is merely an invitation to do more advocacy.

Critical Thinking Questions

1. Define *poor bashing* and give three examples from your experience. Remember you do not have to have experienced poverty personally to see the devastating effects of it around you.
2. Administrative advocacy strategy and tactics are used by Nada and Veata to successfully have Nada's welfare benefits reinstated. Develop legal, legislative, public education, or community organizing strategy and tactics for advocacy action.
3. The network of advocates in the second case study uses public education and organizing strategy to change oppressive cultural beliefs about men who are poor and homeless. Describe an oppressive cultural belief in your community. Which broad strategy area (legal, legislative, administrative, public education, or community organizing) would you choose to try to advocate for change? Justify your answer.

4. Do you think the coalition of advocates in the third case study could have avoided the backlash? Explain why or why not?
5. Find a problem discussed on social media or by traditional media (e.g., racism on a college campus, people with disabilities facing employment discrimination, seniors living in poverty) and develop appropriate strategy and tactics for advocacy action.

Suggested Readings

Gaetz, S., Scott, F., & Gulliver, T. (2013). *Housing first in Canada: Supporting communities to end homelessness*. The Canadian Homeless Research Network Press. www.homelesshub .ca/housingfirstcanada

Guirguis-Younger, M., Hwang, S., & McNeil, R. (2014). *Homelessness & health in Canada*. Ottawa: University of Ottawa Press. www.press.uottawa.ca/homelessness-health-in-canada

Tweddle, A., Battle, K., & Trojman, S. (2013). *Welfare in Canada 2012*. Ottawa: Caledon Institute of Social Policy. www.caledoninst.org/Publications/PDF/1031ENG.pdf

Suggested Videos and Websites

Caledon Institute for Social Policy. www.caledoninst.org/
Canadian Centre for Policy Alternatives. www.policyalternatives.ca/
Conference Board of Canada. www.conferenceboard.ca/
The Homelessness Hub. www.homelesshub.ca/
Canada Mortgage and Housing Corporation. http://cmhc.ca/en/index.cfm

Notes

1. This case, and all the case studies in the text, is inspired by real experiences but does not represent a specific service user or circumstance. It is a fictionalized version of several similar cases and any resemblance to actual events is coincidental.
2. MLA, Member of the Legislative Assembly, is a title used for elected members of the provincial/ territorial level of government. MLA is used in the three territories and every province except Ontario where Member of Provincial Parliament (MPP) is used and Quebec where Member of the National Assembly (MNA) is used.

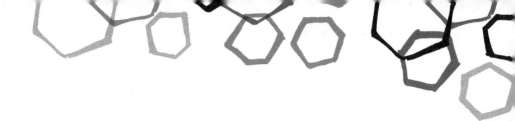

6 Advocacy Stories

Chapter Objectives

After reading this chapter you should be able to:

1. Appreciate that there are many different ways to become an advocate and to do advocacy
2. Understand the influence of advocacy strategy on advocacy action
3. Recognize the effects of oppression and the intersections of oppression on advocacy
4. Appreciate the value of learning from both successes and failures, and understand how to integrate those lessons into advocacy
5. Recognize and value the teachings of experienced advocates and the passion of new advocates

Introduction

Social work operates at the nexus of social structures and human pain. If we are genuinely to assist people with the kinds of problems they encounter in today's neo-liberal, globalized world, radicalism is necessary.

(Baines, 2011, pp. 24–5)

First, I want to sincerely thank the advocates I interviewed for this chapter for sharing their time and their stories with me so that I could share them with you. The following advocacy stories are based on in-depth interviews with eight advocates over approximately six months in 2013. The interviews ranged from one and a half to five and a half hours in length. Even the shortest interview contained far too much material to include in the brief profiles that follow, but I have done my best to present some of the most salient experiences. The stories are presented in random order, and for privacy reasons, the full names of the advocates are not included.

Some of the advocates profiled here have advocacy experiences that could fill a thick memoir if they could drag themselves away from their busy lives as activists and advocates to write it all down. Collecting and telling their stories is a way to examine the thinking, strategy, motivation, and values behind the work of advocates in the real world. While the stories focus on advocacy achievements, I have also included stories of failed efforts to hopefully offer a more realistic picture of advocacy work. I hope many of these stories inspire, but they should not be idealized. In fact, one of the goals of presenting them is to help dispel the common myths and stereotypes associated with advocacy.

Many of the advocates profiled here caution that advocacy can be difficult, time-consuming, and even risky due to the potential for backlash. The advocacy literature, including much of this book, presents the fully formed, professional advocate, but of course becoming an advocate is a process, one that is different for everyone. While some people seem to have advocacy in their genes, others turn to advocacy because of their own personal experiences, or experiences fighting oppression on behalf of a family member, a friend, or within their communities. There is no single way to become an advocate committed to social justice and progressive change. The type of issues advocates take on and the way they fight their battles are influenced by who they are, where they come from, and the serendipity of life. Advocates are human, fallible, and complex; they evolve, change, learn, and grow with experience.

The advocates featured in this chapter are diverse and so are their advocacy experiences. Each of the advocates took up advocacy in two or more cause areas. They recognized the intersections of oppression, such as race, gender, and poverty and the linkages to environmental degradation and national and international political disputes.

- At least five of the eight advocates used some of their advocacy efforts to fight racism.
- Four focused on poverty and workers' rights.
- Four had experience doing advocacy nationally and internationally on behalf of causes around the world.
- Three used some of their advocacy efforts to fight sexism.
- Two worked on environmental causes and one on transphobia.

Their stories include examples of personal, cultural, and structural advocacy. Some of the advocates did advocacy as part of their paid work, others volunteered to participate in advocacy action. All of the advocates profiled saw that opportunities to do advocacy arise regularly in employment situations, while volunteering, or in social situations. Essentially they had an advocacy attitude (discussed further in Chapter 7). I hope you find their stories as compelling as I have.

Mary L.

Sometimes we piss people off but that is OK if we piss them off for the right reason; we are doing the right thing.

– Mary L., February 2013

As a young person, Mary said, she gave her mother grief over the unequal treatment of the boys and the girls in her family. Mary was the middle child, with two older brothers and two younger sisters. She said, "so I was like the ice breaker. . . . I think I drove my mother nuts. . . . I pushed the envelope all of the time." Even then, she could not figure out why, as a female, she could not do what her brothers were doing. That was the start of a common thread running through her life—taking on injustice and fighting for gender equality. Mary had always wanted to be an electrician but she never got there. She explained, "back then women got married and had kids." Yet Mary did not settle quietly into a traditional domestic life, even after the birth of her two children. Instead she took on one important issue after another, earning her the moniker the "cause queen." When her boys had to cross a busy uncontrolled intersection on their way to school, Mary fought to have a stop sign installed so all the children from the neighbourhood could cross safely. Later, when her children were a little older, they brought their friends' advocacy problems to Mary. They affectionately called her "mad dog Mary" because she was such a tenacious advocate. Mary said that advocating for social justice was a necessity, a way to make her way in the world.

For 18 years Mary worked hard as a counsellor and advocate for service users at a family counselling centre. The important services provided by the centre came to a sudden end, ironically on 8 March, International Women's Day. The centre was forced to close the doors because it was deeply in debt. Pay cheques bounced and dental and health care benefits were cancelled. There was no money for vacation pay or severance. Mary led the employees on a campaign to save the 85-year-old centre, and their jobs. They picketed, lobbied, negotiated, and advocated, using the media and political connections, to no avail.

During her time at the centre, Mary's husband, Dick, was injured in an accident at a worksite. His condition was so critical that doctors were unable to help him and Mary made the difficult decision to disconnect him from life support; he died in hospital a few days after his accident. In the weeks and months that followed the accident, Mary started asking a lot of questions about her husband's death, and in the process became an expert on workers' health and safety legislation. She believes that advocates really need to understand the legislation and have "a well-constructed argument for your particular interpretation." Indeed, throughout this period Mary became keenly aware of the relationship between advocacy and legislation. She acquainted herself with Saul Alinsky, a renowned activist and organizer. She particularly liked Alinsky's strategy of keeping the opposition off balance. Mary followed this strategy; at one meeting she was hardline and aggressive and the next pleasant and polite. The opposition (employers, government officials) did not know what to expect from her and this gave Mary an advantage. Mary also liked the Alinsky idea that organizations sometimes don't abide by their own policies and therefore as an advocate you need to make them do just that. Her efforts paid off and she contributed to changes in workplace safety in the province.

Mary's work in the union movement led her to the presidency of the local labour council. She was the first woman elected to the position in its 145 years of existence.

It was a bitter campaign but Mary laid out her priorities and the membership supported her. She moved away from the "old boys" style of "thumping on the table, screaming and yelling, and carrying on." In her role as president she made it a priority to educate the broader community about the labour council and unions. She wanted the community to understand that union membership today is very diverse. The old stereotype that union members are well-paid white men with generous benefits and pensions is no longer the norm. The union movement has changed in recent years, including a trend toward decreasing membership. The demographics of membership have also changed; for example, a union local in Mary's city is comprised mainly of female newcomers to Canada who work as cleaners making just over minimum wage. During her tenure as president of the labour council, she joined many committees in the community in which organized labour had never before participated. In her role as president, Mary advocated for any workers that approached her needing help, including those who were not members of a union. She led rallies in support of striking workers, leafleted neighbourhoods, campaigned door to door, picketed politicians' offices, and participated in political campaigns at the municipal, provincial, and federal levels. She started a food bank and emergency fund for laid-off and striking workers and their families. In our discussion Mary explained that unions are not just a means to acquire higher wages and better benefits for members. They are about "social justice and human rights" for all workers, unionized or not.

Mary offered this advice to new graduates doing advocacy: "live it, breath it, eat it, sleep it. . . . this is what you have to do when someone else's life is hanging in the balance." Understanding the legislation relating to the advocacy work you have undertaken is also key to making a good case. Look for new interpretations, loopholes, and what has been missed. Know what you are doing, do your homework, even use a checklist so nothing is missed. Be confident and passionate about the case. Care about the world and keep trying. "It doesn't always go smoothly, but that doesn't mean you don't go back at it again, and try again, because there is always another way in, there is always another level, and you have to be prepared to exhaust every level of advocacy."

Cole G.

I have always liked being in between the place as far as identity goes, so I am mixed race, I'm trans, I was a lesbian. I have this [working] class thing going on as well.

– Cole G., 2013

Cole is an advocate who has used his comfort in being "in between" to fight oppression and has turned his personal experiences into activism on behalf of others. Cole experienced racism and oppression before anyone should be expected to. He grew up in Scotland in the 1970s, the child of a brief affair his mother had with a south Asian man while she and her husband were separated temporarily. Later, when they reunited, Cole was accepted and loved by his non-biological father. The family moved to Canada together, but the marriage reunion between his parents did not last. After that relationship ended his mother moved back to a small village in Scotland with Cole and his sister. Cole was being raised as a girl at the time and had long, dark, straight hair and black eyes while his sister had frizzy blond hair and blue eyes. Cole's physical appearance was so different from that of his sister that people continuously asked how they were related. Cole was the only racialized person in his entire village and the minute he started school, around the age of five, Cole encountered racism. "Basically my nickname became 'paki' in school, all the way through, and I felt pretty different from everybody." Love, caring, and unconditional acceptance from his mother helped to counter some of the damaging effects of the racism.

Even with an accepting and supportive family, Cole still felt like the "other" in many circumstances. He said he usually felt more comfortable on the margins. At 21 Cole moved to Canada to attend university. At the time he identified as a lesbian. Over the next decade or more, Cole came to understand he was transgender and started to identify as a man. In thinking back, he said he always felt like a boy when he was a child. As Cole began to transition, he chose a new first name, sought medical advice, and started hormone injections—his voice deepened, he started to shave daily, and he presented himself in accordance with his gender. However, Cole's transition was not without challenges; he lost friends and gained others, while some lesbian friends could not understand his "choice". His employers were supportive and so were several old friends, but some still slipped up, misdgendering him by using incorrect pronouns (referring to him as "her"), essentially outing Cole as a trans man.

Advocacy is deeply personal for Cole because of his lived experiences, but it is also political. Trans people face higher unemployment rates, difficulties finding safe housing, and impediments to accessing appropriate health care. They face challenges in their daily lives with regards to parenting and family life, legal issues, travel, identity documents, and everyday routine experiences, such as using the washroom at school or work or the change room at the gym (Todd, 2010).

Cole has spent much of the last 25 years advocating for people who face marginalization and othering because they are poor, disabled, or racialized. He has also done his fair share of advocacy at the cultural and structural levels, by speaking out on trans concerns. In 2014 Cole appeared on local cable TV to discuss his personal experience as a trans man. He patiently and articulately answered the host's probing and sometimes personal questions (Cable 14, 2014). Another example, detailed in his local newspaper, stems from Cole's experiences with the federal organization responsible for immigration, customs, and borders. A few years ago Cole was scheduled to attend a conference in San Diego relating to his work. He had not been to the US since he had transitioned. The problem was that Cole's Canadian passport identified him as "F" for female when he clearly no longer presented as a woman. Cole was concerned about the confusion this might cause at customs and at airport security. Proactively, Cole called the federal border authority to explain his circumstances and to ask about the provisions they had in place for these situations. After being transferred to several different people, as these things go, Cole finally found someone who seemed to be able to answer his questions. According to Cole, the government official asked very personal questions like "do you have breasts" and also made several comments expressing astonishment such as "[that's] too much information." Cole said that he could hardly believe it when the official recommended that he "just dress like a woman that day." Cole explained that this was not possible, that he is not a woman and no longer presented that way, and asked to speak to another authority. Cole said the official explained that there was no need, as he had been there for many years and that his advice was to dress like a woman.

Despite that "advice" Cole did make it to the conference, having sought out useful advice from other trans people who had had similar experiences. He went to the conference in San Diego armed with a letter from both his doctor and his employer explaining that he is a transgender person. Cole continues to advocate for better understanding of the difficulties experienced by members of the trans community. He summed up his story by commenting, "so if I wasn't doing this work, I wouldn't have very much fulfillment in life—I mean I really have to do it."

Elizabeth G.

No one's position, education, training, status, money, or power, intimidates me.
— Elizabeth G., July 2013

Elizabeth radiated joy, energy, and passion as she shared her Aboriginal heritage and teachings. Her advocacy and activism is imbedded in her Aboriginal identity. Elizabeth, however, did not have the advantage of growing up in these traditions and teachings; she grew up in a white, middle-class, suburban community. She said, "it was all about image, your car, your house, your grass, what your lawn looked like was a really significant thing." The parents who raised her told her many times that she was a "white, Anglo Saxon, protestant." They did not tell her she was adopted or Aboriginal; it was not discussed, until Elizabeth eventually confronted them when she was in her early 20s. Elizabeth had been adopted during a time that has come to be known as the '60s Scoop.[1] The news of her adoption confirmed her long-standing belief that she did not belong in that environment.

As a child, Elizabeth felt a longing for nature and the out of doors; she remembers that she would often make her way, on her own, to the woods, the abandoned farms and undeveloped land on the outskirts of suburbia. "I went there for comfort," she said, and she believes that this longing was very much part of her search for her true, Aboriginal identity. Elizabeth explained that where she lived, at that time, going to the woods was not considered normal; in fact it was discussed as a place that should be feared. Elizabeth recounted how she was always drawn to Aboriginal culture—when she was 13 she saved her babysitting money, over a substantial period of time, to buy a buckskin fringe jacket that she wore incessantly. At 14, she skipped school and hitchhiked nearly 70 kilometres to a First Nations reserve to buy beads and a bead loom. Unfortunately, Elizabeth's adoptive parents disparaged and punished these early interests in Aboriginal culture, and as a result the search to discover her identity would take many years.

Once she reached adulthood, Elizabeth tried to find her birth parents but the records had been either destroyed or lost; she was only able to discover that she was adopted from a New Brunswick First Nation. Elizabeth spent years in Ojibwe language classes and sought out the teachings of Elders to make up for the time lost as a child growing up away from her culture. Her passion for learning, especially about Aboriginal spirituality and culture, continued when she enrolled in a unique graduate social work program rooted in a holistic Aboriginal world view. Prior to finding that program, Elizabeth had been reluctant to return to academia following some negative, unsupportive experiences in an undergraduate social work program. Elizabeth explained that given the racism against Aboriginal people, education can result in wounding, though it can also be a powerful way to heal and resist. She was not alone in her experiences of mainstream education. Generations of Aboriginal students have endured poorly funded, substandard public education, including the now notorious residential school system.[2]

Today Elizabeth generously shares her knowledge and understanding of Aboriginal culture and spirituality with both Aboriginal and non-Aboriginal people. She strongly believes that these teachings contribute positively to what she considers to be everyone's personal responsibility to "live a good life, . . . keep a good mind, be of good heart, and carry good teachings." She explained that, for her, studying the advice of Elders and the knowledge of the teachings is the foundation of successful advocacy.

Elizabeth has been called on many times in her life to fight injustice, through quietly supporting and advocating for students in her position as a counsellor in an Aboriginal student centre at a community college, through beading moccasins for a commemorative art installation intended to draw attention to missing and murdered Aboriginal women in Canada, or supporting environmental causes and Idle No More. In the early 2000s, Elizabeth, reluctantly at first, became involved in a fight to stop the indiscriminate spraying of malathion[3] in urban neighbourhoods. At the time, officials, contending with several almost concurrent public health emergencies,[4] recommended spraying malathion to kill West Nile–carrying mosquitos. She said, "I was listening to the radio and they announced that they were going to conduct wholesale spraying from applicator trucks at night, under armed guard, if necessary."

Elizabeth quickly organized a public meeting and about 20 concerned citizens attended. The group's strategy evolved, and for the next six months, when no other leadership emerged, Elizabeth and her friend became the key organizers and leaders of this grassroots group. "We would look at each other and say how did a native woman and a black woman end up leading a campaign in a predominantly affluent, white community?" They had some advantages though; they worked hard, were experienced organizers, and had good skills, great mentors, and experts to call on if needed. Elizabeth also attributed some of the success to her spiritual practices and the help of her ancestors. As leaders, Elizabeth and her friend were well connected in the community and comfortable speaking to anyone, even those with great power and authority. They learned from their mistakes and sought advice when they needed it. In the end the political climate, timing, and good strategy sense, along with Elizabeth's and her friend's personal qualities and skills, prevailed. The city backed down and did not spray malathion and the community was left stronger and ready to take on new challenges.

Elizabeth often prefers to be behind the scenes developing strategy, teaching and mentoring the next generation of advocates in the Aboriginal community, especially young women. She understands that not everyone can be a leader or a marcher, but everyone has a role. Alongside every public action—Chief Theresa Spence[5] fasting in support of Idle No More or Aboriginal women across the country calling for an inquiry into missing and murdered women—there are many unseen acts of resistance supporting the cause for justice and human rights. Elizabeth explained that a lot of what is going on in the Idle No More movement goes unseen, unpublicized. Not everyone is called to be part of the public advocacy. Supporting activities can include helping Elders at home or watching the children of someone taking a more active role. Other supporting acts include round dancing, singing, ceremony, fasting, feasting, and praying. "No one knows how many people were fasting in solidarity to feed [Spences'] spirit."

Elizabeth said that she believes it is her particular challenge and gift that she has the ability to "walk in two worlds." Raised as white and middle class in suburbia and then rediscovering her Aboriginal heritage as an adult, she explained, "I know that world really well, I understand what is going on in a way that a lot of my Indigenous brothers and sisters don't and it makes me a really good mentor." She has been called a bridge walker. "I think that is part of my role in my life is to be a person who goes back and forth, who translates, who helps both sides navigate, because we have a vested interest in everybody doing better."

Ali C.

I am always saying to myself "I'm going to pay for this eventually." . . . we are really getting some people pissed off at us, especially politicians, especially powerful people in the community who have excellent relationships with Ottawa.

— Ali C., January 2013

Helping others and standing up against injustice comes naturally to Ali. In fact you might say it is in his genes. When Ali was a child in Beirut, Lebanon, he recounted, he remembers seeing people line up outside his parent's home before dawn. Many of these visitors were marginalized Lebanese citizens who came from remote areas to seek the advice and help of Ali's father, a respected advocate in the community. Ali's father was carrying on a family tradition learned from his own father (Ali's grandfather). Ali's mother, a strong and assertive woman, also had an important influence on his character. She was always ready with wise counsel such as, "when you are meeting people of grand stature, it doesn't matter whether that person is a king or head of state, always look at that person as your equal."

Canada, and Canadians, also influenced Ali. He said that living in Beirut he had to be tough and aggressive, regardless of the subject or process. One of his first observations when he came to Canada was that city walls are not riddled with bullet holes as they are in Beirut, a city devastated by years and years of war. Ali experienced these dangers first hand as a teenager when he was caught in the crossfire on his way to school and lost part of three fingers. In Canada he learned that he could be a softer, gentler person. Ali explained that early influences and the people with whom you surround yourself in life have a great impact on the shape of your advocacy. These supports are "omnipresent". "So you feel as if they are there guiding you, helping you out, whether that be your grandfather, your mother or your father, your friends, your neighbours, people who have touched you in a positive way and have a positive impact on you growing up." These personal influences and support network are the "reservoir" needed to take on oppression and fight for social justice. Ali internalized these important early influences and values and has upheld them in his life—equality, respect, and advocating for social justice.

For Ali his influences, values, and community really came to the fore on September 11, 2001. The perception of Arabs and Muslims was unjustly transformed almost overnight by Canadian and Western media from that of people who were trustworthy, well-educated, and hardworking, to a dangerous, fanatical "other," worthy of suspicion and distrust. Muslim women wearing hijabs were assaulted and spat on, mosques were vandalized and fire bombed. These attacks led to anger and fear among Arab and Muslim community members and Ali was sought out, as his father and grandfather had been, for advice, counsel, and action. Ali formed and joined committees, organized events, wrote articles, and spoke at and led demonstrations. Over the next dozen years following 9/11, he became a central figure locally and nationally advocating for Arab and Muslim people here and abroad.

In late 2001 Ali was invited to join the community editorial board of a local daily newspaper. Ali used most of his op-ed articles to highlight the conflicts around the world involving Arab and Muslim people especially in Iran, Lebanon, Gaza, and the West Bank. In these articles, he skilfully pointed out oppression, indignities, and violence directed at innocent civilians and advocated for changes. At about the same time, he helped to organize and became president of the local chapter of a national Arab association with a goal to improve relations between Canadians of Arab descent and other citizens. The mayor of his city invited Ali to join a forum to "create a peaceful community that values all its racially diverse parts" (Stepan, 2002). Ali was also active as a volunteer in several community-based organizations working with newcomers. When newcomers were unfairly targeted by police, Ali became active in a committee to bring anti-racist training and to encourage recruitment among the growing multicultural population of the city. Even as Ali advocated for peace, acceptance, and tolerance in Canada, he was regularly distracted by conflicts in the Middle East, as the US government waged war in Iraq and Afghanistan, and Israel enforced harsh conditions and military violence on innocent civilians in Gaza, the West Bank, and Lebanon. On various committees, both informal and formal and through his writing, Ali took every opportunity to enlighten others with his deep understanding of history, cultural context, and current conditions, with an aim to advocate and educate less knowledgeable community members.

In July 2006 Ali was personally impacted when the conflict between Lebanon and Israel flared. Ali and his wife were on vacation in Lebanon visiting family and friends when Israel began an aerial bombardment of Beirut, an offensive that would claim over 1,500 lives. Ali and his wife were among 25,000 Canadian citizens trapped in Lebanon, unable to leave because of the constant shelling. Eventually public pressure forced the Canadian government to send seven ships to evacuate Canadian citizens. Ali and his wife eventually made their way back to Canada. Others may have been filled with hate by the terrifying experience and Ali was angry; however, he said he had witnessed the effects of violence all his life and knew he had to turn away from that approach. In an article published in the local newspaper after his return he said, "I know the dialogue has to continue because I have seen the alternative" (Borcea, 2006).

The "dialogue" to which Ali refers is a reflection of his disturbing experiences in Lebanon, but also a reference to his advocacy work in Canada. With an aim to improve the dialogue, Ali, along with other Arab and Muslim leaders, started to meet informally with prominent members of the Jewish community, to share a meal and develop understanding. Ali received a lot of criticism from the Arab and Muslim community for his involvement in these efforts at communication, but he persevered. To bring the dialogue to the broader community, Ali helped to organize a public forum to bring two groups together. The forum featured a prominent Islamic scholar and a well-known Jewish speaker, as well as a choir comprised of Christian, Jewish, and Muslim children (Carter, 2006). About 800 people attended the forum. Ali and the Jewish organizers considered it a positive step to have members of the various communities together in one room carrying on the dialogue.

A community of support is necessary for effective advocacy according to Ali. He is surrounded by a close-knit group of family, friends, and colleagues that he can call on for guidance and discussion. He said it is important to "listen a lot." "You need to have the connections, the social networks, and you need also to have people around you—I mean I couldn't have done anything if I didn't have those support systems in place, my wife, my mother, and close friends." Ali also recommended that advocates take time away from advocacy to reflect, read, study, question, and soul search—even live in isolation for periods of time. All activists need time away from the intensity of political activism, where the pressure can be intoxicating but also suffocating. Ali also advised that advocates should anticipate the backlash, because it will come. Some advocates may cringe at the expectation, but Ali chooses to look at it in a different way. He thinks some people will find it strange but he said he found closure and reward when the backlash arrived for him. He considered the backlash a sign that he had made a difference, had an impact—"mission accomplished." He explained that no matter how many awards you receive for your advocacy or how much you are celebrated by the community, you do not know if you have pushed hard enough until you come up against the backlash. Ali said that the experience stirs complex feelings, knowing that you can be hurt, knowing that the opposition has the power, but also knowing that you made a difference is both validation and verification. The pain of the backlash is balanced by feelings of gratification. "The project was to bring about change to the social injustice that was taking place, by empowering newcomers, to make sure they understand their rights and their responsibilities. We were able to get things done and to some people this became very radical."

Vivene

Fresh out of university in 1982 Vivene tore into advocacy in a big way, taking on antiquated sexist and racist immigration and labour legislation. In her new job she met women from all over the world who had come to Canada to make a better life for themselves and their families. Some of these women were foreign domestic workers, primarily from the Caribbean and the Philippines. Vivene heard the stories of long hours, poor wages, isolation, loneliness, and abuses. She called their circumstances a form of servitude. Many foreign domestic workers left their own young children behind to be raised by relatives, while they spent years caring for the children of wealthy Canadians. When they wanted to stay in Canada and bring their own children to live with them, they faced many barriers because of Canadian immigration legislation. Yet for decades women continued to come to Canada to do domestic work, as it was one of the few ways racialized people could immigrate to Canada. Until the mid- to late 1960s, Canada's immigration policy gave preference to white European immigrants. Vivene and other activists took up the cause of foreign domestic workers and successfully advocated for changes to immigration and labour legislation.

Vivene's passion for her work was grounded in personal experiences. Her mother had laboured as a domestic worker for four years to save enough to bring Vivene and her five siblings from Jamaica to Canada in 1974. According to Vivene, once she had finally reached her goal her mother said she would no longer have to cry at night, now that her children were with her. Adjusting to the cold and the unfamiliar food in Canada took some time, but the close-knit Jamaican community and some imported goods from the local Caribbean market helped. Starting school in Canada, Vivene was a good student with excellent grades and, in fact, an assessment of her academic abilities recommended the academic stream. However, her high school placed her in the non-academic stream. According to Vivene, a disproportionate number of black students were placed in this stream because of low expectations from their teachers. Vivene's mother objected strongly to her placement in the non-academic stream and she was soon moved. Vivene remembers being so proud of her mother's advocacy. Despite the early challenges, Vivene had pride and confidence in high school. Her mother supported the family of seven through low-wage employment, but the children were well-fed and dressed appropriately.

In the late 1980s, Vivene took a position in a federal government department that focused on technical support and grant administration for community groups to improve the status of women in Canada. Over the next 18 years Vivene managed a number of portfolios including women's equality, disability programs, Aboriginal programs, francophone programs, and multiculturalism. It might be assumed that working for a federal government department would be confining for an activist like Vivene. She explained that there were protocols and regulations, but that most of the people in the department worked from a similar progressive perspective. She called the climate empowering. After the department closed, Vivene was offered another position within government but decided it was time to leave. "We were fortunate to have, at the time, a progressive viewpoint that believed engaging people was a positive thing, a good thing for democracy. It was a department that advocated equality for women. No other department in government was doing that kind of work, and those jobs no longer exist."

Vivene took on new challenges, developing a comprehensive settlement and integration strategy for people new to Canada and then a demanding position as the director of a centre promoting civic inclusion. The centre was formed as part of efforts to heal her city after 9/11-inspired hate crimes rattled the community. Being a single parent with demanding work responsibilities would be sufficient challenge for most, but over the past 25 years Vivene has also used every opportunity to fight racism and sexism and to advocate for greater equality. She has managed her own consulting firm since 2010, providing motivational speaking, community strategy building, and coaching and leadership development. She is a member of a committee that oversees her city's corporate cultural plan. She co-chairs a committee that plans and organizes Black History Month celebrations and educational programs. She has many past affiliations with grassroots organizations and high profile committees such as the chair of a municipal status of women sub-committee. Under her leadership, her city adopted non-sexist language policies. She said, "[the policies] were archaic at the time, this was a big battle." A key avenue for her advocacy for women and racialized people, and others marginalized in mainstream culture, is the biweekly current affairs column in her local newspaper she has had for the last 15 years. She writes about the devastating impacts of racism, poverty, sexism, addiction, homophobia, and disability, to name a few. Her writing is rich with her experiences and the experiences of others. She provides context and history to local, national, and international issues such as the rape of a young female student in India, female genital cutting, and the murder and shooting of young girls on their way to school in Pakistan.

Vivene acknowledged that the women's movement is making efforts to be more inclusive—representing the interests of women from more diverse backgrounds and income levels. But in the past she had to "fight her sisters" in the women's movement on behalf of marginalized women. Vivene explained that "when you are a woman of colour you have to stake out your claim and declare to other women, 'Ain't I a Woman.'"[6] Within the movement her work has been to help other women recognize and understand the intersectionalities of race and gender by "challenging from the margin to centre," as bell hooks did in her famous book (2000). Vivene explained, "I think every woman should do that. It is important to build the movement when everybody is in it, right?"

According to Vivene, the opportunity to do advocacy exists wherever you work, volunteer, or socialize. Even in the most restrictive, oppressive circumstances you can be an advocate. She explained that equity and inclusion can be transformative; however, the current climate, especially the lack of funding, make advocacy work challenging. At one time agencies that received funding from the government were free to critique the government, it was thought of as a way strengthen democracy. Vivene's experiences working under the Harper Conservative government led her to feel that advocates are often seen as a threat and are being silenced. Being strategic tops Vivene's list of skills that an advocate needs to endure and succeed in various political contexts. She said it is important to be comfortable with people in all of their diversity, and to understand and value community empowerment. According to Vivene, advocates should be self-aware, should reflect on their biases, and should seek out anti-oppressive training. Vivene recommended bringing people in to the advocacy who are affected by the issue, helping them to speak for themselves, and not just hearing, but really listening. Remember that everything is political from the small everyday choices to weighty strategy decisions. Vivene encouraged racialized people in particular to take up space and speak up. Also fundamental to Vivene's advocacy work is to have a good support system in place. "You need networks of friends and colleagues you can trust to support your efforts.

Ken S.

Act on your outrage at injustice, don't let injustice pass, do something about it.

– Ken S., April 2013

As a snapshot of Ken's advocacy, he recounted a recent experience. He was resting quietly at home recovering from a recent surgery when there was a knock at the door. Through the window he saw two women dressed formally in suits and surmised they were on a proselytizing mission. Having opened the door, Ken was surprised when they identified themselves as Canadian federal security agents. They said they wanted to ask him about his travels to Iran for a conference on Palestine and an op-ed article published in the local newspaper, where he had been critical of the federal government's foreign policy. When Ken recovered from the shock, he politely asked them for their cards and hustled them away from his door. While these events might intimidate some into silence, Ken was outspoken. He contacted his Member of Parliament, filed official complaints, wrote more articles for the newspaper, and spoke to the media. This was not the first time Ken had received unwanted attention from Canadian security officials for his advocacy and activism. For more than 50 years he has been fighting injustice. A few years before the security agents' visit, Ken had filed an official request for his PROFUNC[7] (Prominent Functionaries of the Communist Party) file. Subsequently he was informed that, as a person of interest, his PROFUNC file was 700 pages long and covered several decades of his advocacy work.

Broadly speaking, Ken's advocacy has focused on anti-war, anti-racist work, trade union, and environmental causes. His work as an activist started in the late 1960s as a student leader at the University of Toronto. However, his introduction to social injustice began long before that when he was a boy attending Hebrew school. "I think that my sense of social justice and my burning indignation at it arises from my Jewish upbringing." For eight years Ken attended synagogue after public school every day to study the Torah, the prophets, and the history of the Jewish people. His parents, both Jewish immigrants from eastern Europe, spoke of anti-Semitism and the pogroms[8] they had witnessed. Ken's parents left Europe before World War II but 70 members of his mother's family were murdered in Poland during the Holocaust. Ken learned at an early age "that it is right to be angry about injustice and to do something about it."

In the late 1960s Ken attended Innis College at the University of Toronto and immersed himself in student politics and socialist ideas. "I think I kept those socialist ideals alive ever since and that is what keeps me going. When things are bad politically, in the advocacy work, I can see that a better world is possible and I see my contribution, however tiny or insignificant, is part of a movement towards that better world." Ken was elected president of the Innis College Student Society and later vice-president of the Ontario Union of Students, which at the time represented 140,000 post-secondary students in Ontario. According to Ken, university administrators at that time did not believe that students should have a say in running post-secondary institutions. Ken and other student activists won a major victory when Innis College became the only academic setting in Canada where half the governing council were students. It is still the case today. Ken was an activist right to his last day as a student at the University of Toronto. At convocation in 1968, Ken boldly tore his BA degree in half in front of a large audience of faculty, students, and their families saying, "[t]his piece of paper is meaningless." In 2008, 40 years after his graduation, Innis College honoured Ken as one of 40 outstanding graduates. Some alumni objected to his nomination but the vice-principal was not deterred saying, "I thought Ken reflected the spirit of Innis College. . . . His defiant act was a principled statement" (Scrivener, 2008).

Ken has been relentless in his activism ever since, taking on racism and discrimination and various environmental issues in his spare time. As a postal worker, Ken was active in the union filing grievances, defending colleagues, and serving on various committees. In the early 2000s, Ken was a leader in a coalition of groups trying to stop the construction of a four-lane, seven-kilometre highway through 1,600 acres of forest and trails situated in an economically depressed section of his city. The planned site is home to numerous varieties of wildlife, a meandering creek, and ancient Aboriginal living and burial sites. The coalition employed various means to try to bring a halt to the construction. They occupied the valley 24 hours a day for months in several encampments, blocked construction crews, fought with police and security, and battled the city in court. Some activists chained themselves to trees while several others climbed high into the canopy to become tree sitters.[9] Ken sought out additional help from the Confederacy Council at the nearby Six Nations (Haudenosaunee) Reserve. Ken recounted how, as he left the meeting, an Elder woman told him that his presentation had had a big effect. That night, the Six Nations encampment started with the lighting of a sacred fire. During the Aboriginal encampment, the coalition built a longhouse and fitted it with a wood stove as the fall evenings were becoming chilly. When an Aboriginal Elder saw the long house for the first time, tears flowed from his eyes and he said that the long house, built by white people, fulfilled an ancient prophecy. The Elder told how for 500 years Aboriginal people would suffer, but there would be a change for the good on the occasion when white people build a longhouse for Aboriginal people. The encampment lasted until early November when a large contingent of 50 heavily armed police officers and private security guards raided the site and arrested 14 protesters, while many others escaped in the woods. Ken said he was personally devastated when the battle was lost, "that one really hurt". But soon he was drawn into new battles for justice and equality. "Life goes on, people are being assaulted in a racial manner, discriminated against by police, and other issues pop up. . . . people came to me with their problems and I was obliged to do something."

For many years Ken has taken up causes that are controversial, and in the process has paid a high personal cost. One such cause is his activism on behalf of Palestinians and Muslims. "It is painful that you lose your best friends and that you are bad-mouthed and shunned in your own community, but it is really small potatoes compared to the oppression of the Palestinians." Ken counselled that advocates must find a way to deal with the difficulties that will inevitably arise. Having a sustaining socialist vision has helped him and so has a broad network of co-activists and a supportive family. Ken said that if his wife were not so "generous this would not be possible." "If you don't have that support network on every single issue you are going to make serious mistakes, you are going to be isolated, and you are not going to win."

Nora L.

You don't even know how much in danger you are, because danger is around you, just learn to live with danger. . . . you don't know where the bullet is going to come from.

— Nora L., 2013

Nora knows what she is talking about. Not many advocates have had their life and the lives of their children threatened because of their advocacy work, but Nora has. She lived through the worst possible reprisals. Later she used her experience and training to advocate for others.

Nora said she was always a bit feisty, even as a child in Honduras. She was the oldest of six children and had a different father than her five siblings. Nora said she always felt like an outsider in her family but this difference made her stronger. She was very bright and her parents paid for her post-secondary education and English classes. About this time Nora met Eduardo and, despite some family opposition because of his "lower" social class, they were soon married and parents to three children.

In the early 1980s, in Honduras, Nora had a good job working for a large hotel as an executive assistant and taught college classes part-time while Eduardo worked as a freelance journalist and human rights activist. Eduardo was well known as a critic of the Honduran government's human rights violations and excessive spending on armaments. In August 1981 Eduardo was detained by the armed forces special unit called the DNI.[10] Nora said when she was informed of his confinement she was in a state of disbelief but also angry and frightened. She found out where Eduardo was being kept and boldly confronted the security officials. She threatened to go on a hunger strike in front of the DNI

facility and attract all types of media attention. Because of her efforts, Eduardo was released. When he came home Nora could see he had been brutally tortured (detailed in an
Amnesty International report). Soon after, Eduardo resumed his human rights work and
was forced to flee to the United States after his life was threatened several times. From the
US he requested asylum in Canada. Canadian authorities rejected his application saying,
"he had failed to prove well-founded fear of persecution in Honduras" (Amnesty International, 2001). Nora still has the rejection letter.

Soon after, Eduardo returned to Honduras and his political activism. That Christmas
Eve Eduardo was to meet Nora at her office but he failed to arrive. She suspected that
he had been abducted again. Nora launched a very public effort to try to have Eduardo
released and her efforts were covered widely by the media. Soon she and her family were
under constant surveillance and received threats of violence and death. Activists urged
Nora to leave the country. In 1985, terrified for the safety of her three children, Nora
applied and was accepted as a refugee to Canada. The family never saw Eduardo again.
He is among many dozens of human rights activists who were abducted, tortured, and
murdered from 1981 to 1984 in Honduras.[11]

Nora continued her advocacy in Canada. She joined Amnesty International and with
their help has continued the campaign for the arrest of those responsible for the torture
and murder of Eduardo. For more than 20 years Nora has told her story and advocated
for justice on behalf of the "disappeared" in Honduras. She has travelled all over Canada
and the world speaking to community groups, church groups, and schools. In 1996 she
spoke to the European Parliament's Subcommittee on Human Rights in Brussels. Because
family members of the "disappeared" have no grave to visit, Nora advocated for a permanent memorial. In 1996, in Ghent, Belgium, a monument was erected to honour Eduardo
and the other "disappeared" around the world. Nora has received many awards for her
advocacy work and after winning the *Latin Presence* (*Presencia Latina*) newspaper's Latin
of the Year Award in 2008, she used the prize money to launch a memorial scholarship
in her husband's name for Canadian students of Latin American descent attending post-
secondary education. Nora says, "I think through this process I have learned that we all
have power, even if it is a tiny little bit of power, but it is not power if we don't exercise it
and sometimes of course we can get killed in the process."

Today Nora is regularly sought out by the media for her deep knowledge and passion
for political and social issues in Canada and around the world, especially Central and
South America. In addition to her political advocacy, Nora has had a long career as a
social worker specializing in advocacy for immigrants and refugees. An example of this is
her work on behalf of a young newly married couple with a small child, originally from
Central America. The young woman came to Nora because her husband had received a removal order from Canadian immigration that required he leave within 30 days or face de-
portation. An unsuccessful attempt to obtain legal status had cost the couple thousands of
dollars in legal fees. According to Nora, the lawyer kept the money and basically did nothing. Nora quickly sent off an Application of Deferral of Removal to Immigration Canada.
She included the baby's birth certificate, the couple's income tax records, a reference letter

from the young man's employer, and a letter from the young woman to support the deferral application. Nora said that this was all work the lawyer should have done. They were able to have the removal order stayed just a day before the husband was scheduled to leave. They then had 60 days to strengthen the application for status in Canada. Nora helped the couple assemble the necessary documents, records, and references and within a month they had approval in principle for his application as a permanent resident. Nora explained, "with advocacy there is nothing much better than when you teach somebody how to advocate for themselves; and then they go and teach other people, so you know it has a ripple effect."

Nora explained that individuals and families struggling with immigration live in turmoil, often taking their fear, anger, and frustration with the system out on each other. She said that they don't know who to fight so they fight here, and emphasized her words with a punch across. Nora reminds them that it is the system that is fighting them. "I say fight here [punching upwards] not here [punching across]." She explains that it is not your partner or family that is oppressing you, it is the system and "together we can fight it."

Meaghan

It is really important to understand that those aren't individual problems that affect a few people, that those are systemic issues based on the way our society is set up under a capitalist, patriarchal, neo-liberal regime. . . .

– Meaghan, 2013

Meaghan can remember when she first became an activist. She was seven or eight years old and she wrote a letter to the local grocery store imploring them to stop selling canned bamboo shoots. Meaghan had learned at school that pandas rely on bamboo as a source of food and shelter. While she doubts that the grocery store changed their merchandizing practices because of her letter, she was undeterred. After all, Meaghan comes from a long line of strong, determined women, qualities she is destined to carry on. She grew up in a middle-class, Catholic household where giving back and helping the less fortunate was expected. Her family instilled caring values, which were a solid foundation for a future advocate. According to Meaghan, her anti-oppressive perspective came much later when she immersed herself in university studies, work experiences, and involvement in community activism.

Soon after graduating, Meaghan started looking for permanent full-time work in the social service field. Like many young workers, she was offered casual, part-time contracts, shifts, low wages, and no health or pension benefits. At the time of my interview with Meaghan, she said she had had up to five jobs in the previous year. One of Meaghan's first jobs out of university was as the only staff person in a group home on a 12-hour shift, responsible for 23 people with mental health issues. The pay was poor, there were no benefits, and little training. This was Meaghan's personal introduction to precarious work.[12] However, Meaghan soon discovered that permanent full-time work could also be oppressive when she started a new position working with low-income tenants and people who were homeless. She was at first enthusiastic about the job, but quickly discovered that working conditions were poor, with regular conflict between the front-line workers and management. Meaghan, along with several other staff members, took on some of the more contentious employment issues. They tried to form a union and initiated a campaign to get health benefits, both of which ended unsuccessfully, though Meaghan learned a lot from the experience. She said workers at the agency made use of critical analysis and practiced advocacy on behalf of service users, but it wasn't enough. These same workers were not willing or able to take a stand on their own behalf and that of their fellow workers. Meaghan said that she believes some of the workers were terrified of losing their jobs, while others gained from the situation.

Meaghan has paid a personal price for her advocacy in the workplace. She was never fired for her strong, assertive manner, but workplaces often find more subtle ways to get rid of so called "troublemakers"—those who ask too many questions about their rights or insist that service users be treated with dignity and respect. Meaghan explained that resistance and activism are often met with subtle and complex management tools used to silence, control, and terminate workplace agitators. Some of the tools are increased workloads, intense surveillance, divide and conquer strategies between workers, and selling people out or setting them up to fail, so that they consistently become those with the problem rather than those who speak out about the problem. Shortly after she was hired, one employer became aware that Meaghan had a reputation for challenging unfair and inequitable employment conditions. So even though she was a new hire, her work was continuously critically scrutinized. "Eventually you just can't do anything right no matter what choice you make. Essentially you fall into their paradigm of understanding you to be—let me think what they said—that I had the skills and the knowledge to do the job but that I wasn't a good fit." Another employer purposefully reorganized and Meaghan was left off the staff roster after the restructuring. This was the same agency where she had fought for benefits and tried to start a union. Meaghan seems to have cemented her reputation early in her career as an advocate for both workers and service users. The social service community in her mid-sized city is small and insular, and the executive directors of agencies share information about so-called troublemakers like Meaghan. Fortunately there are some agencies that actively recruit strong advocates who are willing to speak out, even when they are risking their own security and well-being. Meaghan eventually found paid employment in a social service agency that is congruent with her anti-oppressive approach to advocacy.

A few years ago Meaghan and another activist started a group to help workers fight for their rights. Meaghan acknowledged that this is the type of advocacy she could not practice in most of the places she has worked for pay in the social services. The group is a collective of precarious workers who have had their wages stolen by employers, been fired, or laid off without due compensation. The group is set up to take direct action against the offending employer to get the money owed to the worker. Initially the group issues a letter demanding that the worker be paid and a deadline. If the employer does not comply, tactics are escalated based on the comfort level of the worker. One recent successful action was against a busy bar in the club district. A female employee had been working at the bar for a few months and was owed several thousand dollars in wages. The group issued a letter to the employer demanding the unpaid wages. When it became clear that the club owner was not going to pay the wages, 40 to 50 members of the group rallied at the club on a busy weekend evening. The group members spoke to the patrons of the bar that night and let them know that the owner was not a fair employer, and that he owed one of his employees thousands of dollars. Clearly the group's actions were not good for business and eventually the worker was paid what she was owed. The group has been successful in all of the cases—"five for five" so far—that they have taken on. Meaghan said that precarious workers are used to getting hammered down, but that the group helps them to "hope, win, learn organizing skills" and experience success through direct action. Activism can become tiring and draining and sometimes aggressive. But they aim to be non-violent and even though the cases are serious the workplace rallies are purposefully designed to be fun for the participants.

Based on her experience as a young person just starting out in the field, Meaghan advised new advocates to be strategic and to look for leverage. Employers see young activist workers as a liability, as people who might challenge oppressive workplace policies and practices. "There is a fine line between being strategic and being a risk that agencies feel they can't take."

Conclusion

I hope you have found the advocacy stories in this chapter interesting and inspiring. The intention was to encourage both thoughtful introspection and action. The advocates featured in this chapter are accomplished in fighting oppression at the personal, cultural, and structural levels. Almost all of the advocates at some time or other had to take on a very personal conflict on behalf of themselves or someone close to them. Think of Cole's encounter with Canadian border officials, Nora's desperate fight to save Eduardo's life, and Mary seeking justice for her husband. Meaghan fights for other precarious workers but she also advocates for her own rights. Elizabeth fought to find her identity and later advocated for Aboriginal youth and joined with others in the Idle No More campaign. Ali fought hard to find peaceful solutions through dialogue, even while he and his community were personally caught up in a centuries-old conflict in the Middle East. Vivene took on racism and sexism in grassroots groups, organizations, and government. Ken faced oppression because of his political beliefs but turned his indignation into advocating for others locally, nationally, and internationally. All the advocates naturally made connections between the oppression faced by individuals and oppression at the cultural and structural levels. Many of the advocates acknowledged that they have paid a price for their advocacy and advised new advocates to be prepared with a supportive network and generous amounts of self-care. It is important to take time to rest, read, reflect, and recover so that you will be ready for the next advocacy challenge.

Critical Thinking Questions

1. Some of the advocates in this chapter discussed how they came to be advocates, such as the experience of racism as a child or witnessing others doing advocacy. Reflect on your influences and write at least the first two paragraphs of your own advocacy story.
2. Pick one advocacy story from this chapter and develop an advocacy strategy that the advocate did not use. Explain why you think your strategy might work.
3. Pick an advocacy problem that is important to you and your community. Make use of one or two of the strategies discussed by the advocates in this chapter and apply these to the problem you select. Some examples are the need for more decent affordable housing, better mental health services, childhood hunger, or a war or conflict in another country.
4. Interview someone in the human services field who does advocacy. Ask them how they came to be an advocate, what type of advocacy they focus on, and their recommendations for advocates new to the field (or any other questions you deem interesting or applicable).
5. Many of the advocates profiled here paid a price for their advocacy work: loss of friendships, family relationships, colleagues, salary, promotions, reputation, or worse. Consider what you are willing to sacrifice to stand up to injustice.
6. Briefly review the stories in this chapter and make some brief notes on their advice or recommendations for advocates new to the field.

Suggested Readings

Bishop, A. (2005). *Beyond token change*. Halifax: Fernwood Publishing.

Capponi, P. (1992). *Upstairs at the crazy house: The life of a psychiatric survivor*. Toronto: Penguin Books Canada.

Capponi, P. (2000). *The war at home: An intimate portrait of Canada's poor*. Toronto: Penguin.

Lee, B., & Todd, S. (2006). *A casebook of community practices: Problems and strategies*. Mississauga: CommonAct Press.

Neigh, S. (2012). *Gender and sexuality: Exploring history through the stories of activists*. Halifax: Fernwood Publishing.

Neigh, S. (2012). *Resisting the state: Canadian history through the stories of activists*. Halifax: Fernwood Publishing.

Suggested Videos and Websites

Poor No More (2010), Bert Deveaux and Suzanne Babin. www.youtube.com/watch?v=RQ1ypJ2erpw

The Activist Network. http://activist.ca/

Rabble. http://rabble.ca/

The Dominion. www.dominionpaper.ca/

Notes

1. Elizabeth was adopted during a time that has come to be known as the '60s Scoop. From the late 1950s to the early 1980s, up to 20,000 Canadian Aboriginal children were removed from their homes by child welfare agencies and adopted to non-Aboriginal families in Canada and the United States ("Dispatch," 2015). One source notes that at the peak of the '60s Scoop, 30 to 40 per cent of Aboriginal children in Canada were legal wards (Hick, 2010, p. 227) of the state. Child welfare adoption records were poor or lost, and so many of the children were not able to find their birth parents or First Nations community. Misguided as it sounds today, many adoptive parents did not tell their adopted children about their Aboriginal ancestry. Further, it was common practice at the time to not tell children they were adopted until they were adults. Some were never told. Some adoptive parents of Aboriginal children held deep-seated racist attitudes towards Aboriginal people and felt the secrecy about the child's origins justified their parenting choice to try to socialize the Aboriginal out of the child.

2. Residential schools were a major contributing factor to the destruction of Aboriginal culture and language in Canada. Generations of children were forcibly removed from their families and taken to residential schools. The students of residential schools were removed from the nurturing of their families and left without the ability to nurture the next generation. These schools are considered a type of cultural genocide (Hanson, 2009).

3. "Malathion is commonly found in house and garden pest control products. Health Canada says the risk malathion poses to residents, where it will be sprayed, is low. Some studies, however, have found malathion may cause birth defects, increase asthma rates and attack the nervous system" (Nolan, 2003).

4. In May 2000, in Walkerton, Ontario, seven people died and 2,300 people became sick from drinking water tainted with E. coli. Between March and July of 2003, 400 people became ill and 44 people died of SARS (severe acute respiratory syndrome) with a further 25,000 Toronto residents being quarantined.

5. On 11 December, 2012, Theresa Spence, Chief of the Attawapiskat First Nation, went on a six-week-long hunger strike in a teepee on Victoria Island in the Ottawa River. The site was chosen because of its close proximity to the Parliament Buildings and Chief Spence's goal was to draw attention to the detrimental impact of Bill C-45 on Aboriginal people and support the Idle No More movement.

6. "Ain't I a Woman?" is the title given to a speech delivered by Sojourner Truth, a former slave, in 1851 at the Ohio Women's Rights Convention in Akron, Ohio. Sojourner Truth became a well-known anti-slavery activist after she gained her freedom in 1827.

7. From the 1950s to the 1980s the RCMP collected information on 16,000 communists and 50,000 people sympathetic to the communist cause. Many well-known Canadians were included in the PROFUNC records including Tommy Douglas, the premier of Saskatchewan, long considered the father of public health care. PROFUNC also had plans to intern suspects in arenas and stadiums where they could be severely disciplined, even shot ("Secret Cold War," 2010).

8. "Pogrom is a Russian word meaning 'to wreak havoc, to demolish violently.' Historically, the term refers to violent attacks by local non-Jewish populations on Jews in the Russian Empire and in other countries. . . . The perpetrators of pogroms organized locally, sometimes with government and police encouragement. They raped and murdered their Jewish victims and looted their property" (United States Holocaust Memorial Museum, 2014).

9. Tree sitting is an act of civil disobedience. The tree sitters climb high into trees and usually build some type of platform. Supporters bring food and water.

10. "One of the agencies most frequently implicated in politically motivated arrests and 'disappearances' was the *Dirección Nacional de Investigaciones* (DNI). The DNI was the plainclothes investigative division of the *Fuerza de Seguridad Pública* (FUSEP), Public Security Force, a specialized branch of the armed forces with wide law enforcement responsibilities" (Amnesty International, 2001).

11. "In the early to mid-1980s the armed forces of Honduras carried out dozens of extrajudicial executions, as well as torture, unjustified arrests, and widespread harassment of individuals from left-wing groups such as trade unions, cooperatives, and human rights activists" (Amnesty International, 2001).

12. According to the International Labour Rights forum, precarious workers toil in unsafe, unstable working conditions for low wages. They do not receive employment benefits and are not unionized. They are often young inexperienced workers, from minority backgrounds, and migrant workers. Full-time permanent work has moved to independent contractors, outsourcing, and temporary employment agencies.

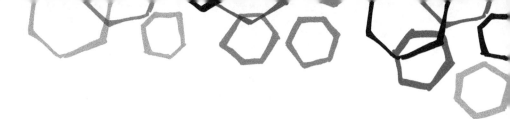

7 Challenges, Trends, and Going Forward

Chapter Objectives

After reading this chapter you should be able to:

1. Anticipate the trends in anti-oppressive advocacy practice
2. Understand the core traits of an advocate working for social justice and equality
3. Appreciate the importance of relationships in advocacy practice with individuals, families, groups, and communities
4. Adopt an advocacy attitude

Introduction

> Every person has to find her or his own way to consciousness and healing. Sometimes it is
> important to work at it in a solitary fashion or with one other person; sometimes the process
> requires healing through activism or group dialogue. Both are necessary.
>
> (Bishop, 2002, p. 98)

The goal of this book is to help build the potential to do anti-oppressive advocacy. It will require a critical perspective, creativity, and risk, but it is difficult to pursue any type of social justice without those things. The book started with a description of an anti-oppressive advocacy model based on the experiences of human service workers. In Chapter 2, the focus was power, politics, conflict, and the need for ethical advocacy practice. The background, history, and development of advocacy and anti-oppressive practices were discussed in Chapter 3. Chapters 4 and 5 used case studies to illuminate the importance of planning, strategy, and action at the personal, cultural, and structural levels. Chapter 6 profiled the stories of eight experienced advocates. This final chapter will first highlight some of the ongoing trends in anti-oppressive advocacy, and then review the important traits and key relationship features for advocates. The chapter concludes with a discussion of the need for an anti-oppressive advocacy attitude.

Trends

Fifteen years ago when I started teaching in the social work field I thought environmental advocacy important but considered its connection to advocacy in the human services as tangential. In the last ten years, Dominelli (2011, 2012, 2013) has made a significant contribution in drawing the links between climate change and social justice for human beings. The state of the environment and the social well-being of people in Canada and around the world is, and will continue to be, a concern for advocates in the human services. Technology has clearly had a significant impact on every aspect of our lives, including advocacy work. The challenge is to use new technology wisely and effectively, and be mindful of those who are excluded from web-based advocacy efforts because of income or ability. That so many services users are increasingly knowledgeable and politicized is a trend that can only strengthen advocacy if mainstream human service workers make efforts to collaborate respectfully as equals. Human service work will be greatly diminished and much less effective unless the efforts and power of service users are taken seriously and valued. In my estimation, based on current social, economic, and political circumstances in advocacy practice in the social services, the three trends discussed in this section are the ones to which new advocates would do well to pay attention.

Advocacy and the Environment

An emerging trend in advocacy in the social services is the fight against environmental degradation and this section highlights the growing significance of the environment for human service workers in a global context. Advocates in the social services should be very concerned about the devastating effects that environmental damage is having on marginalized people in Canada and the world. Human service workers are trained to consider the context of social problems, including the physical environment, and therefore are in a strong position to do advocacy in this area. As we saw in Chapter 3, in the past Settlement House workers advocated for better housing, sanitation, and a healthy supply of food for people with low incomes. In *Green Social Work* (2012), Lena Dominelli revitalizes a fundamental principle in the human service field, to link social inequality and the environment. She challenges human service practitioners to advocate for the alleviation of poverty and a cleaner, healthier environment (Dominelli, 2011, 2013). "Environmental justice requires practitioners to tackle structural and individual forms of oppression that impact upon people and destroy the environment in the process of creating a privileged life for the few" (Dominelli, 2013, p. 432).

Concern for the environment is an area where a clear link can be made between the personal and the political (see Chapter 2). While all citizens are hurt by environmental degradation, those with a low income and those who are racialized, disabled, or in poor health are more adversely effected. There are many examples in Canada of the differential impacts of environmental degradation. Think about where the poorest families and individuals in your city live. If yours is like most cities in Canada, the people who are economically disadvantaged live on busy arterial roads and near polluting industrial sites. Canada has seen its share of examples of polluting industries partnering with political powers to foist damaging industrial projects on poor and powerless communities. For example, over a period of about 150 years the small community of Africville,[1] Nova Scotia, was neglected and actively degraded. In 2013 managers in the city of Abbotsford, British Columbia, approved the dumping of chicken manure on a natural area to dislodge a homelessness encampment ("Many Implicated in Manure Dump," 2013). In September 2014 close to half of the First Nations reserves in Ontario had boil water advisories because of polluted water (Porter, 2014). A First Nations community near the Alberta oil sands projects is coping with abnormally high levels of rare cancers and autoimmune diseases due to air and water pollution (Ambrose, 2015). These are examples of how those with political, economic, and social power in Canada have neglected and deliberately fouled the natural environment of marginalized people. The connection between the environment and human well-being is increasingly clear and the need to act is imperative.

The burning of fossil fuels over the last 50 years has resulted in climate change. Around the world severe storms, heat waves, smog, droughts, forest fires, and flooding have the greatest impact on children, older people, the poor, and those with frail health (Waldie, 2013; World Health Organization, 2012). Climate change has already forced large numbers of people to leave their homes temporarily or permanently. In developing countries people have moved from areas of drought to coastal areas more susceptible to flooding and storms (Kalaugher, 2013). A recent article in the *New York Times* reports on a causal relationship between climate change and violent conflict.

> Drawing one of the strongest links yet between global warming and human conflict, researchers have said that an extreme drought in Syria between 2006 and 2009 was most likely due to climate change, and that the drought was a factor in the violent uprising that began in 2011. (Fountain, 2015)

In the coming years, advocates in the social services will increasingly find that more of their efforts will be directed at helping climate migrants and refugees with resettlement and access to food and health care in Canada and around the world. Efforts should also be directed at structural level advocacy to help reduce or eliminate the devastating impact of environmental damage and climate change. Here are just five good reasons for human service providers to become active environmental advocates (Dominelli, 2011; 2012; 2013):

- Prevent illness, injury, and deaths in Canada and around the world;
- Ensure compensation, financial assistance, food aid, and medical care for the victims of environmental degradation including climate change;

- Safeguard that all migration and immigration is freely chosen and not forced by environmental disasters and climate change;
- Make certain that environmental refugees to Canada and around the world receive appropriate, adequate resettlement services including health care, housing, social services, education, and language training; and
- Preserve flora and fauna for future generations. Some Aboriginal people believe that decisions we make today should take into consideration the impact on the next seven generations (or about 140 years) into the future. This is far superior to the current political decision-making cycle of approximately four years.

Information and Communication Technology

Advocacy, not too long ago, meant writing petitions (on paper) and walking door to door asking for signatures. It also involved sending letters of advocacy (written on paper) to politicians, calling other activists by telephone, or sending them a (snail) mailed notice to attend a meeting or demonstration. Today advocates use texting, email, message boards, and websites (social media platforms and chat rooms) to exchange information, organize, and take action. Information and communication technology has become a powerful tool for advocates and activists. Advocates can access current and historical information nearly anywhere at any time on a smartphone (*telephone* is really no longer an adequate term for our communication devices). They can organize a demonstration in a matter of hours by messaging other activists and gather thousands of names on a petition in just a few days.

Advocates have been quick to take up new technology and use it in unique and creative ways to bring attention to important causes. Each year, more and more people have access to the internet using smartphones, tablets, or any variety of devices. Today about 83 per cent of Canadians use the internet in their home and 97 per cent have high speed internet access (Statistics Canada, 2012). The growth in internet use has been nothing short of remarkable. The International Telecommunication Union (2014) estimated that there would be nearly 3 billion internet users worldwide by the end of 2014, with approximately two-thirds coming from developing countries. Apart from the sheer growth of internet users, the significance of this technology for the protection and spread of human rights has been officially recognized by the United Nations. In 2011 the Human Rights Council of the United Nations declared internet access a human right (United Nations, 2011). The report explains that access to the internet helps to achieve equality, fight oppression, and aid in economic, social, and political development. Many recent examples locally, nationally, and around the world can attest to the significance of internet access for fighting oppression.

The evidence for the use of the internet in advocacy and activism seems unequivocal and growth in use is indisputable. However, no method, process, or theory should go unexamined. The use of the internet and associated technologies must be critically examined within the context of the privilege analysis, P/C/S, and the anti-oppressive advocacy model discussed in Chapter 1, as well as with regard to planning priorities and action strategies, as discussed in Chapters 4 and 5. Even in Canada there are still individuals, groups, and communities that have limited or no access to a reliable internet connection. The so-called digital divide particularly affects people with a low income and those in remote and rural areas. A CIRA report found that 95 per cent of the highest income earners in Canada had access, compared to 62 per cent of low income earners (Canadian Internet Registration Authority, 2014). Further, 100 per cent of Canadians in urban areas had access to the internet compared to 85 per cent in rural areas.

Experience tells us that the low-income category includes people with mental and physical disabilities, seniors, racialized people, and single parents, among others. Steyaert (2002) makes this point "technology replicates the existing social stratification, rather than creating a new social divide" (p. 199). The concern is that the exclusive use of internet-based strategies will categorically exclude marginalized people. Ironically these are the same people many advocates aim to mobilize against oppression. A few examples include the homeless woman sleeping under a bridge, the mentally ill senior begging for money on the corner, or the single parent with no money for her internet connection. Face-to-face or other low-tech communication processes will need to be used when doing advocacy with certain communities. Advocates should not assume service users are computer literate or that they have access to a computer and the internet. Indeed some service users may not be able to read and write in English or any language. So while information and communication technology can be exceedingly beneficial to advocacy, it can also be exclusionary and therefore counter to the goals of equality and social justice. Table 7.1 lists some of the strengths and weaknesses of using information and communication technology in advocacy.

One additional weakness of heavily focused internet-based advocacy that requires additional discussion is the absence of holistic community approaches. Advocacy, at the cultural and structural levels in particular, is underpinned by community organizing strategy. While some community organizing can be facilitated by information and communication technology, a solid grounding in the values and goals of a healthy, caring community is vitally important if positive change is to be sustained. Net-based communities multiply and thrive. As a result, many individuals consider themselves part of numerous communities in the virtual online domain. However, regardless of an individual's involvement in virtual communities, everyone is still part of a community with housing, grass, trees, water, air, streets, services, businesses, and of course flesh-and-blood people. So even though we may feel "connected" online, we are also all connected to the living, breathing natural world.

Perspectives on community organizing inspired by Aboriginal views of community emphasize the importance of a holistic approach (Baskin, 2011; Brown & Hannis, 2008). That approach encompasses the "four aspects of a person" (spiritual, physical, emotional, and psychological), the "interdependency of individuals, families, and communities," the "interconnectedness of all creation" and "healing" (Baskin, 2011, p. 108). Advocates are wise to be wary of strategies that depend solely on online tactics and community building. Instead advocates should be mindful of holistic, Aboriginal-inspired perspectives on community and use information and communication technology to facilitate healthy, caring community development.

Table 7.1 Summary of the Strengths and Weaknesses of Information and Communication Technology

Strengths	Weaknesses
• Influence a large audience • Worldwide circulation • Instantaneous feedback on issues • Spread information quickly • Cost-effective • Environmentally friendly (no paper) • Anonymous and convenient participation • Rapid membership recruitment • Fundraise efficiently • Network effectively • Receive numerous diverse opinions and points of view • Inspire ingenuity and creativeness • Efficiently disseminate educational information	• Highly competitive and over-used • Concerns about security, confidentiality, and privacy • Unreliable or untrustworthy information • Limited or poor access (for some users in some areas) • Risk of miscommunication • Deception, fraud, and misrepresentation • Difficulty communicating emotions and compassion • Lose control of the message (mockery or violence) • Viewed as lazy (slacktivism, hacktivism) • Technical problems and viruses • Absent or inaccurate culture/language translation • Neglect of maintenance • Lack of face-to-face contact • Historical and contextual data is missing • Effectiveness not well-researched

Knowledgeable, Politicized Service Users

A trend in advocacy in the human services is that service users are more knowledgeable and politicized then every before. Service users are no longer merely passive and compliant; they are asserting themselves, organizing, and challenging the professionals and mainstream services that purport to help them. Many service users have suffered at the hands of professionals who discounted and disparaged their lived experiences as exaggerated, invalid, or overly emotional. In some of these circumstances human service workers may have labelled service users as clients with a bad attitude or as resistant (to treatment or the advice of professionals). However, Taylor (2011) considers resistance a normal way to cope with difficult life circumstances. He explains that resistance is a "client's conscious or unconscious attempt to protect themselves emotionally from interactions or events which challenge the coping mechanisms or defenses they have created to manage how they feel about, or understand, their world" (Taylor, 2011, p. 139).

The mental health "survivor" movement is an example of service users reacting to their treatment by mental health professionals. The movement rejected the label "victim" as they became more organized, politicized, and active. Other service users, such as the so-called "victims" of domestic violence, have since adopted "survivor" for similar reasons.

Some service users are angry, often justifiably, because of their treatment. Sometimes they use the anger to learn how to advocate for themselves and organize others who have had similar experiences into political and social movements. Years ago I worked briefly with a group of incest survivors on a research and community organizing project. They came together because of their common experience of childhood incest and their frustrations with the lack of community services. Bishop (2002) provides the following description of the process.

> The spiral of human liberation is well documented. It begins with breaking the silence, ending the shame, and sharing our concerns and feelings. Story-telling leads to analysis, where we figure out together what is happening to us and why, and who benefits. Analysis leads to strategy, when we decide what to do about it. Strategy leads to action, together, to change the injustices we suffer. Action leads to another round of reflection, analysis, strategy, action. This is the process of liberation. (p. 100)

This new political awareness and activism is growing and is supported and influenced by progressive social movements fighting for Aboriginal, disability, and LGBTQ rights, among others, as well as the women's and civil rights movements. Self-help, consumer rights, and victim rights organizations have also helped to raise consciousness and build political analysis among marginalized groups.

The widespread use of information technology, as discussed above, has also contributed to knowledgeable, politicized service users. Service users now arrive at agencies informed about the services and benefits provided. This information was once deeply buried in thick policy manuals and legalistic language. Service users had to rely on the service provider for information, which could be withheld or shared at the worker's discretion. Today service users can access policy information in plain language from a plethora of online consumers' rights organizations such as Canada Without Poverty (formally NAPO), Council of Canadians with Disabilities, and Egale Canada. They can also access federal and provincial legislation online if they so choose. They can find information, advice, and solidarity online and in their communities.

Service users are developing a political consciousness and challenging paternalistic, bureaucratic service providers who perpetrate oppression. Sometimes that challenge takes the form of an individual act, born out of frustration, such as a youth with a mental health problem swearing at a counsellor, or a single parent on social assistance complaining about the unhealthy food at the food bank, or a senior living in a social housing building angry at the housing provider because the elevators are not working again. These service users may find others who share their frustrations, and may put that frustration into action via tenant's associations, anti-poverty groups, or alternative services. Mullaly (2010) explains that anti-oppressive work involves supporting alternative services that are managed by and serve groups that are oppressed. Alternative services are generally developed and controlled by a specific group of oppressed people. Women, Aboriginal peoples, and more recently people with mental health problems have developed their own services.

Knowledgeable, politicized service users have been developing alternative services as a reaction to the neglect and mistreatment by professionals in mainstream organizations for more than 60 years. As an example, Ishtar House, a shelter for abused women, opened in the Central Fraser Valley of British Columbia in 1973 (Ishtar Transition Housing Society, 2015); it was the first transitional housing of its kind in North America. It was developed, managed, and staffed by women for women. Since then advocates and especially supporters of the women's movement have worked hard to develop a network of of domestic violence shelters, women's counselling centres, rape crisis centres, and medical centres specializing in birth control and abortion counselling and referrals across Canada. Other groups have done the same. Native Friendship Centres across Canada are developed and managed by Aboriginal people. The first centre was opened in Toronto in 1951 and today there are 118 across Canada (National Association of Friendship Centres, 2014). In addition, Aboriginal groups have developed emergency shelters for the homeless, social housing, community medical care, seniors' centres, and daycares. These alternative services are a reaction to the sometimes oppressive service conditions in mainstream organizations delivered by professionals such as doctors, psychiatrists, lawyers, police, judges, politicians, government bureaucrats, and human service workers. Carniol (2010) provides the characteristics of alternative services:

- Service users control the service not professionals
- Non-hierarchical, non-bureaucratic (e.g., collectives, co-ops)
- Staffed and managed by people sharing the same problems and issues as the service users
- Policies and rules are flexible
- Welcoming environment with an emphasis on relationships
- Positive space and cultural pride
- Precarious funding
- Often supported by social movements

In addition to forming advocacy groups using technology and developing alternative services, politically active service users are filing complaints and appeals and demanding a say in how mainstream services are delivered and managed. They want to be on committees and boards of directors. They want a say in policy making and budgeting. They no longer want to be merely consulted or left out of the decision-making process entirely. They want their experiences to be heard, valued, and considered relevant, even privileged over professional opinions. An example is the Mental Health Rights Coalition (MHRC) project called Voices of Experience. The MHRC is a community-based alternative service managed and staffed by consumer survivors. The Voices of Experience project charges mainstream agencies to train and support service users who volunteer to sit on boards and committees of mainstream addiction and mental health services (Mental Health Rights Coalition, 2013). Anti-oppressive advocates in the human services should encourage and respect knowledgeable, politicized service users and support and partner with them on the causes they take up. In addition, advocates should work to help service users who are not yet actively involved to become so, through anti-oppressive work and connecting them with groups and organizations.

Access to information and communication technology is differentiated by income and ability; however, overall, increased freedom of information will continue to foster anti-oppressive advocacy efforts. Service users are fighting back by becoming informed, empowered, and politically active. They have and are continuing to demand better services from mainstream organizations and are developing their own services. Anti-oppressive advocacy means attending to trends and working with service users in Canada and around the world at the personal, cultural, and structural levels, and certain personal strengths and skills will facilitate doing that work. These will be the focus of the next section.

Strengths and Skills: Fostering the Personal Traits Needed for Advocacy

This section provides an overview of some of the key personal strengths and skills associated with anti-oppressive advocacy. These are qualities, behaviours, or characteristics that, when combined with planning (Chapter 4) and action (Chapter 5), enrich, embolden, and inspire advocacy work. The reason they are highlighted in this section is because they are the ones most closely associated with anti-oppressive advocacy practice. Most human service workers will already possess these strengths and skills to a greater or lesser extent. Do not be discouraged if you believe you are not terribly creative, courageous, or pragmatic (or a critical thinker, reflexive, resilient, or compassionate). There are many ways to improve the strengths and skills discussed in this section. Everyone is different so I will not suggest a single pathway, but experience, reflection, and study are some of the more helpful ways; indeed, periods of hands-on experience followed by reflection and study under the helpful support of a respected mentor was recommended by some of the experienced advocates profiled in Chapter 6. Experienced advocates are often very willing to share and pass along what they know; several of the advocates from Chapter 6 were mentors for new, less experienced advocates. The following section focuses on seven traits important to anti-oppressive advocates. Examples are drawn from the advocacy stories in Chapter 6.

Creativity

Creativity as we will discuss it here—perhaps more accurately *creative thinking*—means departing from established practices and inventing new approaches, novel ways of thinking, and original understandings and analyses. It can be defined as "the process we use to develop ideas that are unique, useful, and worthy of further elaboration" (University of Michigan, 2010, para. 2). Anti-oppressive advocacy can be enhanced significantly with creative thinking. For example, creative thinking might suggest using drama and art to support a tremendously serious advocacy issue. Most years I have attended the Take Back the Night march in my hometown. Women typically hold signs and chant during the march, but the last few years have also featured several large street puppets to bring attention to missing and murdered Aboriginal women. The beautifully painted puppets, more like works of art, move rhythmically and dance thanks to the efforts of the puppeteers below them. The cause they represented was very serious but it was presented beautifully through drama and art.

There is more than one way to be effective and bring attention to an advocacy cause using creativity, surprise, and unconventional presentations. Saul Alinsky (1989) was masterful at designing unique and creative approaches that did not violate any laws and often simply required those in power to follow their own rules. In his book *Rules for Radicals*, Alinsky recounts creative and effective advice he provided to students attending (as he describes) a conservative, fundamentalist Protestant college. The students explained that they could not have any fun on campus, where they were not permitted to "smoke, dance or have a can of beer" (p. 145). Alinsky asked the students what they *could* do, and they responded that all they were allowed to do was chew gum. He said, then "gum becomes the weapon." He recommended that two to three hundred students chew gum and drop it on the campus walks. The students thought Alinsky had taken leave of his senses, but a few weeks later he received an "ecstatic" letter saying that his tactic was a success—they were finally able to do just about anything, except chew gum (p. 146).

Creativity, imagination, and originality are too often an afterthought in advocacy rather than integral. Truthfully much of this text stresses the logical and customary methods associated with advocacy practice. While the five broad strategy areas (see Chapter 4) are important starting points, the specifics are limited only by the advocate's imagination and creativity (and resources of course). As an example recall the advocacy stories in Chapter 6. Meaghan and a group of precarious workers held a rally at a busy nightclub on a Saturday night to demand justice for a worker. The demonstration was intentionally designed to be fun for the participants. Ken S. and a coalition of environmentalists supported tree sitters and constructed a long house as a way to draw attention to the proposed destruction of a beautiful urban wilderness area. Nora L. threatened to go on a hunger strike to save her husband from torture and death. Some creative actions are carefully planned while others spring from frustration or desperation. Creativity helps advocates discover unique approaches that attract attention to a cause and keep the opposition off balance.

Critical Thinking

Critical and creative thinking are complementary traits, not opposite as is often believed. These two traits work together, with critical thinking used to evaluate and improve on what was created (Vaughn & MacDonald, 2013). Critical thinking is "the systematic evaluation or formulation of beliefs or statements by rational standards" (Vaughn & MacDonald, 2013, p. 550). Those who think critically continually examine, analyze, and deconstruct the context of the advocacy in light of changing circumstances. Much of this text has emphasized critical thinking and analysis. Critical analysis is discussed in Chapter 1 as an integral part of the anti-oppressive advocacy model. Suffice it to say advocacy requires keen critical thinking skills. After much careful critical analysis, Elizabeth G. and a group of activists targeted malathion spraying, rather than trying to have all chemical spraying halted. Cole G., hemmed in by bureaucratic forces, used critical analysis and strategy to fight for service users. For advocates, critical analysis is not an academic exercise, instead it is the springboard for action and resistance.

Courage

bell hooks explains that in southern black communities "speaking as an equal to an authority figure" is considered a "courageous act—an act of risk and daring" (1989, p. 5). Courageous people find an inner strength that allows them to confront threats, struggles, and fear. Advocates who are courageous may be fearful or intimidated by authority, but they do not let that stop them. They will stand up or speak out even when it involves some personal risk or likelihood of reprisal. The advocates featured in Chapter 6 were courageous in the face of opposition or a daunting undertaking. Ali C. spoke out on behalf of Arab and Muslim people in his community and around the world after 9/11. Vivene championed a non-sexist language policy in her city government. Cole G. advocated for trans rights in a television interview. All of the advocates profiled in Chapter 6 experienced direct and indirect reprisals because of their advocacy work. Three said that they had an official file or record on their activities, or believed that they had a file, meaning that the police or other security forces were deliberately monitoring their advocacy activities. Despite the intimidation the advocates persisted.

Pragmatism

Advocates are pragmatic in the sense that advocacy work is complex and rarely finished, especially at the cultural and structural levels. Pragmatic advocates have ideals and visions of social justice and equality, but they know that time, energy, and resources are limited. Pragmatic advocates frame their ideals and visions within the possible. Both Vivene and Elizabeth G. spoke of a kind of fine balance, of weighing options and assessing resources. Pushing too hard can result in alienating potential allies and supporters while not pushing hard enough can reduce the potential of the advocacy. Being resourceful and reasonable is also part of being a pragmatic advocate. Scrounging, borrowing, and calling

in favours are all elements of resourcefulness. Resourceful advocates do not wait for a generous grant to fund the advocacy, instead they start small, within the means of the group,
and gather resources like a snowball rolling down a hill. Having reasonable expectations
and making reasonable demands on participants can greatly increase the potential of the
advocacy. Advocates who are over-worked burn out and those who are under-used lose
interest. Elizabeth G. explained the importance of ensuring that everyone who attends
a meeting leaves with something to do, a meaningful task that contributes to the cause.

Reflexivity

Related to critical thinking is the importance of being a reflexive advocate. Personal reflexivity is discussed within the framework of the anti-oppressive advocacy model in Chapter
1. "Reflexivity is about continually thinking through how our values, beliefs, location, and
social difference from our clients, as well as our access to various forms of power, affect
client–worker interactions" (Strega, 2007, p. 77). Reflexivity is included in this section on
advocacy strengths and skills as a reminder of the importance of a reflexive stance. A reflexive advocate turns the critical analysis inward to continually analyze their personal position
relative to the advocacy context and to look for opportunities to act. All of our personal attributes offer advantages and disadvantages depending on the context of the advocacy. The
reflexive advocate is intensely aware and looking for, or making, opportunities to contribute
to social change. Vivene's advocacy for the rights of women and the black community is an
excellent example of how she framed the message depending on the context. Meaghan spoke
about the privilege she held in certain circumstances and how this allowed her to speak out
on behalf of other workers in more precarious positions. Reflexivity is a micro-level position
but ultimately all advocacy is comprised of numerous interpersonal interactions that can
contribute to or take away from the success of the advocacy. These interactions culminate in
advocacy action at the personal, cultural, and structural levels.

Compassion

There are many definitions of compassion in popular and academic literature. Some lean towards a spiritual definition while others are associated with the caring professions of nursing,
teaching, and social work. Germer and Siegel (2010) define compassion as "the experience
of suffering with the wish to alleviate it" (p. 12). In advocacy, compassion is a sense of deep
caring and understanding coupled with a non-judgmental stance. Caring means the advocate is willing to get involved and be engaged in the difficulties of others. Understanding for
advocates is to go beyond the superficial and probe for context, meaning, and historical influences. Finally, being non-judgmental is to acknowledge your personal biases and try as much
as possible to put them aside. In Chapter 6, Ali C. and Ken S. dismissed the backlash directed
at them, explaining that their suffering was nothing compared to the suffering of Muslim and
Arab peoples around the world. Some of the literature warns against compassion fatigue or
burnout, which can be a danger for advocates if they neglect their self-care.

Resilience

Resilience is a trait that allows advocates to recover and respond with force after a defeat. Lee (2011) describes the resilience of Aboriginal communities after hundreds of years of oppression. "The sources of resilience infuse the community life with the energy to take on the tasks of struggle and healing that must go on in order to retain a high degree of community empowerment" (Lee, 2011, p. 80). Elizabeth G. tapped into community resilience to help power a campaign to stop pesticide spraying. Resilience is also a personal trait as evidenced in Mary L.'s story. She experienced the death of her partner and turned her pain into a fight for improved health and safety standards. Likewise, Vivene showed resilience when she turned her personal experience as the daughter of a foreign domestic worker into a fight for better immigration and labour legislation for all foreign domestic workers. Communities and individuals may both suffer trauma and oppression. Healing and resilience help to power advocacy for change. Advocates with resilience recover from defeats and use their failures to carry on and fight harder.

While this is probably not a complete list, I believe, based on the literature, discussions with experienced advocates, and my own experiences, that the section above includes many of the strengths and skills associated with effective anti-oppressive advocates.

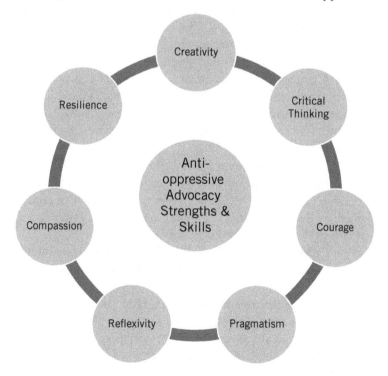

Figure 7.1   Strengths and Skills of an Anti-oppressive Advocate

These were not presented in any particular order because they are all equally relevant. It would be remarkable for one advocate to be strong in all of these areas. This is why advocates should have a strong, diverse network of advisors and mentors, and a solid support network. So if you are not particularly creative or pragmatic, draw on your contacts for advice, ideas, and, of course, constructive criticism. The relationships an advocate has with colleagues, friends, family, and community are key to their health, well-being, and long-term effectiveness. The next section will address the significance and meaning of relationship development in anti-oppressive advocacy.

Relationships

It may seem odd that this section falls so close to the end of this book because it is one of the most important. I decided to place it here with the thinking that, if it is read last, it will be remembered the most. Advocacy work is about working with others, which means a text is unfinished if it does not include a discussion of the importance of relationships in anti-oppressive advocacy. In fact, human service work in general, at its core, is dependent on the quality of relationships. Theory, models, processes, and technology aside, the quality of relationships is primary to the work. According to Morgaine and Capous-Desyllas, strong relationships are "a solid foundation for collaboration . . . change and transformation" (2015, p. 142). Indeed, strong working relationships are interdependent with healthy caring communities—relationships between service users and advocates are developed and sustained within the context of community. Whatever the level of practice—personal, cultural, or structural—it takes place within a community. Dialogue, critical consciousness development, and praxis (established practice) all develop and change within the community context of the actors. "The teachings are clear: A person cannot be viewed as separate from a community, however that community may be defined" (Baskin, 2011, p. 130).

This section will not repeat the many excellent resources available to human service workers that outline good general practices such as using an open posture, making eye contact (when culturally appropriate), showing warmth and empathy, and being genuine and non-judgmental (Hennessey, 2011). Instead the focus here will be on some key elements of relationships within anti-oppressive advocacy work.

Anti-oppressive advocacy with individuals, families, groups, communities, or social movements at any level is dependent on the quality of relationships. *Relationship* within this context means a commitment to dialogue, critical consciousness, and praxis. This section will highlight these three elements as inspired by the writings of Paulo Freire, a Brazilian academic and educator. Freire developed a method called conscientization, "[t]he process of developing a critical awareness of one's social reality through reflection and action. Action is fundamental because it is the process of changing the reality" (Freire Institute, 2014, para. 5).

Dialogue

The first element of anti-oppressive advocacy relationships is dialogue. In *A Glossary of AOP Terms*, *dialogue* is defined as "[a]n exchange of knowledge and a process of co-learning which assumes an intrinsic equality between and among the people involved" (2014, p. 13). Service providers and service users come together to share "information, thoughts, and ideas" to co-create meaning (Morgaine & Capous-Desyllas, 2015, p. 149). The interaction is genuine, open, and honest. The service provider and service user have different types and sources of knowledge—one is professional while the other is experiential—but both are valued and respected. Mutual learning and teaching come together in the form of new shared knowledge. Dialogue also involves working with service users to examine their life narratives and to discuss how oppression has contributed to their views (Freeman, 2011), and then helping service users to retell their stories in light of the analysis of oppression. The dialogue will also involve what Mullaly calls normalization (2010). Normalization is a process of reassuring a service user that their personal circumstances are the logical outcome of oppression and that what they are experiencing is normal.

Critical Consciousness

Critical consciousness development, the second element, is clearly related to dialogue as we have discussed above. Morgaine and Capous-Desyllas (2015) explain that critical consciousness "is firmly grounded in participatory dialogue as a way to engage community members to tap into their own knowledge through their lived experience" (p. 149). Service users develop agency in a process that involves linking personal experiences of oppression to cultural and structural issues. The service user and the advocate "assume roles of mutual sharing and learning" (Mullaly, 2007, p. 304). Service users develop a critical consciousness and become politicized as they examine the interconnections between their personal experiences of oppression and the political, economic, and social structures that contribute to and recreate oppression. Service users developing a critical consciousness are less likely to feel themselves to be responsible for their situations and more able to identify the structural causes. Critical consciousness helps to focus service users on cultural and structural level resistance and action, rather than feeling they must change themselves to cope with oppressive conditions.

Praxis

Advocates working from an anti-oppressive perspective will assist service users in developing a critical consciousness through dialogue, but while important, "[i]t is not enough for people to come together in dialogue in order to gain knowledge of their social reality. They must act together upon their environment in order to critically reflect upon their reality and so transform it through further action and critical reflection" (Freire Institute, 2014, para. 1). In other words, meeting to discuss and analyze social problems is incomplete unless the process involves action. Freire calls this praxis. This final relationship element is about helping service users to find and join with others who are also oppressed—to see their commonality and to work together in groups, or with larger movements, towards transforming the oppressive conditions. Services users will no longer feel "guilt, shame, and blame" for their situation; instead they will feel pride and find solidarity with others (Mullaly, 2010, p. 238). This final element is about inspiring resistance and taking action. Case Study 7.1 brings the three elements together: dialogue, critical consciousness, and praxis. See if you can find examples of each in the story.

Case Study 7.1   Anti-oppressive Relationship Development: Collaboration and Transformation

When Luke first came to the youth mental health centre for his appointment with a counsellor he shuffled in wearing heavy, untied work boots, slouched deeply, and wore a cap and a hood that concealed his eyes. Loud music bled from his headphones.

Luke admits now that when he first started seeing Sharon, his counsellor, he was "f---ed up." He had a lot of suicidal thoughts and was living in a youth shelter after being thrown out of his parents' house for drug and alcohol abuse, fighting, and skipping school. He did not want to see Sharon but the youth shelter made it a condition of his stay after he got into a fight with another resident. The other resident had allegedly stolen Luke's stash of OxyContin tablets, which Luke felt were the only thing that relieved his depression and anxiety. Luke knows that if he does not get help soon he is going to die either by suicide or some violent interaction on the street.

At the first appointment Luke is glad that Sharon does not act like a know-it-all expert. She is genuinely interested in supporting him and she helps Luke to tell his story slowly, when he is ready, when he feels comfortable. Over time, Luke grows to trust Sharon and feels that she values and respects him.

Sharon really listens and asks questions that sometimes are difficult to answer but help him to think about his life in a different way. Slowly she assists him in taking control and responsibility for himself and in seeing his experiences from another perspective. He sees that the poverty in his home had caused a lot of stress in his life and that of his parents. He remembers his parents fighting constantly when they could not pay the rent or buy groceries. When he was young he cowered in another room when they started yelling; as he got older he got involved in the fighting. The anxiety and stress led to drug and alcohol use, and then abuse, and then more fighting until he was finally kicked out of the house. He feels a lot of shame and guilt about his anger and addiction. Sharon helps him to see his circumstances in the context of how our society heaps blame and stigma on people who are poor and mentally ill and that he is not alone. Many other young people and their families live in similar circumstances. He notices that many of the youth in the shelter have similar stories to his; they come from poor families and experienced lots of fighting over money and substance abuse.

With Sharon's help Luke starts to consider the bigger picture: the many social, economic, and political factors that contribute to poverty and the impact this can have on families and individuals. He starts following the news locally and around the world. Luke also decides that he wants to return to high school and Sharon advocates with the school to get Luke readmitted. She also helps him to reconnect with his parents.

Luke works hard to first cut down and then quit his drug and alcohol abuse. Sharon helps Luke find a family doctor specializing in managing withdrawal symptoms and after several months he is no long abusing drugs or alcohol. In the process Luke learns a lot about the reasons for his addictions and the best ways to stay clean in the future. He feels stronger mentally and physically.

Luke starts to ask Sharon a lot of questions about what is being done to change things for poor families under stress. He wants to know how he can get involved in the change efforts. Sharon tells Luke about an anti-poverty group she is involved with and invites him to come to their next meeting. The group is in the middle of a campaign to get the provincial government to increase welfare rates by 25 per cent. Luke is very interested and brings two friends from the shelter to the meeting. He participates actively in the meeting and signs up for several upcoming anti-poverty events.

About a week after the meeting Luke meets again with Sharon. He is different. The guilt and shame about being poor and mentally ill is almost gone. His whole posture has changed. He walks straight, head up, eyes alive. He tells Sharon that he realizes that the family circumstances that had led to his depression and anxiety are not his fault. He now knows that his parents are not lazy or stupid or any of the other stereotypes heaped on the poor by those with economic privilege. He sees his situation and that of many others as part of the personal, cultural, and structural oppression of the poor. Hope and activism have replaced his depression and anxiety.

This case study illustrates the possibilities and opportunities for anti-oppressive advocacy work and the connections to advocacy work at the cultural and structural levels. The development of solid, caring relationships between service providers and service users is the foundation of anti-oppressive advocacy.

Conclusion: Having Advocacy Attitude

Attitude is one of those words that really needs a qualifier to be understood, for instance good attitude or bad attitude. As we saw in the stories in Chapter 6 and from my own experience, it is not uncommon that anti-oppressive advocates are described as having a bad attitude. This criticism comes from employers in situations where an advocate asks for better working conditions, social benefits, or improved programs for service users. It comes from politicians and bureaucrats who do not like to have their decisions and policies challenged. The criticism comes from those in authority in business and the social services who deny people's rights and dignity. If an advocate is receiving this type of criticism, for these reasons, it means they are doing exactly the right thing. This is the type of criticism that means the advocate is making a difference and contributing to positive social change. Essentially, the label of bad attitude is good in these circumstances.

Having an advocacy attitude means looking for opportunities to speak out against injustices in every context. It means bringing together anti-oppressive advocacy practices, planning, strategy, and action to achieve greater social justice. It means taking on unfair practices in the social services. It means going after slum landlords and stopping other human service workers and government bureaucrats from discriminating against service users. It means fighting to change unjust policies and legislation. It also means challenging our friends, families, and colleagues. Anti-oppressive advocacy attitude is being politically alive, seeing that everyday interactions between friends, colleagues, and the public are connected to oppressive cultural and structural conditions. The ordinary choices that we make can contribute to human rights, equality, and social justice, or not. "We need to have harmony between our political beliefs and our personal lives" (Mullaly, 2007, p. 362). An anti-oppressive advocacy attitude is joining with others in a culture of progressive change that honours human rights, equality, and social justice. This attitude is the heart of advocacy practice, and, allied with and supported by the theory and practice skills discussed in this text, will set you in good stead to create social change.

Without a struggle, there can be no progress.

– Frederick Douglass, 1857[2]

Critical Thinking Questions

1. How may your advocacy practice be affected by the trends discussed in this chapter?
2. Of the seven anti-oppressive advocacy strengths and skills identified in this chapter which do you feel are your strongest traits and which will you need to work on?
3. Assess your own advocacy practice in light of the section in this chapter discussing relationships in anti-oppressive advocacy work.
4. What do you need to do to develop your advocacy attitude?

Suggested Readings

Rather than recommending specific books or articles here, instead I would like to suggest some prominent Canadian authors who through their writing are important advocates for various progressive causes. Recommended authors include: Thomas King, Naomi Klein, Irshad Manji, Linda McQuaig, Raheel Raza, and Judy Rebick.

Suggested Videos and Websites

Greenpeace Canada. www.greenpeace.org/canada/en/home/
Council of Canadians. http://canadians.org/
Make Poverty History. www.makepovertyhistory.ca/
PovNet. www.povnet.org/
Canada Without Poverty Network. www.cwp-csp.ca/
Stop Racism and Hate Collective. www.stopracism.ca/
Canadian Council for Refugees. http://ccrweb.ca/
Council of Canadians with Disabilities. www.ccdonline.ca/
Disabled Women's Network Canada. www.dawncanada.net/
Egale Canada. http://egale.ca/

Notes

1. Africville, a primarily black community, lacked clean water and basic sanitation. According to Ward (2002). the nearby city of Halifax located several less than desirable facilities in Africville including a prison, a contagious infection hospital, a slaughterhouse, a fecal waste reservoir, and a garbage dump. During the 1960s the residents of Africville were evicted from their community by officials and relocated using Halifax city garbage trucks.

2. Douglass, Frederick. [1857] (1985). "The Significance of Emancipation in the West Indies." Speech, Canandaigua, New York, August 3, 1857; collected in pamphlet by author. In *The Frederick Douglass Papers. Series One: Speeches, Debates, and Interviews. Volume 3: 1855–63.* Edited by John W. Blassingame. New Haven: Yale University Press, p. 204.

Appendices

Explanations, templates, and samples for the following appear on the pages as noted.

Appendix 1
Advocacy Agreement Form

Purpose: To ensure that the service user and the service provider are both clear about the advocacy work to be done. The agreement should
- Provide the name, address, and contact information of the organization provider.
- Provide the name, position, and contact information of the advocate.
- Clearly state what advocacy work is to be done and in what order the advocacy actions will be carried out.
- Outline the responsibilities of the advocate and the service user.
- Provide a timeline for each advocacy action.
- Discuss confidentiality and service quality.
- Be signed and dated by the service user.

Template: Advocacy Agreement Form

Name of social service organization
Address
Phone number
Email and website

Advocate's first and last name and position name
Phone number
Email

I, *service user's name* agree to participate in advocacy planning and actions with support and assistance of *advocate's name, position and organization name*. The following actions will be carried out in the order given below, by the individual[s] listed, within the noted time frame.
1. Describe first advocacy action, name[s] of who will carry out the action, date the action will be completed
2. Second advocacy action; include the same details as in step 1. If two actions are to be completed simultaneously this should be noted.
3. Third advocacy action; include the same details as in step 1.
4. List as many as necessary.

Your personal information and participation in advocacy is kept confidential by *name of organization* unless you specifically agree to the release of your information and this will only be requested for the purposes of the advocacy. The *name of organization* makes every effort to ensure that service users receive quality service and respectful treatment. If you have any concerns about the advocacy service at *name of organization* please contact *name of supervisor/manager, position name, phone number and email*.

_____   _____
Service user signature   **Date**

Sample Advocacy Agreement Form

The following is based on a case study inspired by real experiences but does not represent a specific service user or circumstance—all names and contact information given are for illustrative purposes only.

Community Advocacy Services & Programs
194 11 Ave. S.W.
Calgary, Alberta
T4J 6G8
(403) 918-2736
http://casp.calgary.com
casp@shaws.ca

Jin Nam, Advocate
(403) 546-8193
Jin.nam@cogo.ca

I, _Abby Roos_ agree to participate in advocacy planning and actions with support and as-sistance of _Jin Nam, Advocate, Community Advocacy Services & Programs_. The following actions will be carried out in the order given below, by the individual[s] listed, within the noted time frame.

1. Contact Students Association Lawyer for free legal advice, Abby Roos, May 1, 2017.
2. Meet with Crown Attorney, Abby Roos, May 5, 2017.
3. Write letter of case advocacy addressed to Crown Attorney, Jin Nam, May 6, 2017.

Your personal information and participation in advocacy is kept confidential by _Community Advocacy Services & Programs_ unless you specifically agree to the release of your information and this will only be requested for the purposes of the advocacy. The _Community Advocacy Services & Programs_ makes every effort to ensure that service users receive quality service and respectful treatment. If you have any concerns about the advocacy service at _Commu-nity Advocacy Services & Programs please contact Yara Souza, Executive Director, (403) 918-527, yara.souza@cogo.ca_.

Abby Roos   _April 25, 2017_

_____   _____
Service user signature   **Date**

Appendix 2
Letter of Case Advocacy

Purpose: To advocate with and on behalf of an individual or family for something they need or have a right to. The letter is written with, or on behalf of, the service user(s) to the person with the authority to make the change for the service user. The tone of the letter should be courteous, polite, and respectful to all concerned. Spindel (2001) recommends not to overly embellish, ramble on, or become excessively detailed. Be brief, specific, clear, and stick to the evidence.

Template: Letter of Case Advocacy

Name of social service organization [sending the letter]
Street address, city, postal code

Date

Recipient's first and last name, position title
Name of social service organization [receiving the letter]
Street address, city, postal code

Dear Recipient first and last name: [send to the key decision maker, and "cc." one or two others]

   1st paragraph . . . Identify yourself and describe your relationship to the service user.
   2nd paragraph . . . Briefly describe the problem and the desired outcome.
   3rd paragraph . . . Address each issue separately, precisely, and logically. It may be a good idea to order events or facts chronologically and use precise dates to explain the service user's situation. Detail the evidence or support you have to validate claims by the client e.g., doctors' notes, job search records, daycare records, and so on. Include exact dates and locations.
   4th paragraph . . . Review and make reference to relevant procedures, policies, and legislation. Use the applicable policy (you may use direct quotes from the policy here) to defend the service user. Explain how the policy is relevant to your client's case.
   5th paragraph . . . If the service user has a very good record then use this to talk about how their current situation is an exception. If the service user has a poor record you need not bring it up here or you might acknowledge it briefly and also explain how they are trying to change (what supports have you helped them put in place to change).
   6th paragraph . . . Make a direct request and ask for a written response. Give a reasonable deadline (so you can take it to another forum if your deadline is not met).
   Sincerely,

Signature of advocate
First and last name of advocate
Position title
Phone number
Email
Attachments:
Date, Name of the item, why it is included

Sample Letter of Case Advocacy

The following is based on a case study inspired by real experiences but does not represent a specific service user or circumstance—all names and contact information given are for illustrative purposes only.

Centre for Community and Legal Advocacy (CCLA)
1890 Upper Walker Street
Halifax, Nova Scotia
B3F 1S4

November 2, 2017

George Green, Caseworker
Community Services
1342 Flood Avenue
Halifax, Nova Scotia
A1B 2C3

Dear Mr. Green, Caseworker:

My name is Veata Pang, Community Advocate at the Centre for Community and Legal Advocacy. The Centre provides information and advocacy for families and individuals with low incomes. I met and spoke at length with Nada Aziz on November 2 of this year and will be representing her on an urgent matter regarding her October welfare deposit. I have attached a form authorizing me to represent Ms. Aziz (Attachment 1).

Ms. Aziz, a new recipient of welfare, did not receive her benefits in October of this year. We ask that you review her case in light of the information below and reinstate her welfare assistance as soon as possible as she has no other means of support.

Ms. Aziz has been in receipt of welfare benefits for approximately four months. She signed an agreement with Community Services to attend English language classes (ESL) daily with a goal to improve her English and find full-time paid employment to support herself and her two young children. Apart from her time away to care for her sick children, Ms. Aziz attended ESL classes regularly and was an excellent student. Her ESL attendance records are attached for July, August, September, and October (Attachment 2). Ms. Conner, Director of ESL classes, has provided a record of Ms. Aziz's grades (Attachment 3). The ESL attendance records indicate that Ms. Aziz was absent from classes from September 4 to 16, missing a total of nine days of classes. During her absence Ms. Aziz was caring for her children, ages eight and ten, who were both ill with influenza. During this time she was unable to attend classes as she is their sole caregiver. Please see attached doctors' notes indicating the diagnosis and dates of confinement (Attachment 4). Unaware of the impact her absence would have on her welfare benefits, Ms. Aziz temporarily suspended her participation in ESL classes to care for her two children.

As an explanation, Ms. Aziz only recently started to collect welfare benefits and is unfamiliar with all of her responsibilities. Ms. Aziz is trying to improve her English but her first language is Arabic, so she was not able to read the correspondence sent from your office indicating a suspension of benefits (Attachment 5). I have reviewed the letter with Ms. Aziz and she now understands that she should have contacted your department immediately when her children became sick and she could not attend ESL classes. Welfare policy allows recipients to apply for short reasonable absences from participation in work-seeking activities to care for sick dependents. Ms. Aziz now understands she should have notified your office of her temporary absence. She regrets that she has neglected her responsibilities to your department and promises that she will not let it happen again.

Ms. Aziz is a dedicated parent and is committed to working hard to improve her English and to find paid work. She has assured me that in the future she will contact your department if she is unable to meet her commitments. Ms. Aziz is available to meet and complete any additional forms or documentation you require.

On behalf of Ms. Aziz I am asking you to reinstate her welfare benefits immediately as she is behind in her rent and unable to buy food for her children. Contact me if you require any additional information to make your decision. Please respond to my phone or email within three days as the matter is urgent.

Sincerely,

V. Pang

Veata Pang
Community Advocate
902-627-4289
pang.v@globalmail.com

Attachments:
1. November 2, 2017. Representation Authorization. A form allowing Ms. Pang to communicate on behalf of and represent Ms. Aziz.
2. July–October 2017. ESL Attendance Records. Attendance records indicating Ms. Aziz regularly attended classes except when her children were sick.
3. October 31, 2017. ESL Grades. The record of Ms. Aziz's grades indicates she has good marks and is progressing well in her ESL program.
4. September 5, 2017, and September 10, 2017. Doctors' notes. The notes indicate that Ms. Aziz took her children to their family physician and include the recommendations for health care and medication.
5. October 16, 2017. Letter from Welfare Department. Notification (in English) that Ms. Aziz's benefits have been suspended.

Appendix 3
Letter of Cause Advocacy

Purpose: To bring about change at the cultural or structural level for individuals, groups, and communities. The letter may be part of a letter writing campaign where organizers encourage large numbers of people to write letters of cause advocacy. The letter may be addressed to the media with the goal of garnering widespread coverage or addressed to politicians at the municipal, provincial/territorial, or federal levels of government.

Template: Letter of Cause Advocacy

Advocate's first and last name
Street address, city, postal code

Date

Recipient's first and last name, position title
Name of organization (receiving the letter)
Street address, city, postal code

Dear recipient first and last name, [include title MP, MPP, MLA, MNA, Honourable for ministers]
 1st paragraph . . . Identify yourself (your professional and personal experiences) or describe the group on behalf of which you are writing. You many include a brief history of the group, purpose and goals of the group, and information about group membership.
 2nd paragraph . . . Explain briefly and precisely why you are writing and exactly what you want.
 3rd, paragraph [this section may actually consist of 2 to 3 paragraphs] . . . Systematically but briefly outline the relevant, credible evidence that supports your position. Data, statistics, studies, expert opinions, and so on should be included. These paragraphs may include some brief background/historical information that pertains to the cause.
 4th paragraph . . . Briefly restate your position and what you want the recipient of the letter to do about it.
 Sincerely,

Signature of advocate
First and last name of advocate
Position title
[only if you are representing a
social service organization]
Phone number
Email

Sample Letter of Cause Advocacy

The following is based on a case study inspired by real experiences but does not represent a specific service user or circumstance—all names and contact information given are for illustrative purposes only.

Adele Turner
25 Eastlake St
Saskatoon, Saskatchewan
S7H 4G9

August 8, 2017

Honourable [name of minister]
Minister of Social Services,
Responsible for Status of Women,
and the Saskatchewan Housing Corporation
Room 303, Legislative Building
2405 Legislative Drive
Regina, Saskatchewan
S4S 0B3

Dear Honourable [name of minister],

I am writing you on a matter of great concern to me—the affordable housing crisis in Saskatchewan. I have worked in the social service field for over six years helping families and individuals find housing. The long waiting lists for social housing and the high and increasing cost of market housing have had troubling impacts on tenants with low incomes. I have personally seen families separated by homelessness, children taken into care, and youth sent to detention as a consequence of the lack of affordable housing.

Based on my experience and my study of housing policy I implore you to build 30 to 50 new social housing units each year for the next 10 years to try to accommodate the more than 550 families, individuals with disabilities, and seniors on the waiting list for housing. Social housing has many short- and long-term benefits for the community. Morel Caissie, President of the Canadian Association of Social Workers, says affordable housing reduces the costs of health care and the harm suffered by people with a low income.

Since 1978 the Saskatchewan Housing Corporation has developed and supported more than 24,200 social and affordable housing units (Housing Service Corporation, 2014). The recent economic boom and bust cycle has put pressure on the affordable housing supply as many citizens are now forced to turn to unemployment insurance and welfare. Families and individuals, through no fault of their own, are now unable to pay their rent or mortgage. Further, the rising income inequality has hit some groups harder than others such as seniors, people with mental or physical disabilities, Aboriginal people, and single parents. It is imperative that the province continue to support its most vulnerable citizens by building more social housing.

Safe and adequate housing is a prerequisite for mental and physical health, education attainment, and social well-being. Social housing for people with a low income provides the best possible basis for equal opportunity for individuals and families. Further, the Federation of Canadian Municipalities call affordable housing the "cornerstone" to a healthy economy. They explain that the economy is dependent on a good supply of affordable housing and "is a vital part of the economic and social wellbeing of a community." Social housing is by far the least expensive solution to the affordable housing problem. Recent studies report the costs each year per person for emergency shelters (men, youth, women, families, victims of domestic violence) is between $13,000 and $42,000, supportive and transitional housing costs between $13,000 and $18,000 and institutional (psychiatric hospital, prison/detention) between $66,000 and $120,000 (Pomeroy, 2005). Comparatively, social housing with supports (singles and families) costs between $5,000 and $8,000 per year. The best social and economic solution to the affordable housing crisis is building more social housing.

I strongly urge you to substantially increase the supply of social housing. The recent economic downturn has left many Saskatchewan citizens in dire straits. Decent, affordable social housing is an essential part of a healthy community. Social housing is also a way for communities to avoid more expensive consequences in the long term. Building social housing is the reasonable, fair, and cost effective solution to the affordable housing crisis.

Sincerely,

Adele Turner

(306) 778-9824
turner.a@gmail.com

Appendix 4
Letter to the Editor

Purpose: Letters to the editor are written by readers to express their opinions or perspectives on articles previously published in the newspaper or journal. Advocates should consider the following points when writing a letter to the editor:

- Choose an issue that your care about passionately.
- Use a tone that matches that of the publication (informal to very formal).
- Speak in first person.
- Connect your issue to a recent article in the publication (three days to a week at most).
- Make interesting and unique points, arguments, and solutions. Take a supportive or oppositional position to the previous article.
- Make your main points at the start of the letter; include data, statistics, experts, and studies to support your points. Then briefly restate your opinion at the end.
- If you are an expert or have specific affiliation with the issue identify this.
- Try to avoid technical jargon.
- Be clear, concise, and don't ramble. Write in a lively, funny, and/or rational style but remain respectful. Use correct spelling, grammar, and punctuation, and proofread.
- Stick to the word limitations stated by the publication for letters to the editor. The *New York Times* recommends about 150 words.
- Include your first and last name and contact information as most publications will contact you to authenticate the letter.

Sample Letter to the Editor

This letter to the editor is responding to an imaginary article about how homelessness is negatively impacting tourism.

Time to End Homelessness

An August 18 news article reported that tourism is being hurt by frightening, unsightly homeless people begging for money.

It is time to implement solutions to homelessness rather than disparaging people that are poor and perhaps mentally and physically unwell.

Researchers tell us that on any night in Canada 30,000 people are homeless. It is reprehensible that communities across our wealthy country tolerate this disgraceful treatment of other human beings.

I have worked in the social service field for many years and know there are ethical and cost effective ways to solve this problem.

First, drop-in centres for people who are homeless, street outreach programs, hot meal programs and emergency shelters need to receive reasonable funding.

Second, build more affordable, adequate social housing for people who are homeless.

Third, housing and service providers should subscribe to a "housing first" policy that moves people who are experiencing homelessness directly into independent, permanent housing and provides supports when needed.

Reasonable, humane, cost-effective solutions to homelessness are available. All that is needed is willing political leadership.

Lami Sesay, Community Outreach Worker
End the Seven-day Rule Network

Appendix 5
Op-ed

Purpose: An op-ed is written, usually by a person who is an authority on a subject, to inform the readership about an important newsworthy topic. The op-ed is written to articulate a particular perspective on the topic and to prompt debate, inform policy, and shape opinions. It is recommended that the advocate contact the newspaper or media outlet to pitch the op-ed idea. Op-eds take time to research and write and therefore you want to do everything you can to ensure it is published. Advocates should consider the following points when writing an op-ed:

- Timing is important—pitch an op-ed when the topic is current.
- Articulate one clear opinion or point.
- State your opinion at the start—if you can, think of an interesting hook.
- Explain why the readership should care.
- Use your personal style in your writing and a respectful tone.
- Use basic language, about grade 10 level, and avoid jargon and technical terms.
- Short, clear sentences and short paragraphs work best.
- Offer solutions or recommendations.
- Include facts, stats, examples, and experts to back up your point.
- Include case studies, stories, and personal experiences to appeal to the reader's feelings or sense of nostalgia.
- Be brief—about 500–750 words.
- Provide a strong summary with an interesting conclusion that restates your main point using different words.
- Include your first and last name and contact information.

Sample Op-Ed

It Is Time to Legalize Marijuana

No I am not a weed smoking youth, a member of a drug dealing gang, or an owner of a marijuana grow-op. I am a parent, social worker, teacher, taxpayer, and citizen, concerned with the irrational, costly, and discriminatory approach to controlling marijuana consumption in Canada.

It is time to put an end to the criminalization of casual marijuana users. They and their families have paid dearly through lost potential, narrowed opportunities, and diminished prospects. The punishment is completely out of proportion compared to the crime. According to *Maclean's* magazine, sometime in 2013 the millionth Canadian was arrested for marijuana possession (MacQueen, 2013). That is over a million Canadians limited perhaps for life because of simple marijuana use.

Various levels of government waste valuable tax dollars on policing, courts, and correctional facilities, money that could be better spent on health care, education, and social services. Up until 2008 the federal government seemed to be moving towards decriminalization of marijuana possession. However, after the 2008 election the new Conservative government, with a misguided law and order agenda, slammed the door shut on the decriminalization of marijuana possession.

Ironically, the law and order agenda coincided with dropping rates of crime across the entire country. This gave law enforcement agencies ample time to focus on the "easy pickings"—recreational marijuana users. In the six years following the 2008 election arrest rates for marijuana possession increased by 41 per cent, or about 405,000 individuals (MacQueen, 2013). In 2011 simple marijuana possession comprised 54 per cent of all drug arrests (Carter & Macpherson, 2013). Police are spending valuable time and resources on busting teenagers with joints rather than focusing on more serious crimes. These marijuana busts allow police agencies to report arrest statistics that keep the pro law and order agenda folks happy and keep the money flowing from the federal and provincial governments for enhanced enforcement.

Interestingly, a study found that "control policies, whether harsh or liberal, appear to have little or no impact on the prevalence of its consumption" (Carter & Macpherson, 2013). So Canadians will still use marijuana almost regardless of the penalty.

Carter & Macpherson explain in their 2013 report *Getting to Tomorrow: A Report on Canadian Drug Policy* that considerable enforcement energy is put into the control of a substance that the prestigious journal *The Lancet* ranks eighth on a list of 20 harmful drugs. Many readers may be surprised to learn that alcohol is the number one most harmful drug, greater that heroin and cocaine (Carter & Macpherson, 2013, p. 84).

Recreational marijuana use should not be a crime. It is time for our federal political representatives to remove this charge from the criminal code and regulate the sale of marijuana as they do alcohol. There are three good reasons to follow this course of action.

1. There is widespread and growing support. A 2012 poll found that 66 per cent of Canadians support the decriminalization of marijuana and 57 per cent support legalization (Grenier, 2013, 29 August). Support has been increasing steadily. Three out of four federal parties—the Liberal Party, the New Democratic Party, and the Green Party—include the legalization and regulation of marijuana as part of their proposed policy platforms.

2. Legalization would improve public health outcomes. Experts recommend a public health approach as the best way to limit harm and improve responsible consumption of marijuana. Canadian authorities have plenty of experience regulating tobacco and alcohol, using methods including "price controls through taxation, restriction of advertising and promotion, controls on age of purchaser, driving restrictions, limited hours of sale, labelling that contains information on potency and health effects, plain packaging, and licensing guidelines" (Carter & Macpherson, 2013, p.89). These methods have been very effective in limiting the sales of tobacco to minors and reducing the number of smokers, and could be applied to the sale of marijuana.

3. The rates of crime in Canada will fall and law enforcement agencies will be able to focus their efforts on more serious criminal activities instead of chasing pot smoking teenagers down in the parks. Unregulated consumption of marijuana hands regulation powers to organized crime groups that use violence and guns to fight turf wars and have no regard for the age of the consumer or the strength and quality of the product (Carter & Macpherson, 2013). The cost of law enforcement is way out of proportion to the harm of the substance.

Countries that have legalized pot experienced no increase in consumption. In fact, those countries all have lower rates of consumption than Canada where it is still illegal. Legalization means that over a million Canadians will no longer face restrictions and have their future potential cut short for simple marijuana possession. It is time to do the right thing—legalize and regulate possession of marijuana in Canada.

Dr. Alex Larsen
alex.larsen@citycollege.ca
(704) 357-9802

Appendix 6
Media Release

Purpose: To use the media to inform a large number of people about an event or an opinion. Advocates should consider the following points when writing a media release:

- Use a strong headline.
- The release should not exceed one page in length, double spaced.
- The opening paragraph should provide all of the important information and a reason to read the remainder of the media release.
- Explain why it is special, important, and worth it!
- Describe the effect on individuals or the community.
- Write clearly and concisely, use short sentences and paragraphs.
- If you want the public to attend an event, accuracy is paramount with regards to places, dates, times, and contact information.
- Use quotes to provide an opinion about the event or topic and use the person's name and their title or position.
- State which organization(s) is involved.
- Explain precisely what activities will be going on and when.
- Provide the date and time (a.m. or p.m.), location, directions, and public transportation and parking information.
- Provide contact information—name, email, phone number (make sure this information is correct).
- Provide a brief bio of the organization at the end.
- Always end with "– 30 –" or "###" this indicates to the media outlet the end of the media release.

Sample Media Release

The following sample media release is promoting an event and is inspired by real advocacy organizations but does not represent a specific circumstance—all names and contact information given are for illustrative purposes only.

For Immediate Release:

LGBTQ Rights Coalition
5450 Main Street West
Hamilton, Ontario
B8G 2T9
lgbtqrights@ourgroup.ca
(905) 593-4523

Stand Up Against State Sanctioned Violence Against LGBTQ Communities Around the World

The Hamilton LGBTQ Rights Coalition is joining forces with members of the arts, entertainment, and culinary communities to present the fifth annual "Stand Up" day to fight against state sanctioned violence against LGBTQ communities around the world. The event will feature an art exhibit, poetry readings, dancing, musical entertainment, and vendors featuring food from around the world. Please join us at the West End Community Centre from 10 a.m.to 4 p.m. on Saturday, October 18, 2015. Visit the lgbtqrights.ca website for directions, parking information, an events schedule, and a complete list of the vendors.

"Stand Up is a thought provoking and lively event that helps to highlight the violence and terror experienced by members of LGBTQ communities around the world," said Francis Gagnon, a local LGBTQ activist.

Last year's Stand Up event attracted over 5,000 people and raised $20,000 to help support LGBTQ refugees in Canada and around the world.

"It is important for our community to stand up against state sanctioned LGBTQ oppression," said Tulu Okeke, President of the LGBTQ Rights Coalition. "We need to understand that people from LGBTQ communities around the world live with the fear of torture, imprisonment, and death every day because of their sexual orientation."

Stand Up is a free event and provides a welcoming environment for all, including children, youth, families, and seniors.

For more information contact Emanuel Curtis at (905) 529-2085 or emanuel.curtis@gmail.com.

LGBTQ Rights Coalition of Hamilton is a diverse network of over 30 individuals and organizations working together to end the persecution of members of the LGBTQ community in Canada and around the world. The Coalition helps resettle LGBTQ refugees, promotes public awareness, and advocates for LGBTQ human rights. The Coalition is an active member of a worldwide network of LGBTQ human rights groups in more than 40 countries.

###

Appendix 7
Petition

Purpose: To try to change institutional or government policies, regulations, or legislation by collecting signatures and contact information from individuals who support the proposed change.

Petitions may be very formal and official or informal. Formal petitions, to be presented in the House of Commons, must follow specific rules precisely. See *Formal Content of Petitions Guidelines*, www.parl.gc.ca/About/House/PracticalGuides/Petitions/petitions PG2008__Pg02-e.htm#addressee

The points below are for writing more informal, paper-based petitions. Informal petitions are often launched as e-petitions as well. Informal petitions are aimed at raising public awareness, and pressing those in authority to make changes. Advocates should consider the following points when writing an informal petition:

- Develop a very clear, specific statement about what you want people to support. Then follow up with a brief explanation of the reasons for the petition.
- Choose a title for your petition and write it at the top of each page above the petition statement.
- Try to contain the petition to one paragraph as people will not want to spend a lot of time reading before they decide to support and sign.
- Create a signers' sheet with columns for: name, address, email (optional), phone number (optional), and signature.
- Include only 15 to 20 lines for signers per page.
- Each signers' sheet should have the petition statement printed at the top.

Sample Petition

PETITION – End Poverty in Canada Now

We, the undersigned Canadians, object to poverty in Canada. Today nearly 1 in every 10 Canadians is considered poor. That is about 3.2 million people, including 634,000 children. More than 833,000 people, about one third of them children, rely on food banks. Nearly 200,000 individuals are homeless each year, approximately 30,000 on any given night. Around 1.5 million Canadians or about 13 per cent, live in housing that is unaffordable, in poor repair, and overcrowded. Therefore, we call on the Canadian government to adopt legislation today to put an end to poverty and the associated problems of food insecurity, homelessness, and lack of affordable housing.

Name	Address, Phone Number, Email	Signature

Appendix 8
Poster

Purpose: To encourage the general public to attend or participate in an important event or activity. The poster provides the most essential information (like an invitation) for interested participants. Most posters are made using some type of software, often Word, but it is still good to create some handmade posters. Poster making parties are a great way to involve young children (bring lots of art supplies). Regardless of the format (computer or handmade) the same basic guidelines apply. Advocates should consider the following points when making posters:

- The top of the poster should have a short, informative title in large lettering to capture the attention of the reader.
- Use colour, pictures, and different sizes and themes of font but keep it simple and clear.
- The central area of the poster may contain information about events, speakers, or activities.
- The bottom of the poster should contain information about what you want potential participants to know or do and contact information for people who want additional information.
- If someone in your advocacy group has graphic design experience, encourage them to take the lead in designing posters for your group's event.
- The most important thing to remember is to have the essential information on the poster: who, what, when, where, how, and why.

Sample Poster

National Housing Strategy
Day of Action

Housing is a right and a basic human need.
Come show you want to end homelessness now.

Join us: City Hall Square, 6:30 pm
Bring demonstration signs and comfortable shoes.

Keynote Speakers
Alma Torres and Riya Malik

Musical Guests
Rap/R&B star: Tarnished Foe
and
Country artist: Garth Jackson

For complete details visit:
housingactionnow@ourgroup.ca

House art © photka/Fotolia

Appendix 9
Demonstration Signs

Purpose: To quickly and clearly inform the public about an important cause. Signs are made to be carried at demonstrations, protests, and pickets. Signs are often handmade, usually during a special group meeting specifically organized for the purpose. If you belong to a union or other well-funded organization, signs may be professionally designed and printed and distributed at the picket site. Advocates should consider the following points when making demonstration signs:

- Gather bristol board, markers, rulers, sturdy cardboard tubes (for handles).
- Use three to five words only on a sign (something that can be remembered when read quickly).
- Print the same message on the front and back of the sign.
- Print in dark ink and use large, clear letters.

Sample of Demonstration Signs

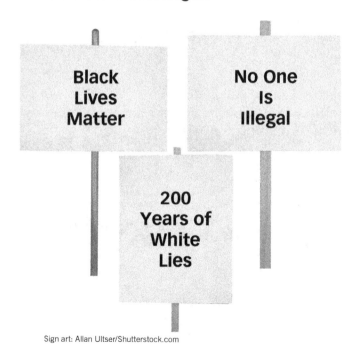

Sign art: Allan Ultser/Shutterstock.com

Appendix 10
Demonstration Chants

Purpose: Chants are easy, short, rhyming verses created to draw the public's attention to a cause. They are recited together by people attending a demonstration. Advocates should consider the following points when creating chants:

- The chants should be created by the people that will be attending the demonstration.
- Consider making up chants while your group is making posters and signs (see above) and don't forget to write them down.
- The cause is serious and so are many chants, but chants can also be humorous, ironic, or even sarcastic or mocking.
- Create new chants or adapt ones used in other demonstrations.

Sample Demonstration Chants

"Women Unite Take Back the Night!"

"Gay, Straight, Black, White, marriage is a civil right!"

"One, two, three, four, this is class war!"

"Hey hey, ho ho! This racist war has got to go!"

Glossary

'60s Scoop is a term used to describe the period from the late 1950s to the mid-1980s during which approximately 20,000 Aboriginal children were taken from their birth families and adopted or fostered to mostly white, middle-class families. Aboriginal leaders protested the policy, labelling it a continuation of colonialism.

Administrative strategy is advocacy that targets agency policies. It can be carried out by those who work within the agency in question or those who work in a different agency and involves a worker or several workers advocating for changes that need to be made to a social service.

Advocacy is, at its simplest, a set of skills and techniques used to bring about a change for individuals, families, communities, and society.

Anti-oppressive theory and practice (AOTP) is a form of social work practice that focuses on combatting social injustice and inequality at the personal, cultural, and structural levels. The practice is grounded in the analysis of power, privilege, and oppression. AOTP is highly politicized and reflexive. Service providers are not neutral; they take the side of the service user. AOTP is empowering, holistic, and transformative.

Bills are proposals for new legislation or for changes to current legislation. Bills are most often written and introduced for consideration in the House of Commons by a minister of the party in power.

Casework grew out of the practices of the Charity Organization Society. The process involves investigating a client and providing counselling, referrals, and programs. Traditionally, casework focused on helping service users to adjust to their circumstances, such as poverty or unemployment.

Charity Organization Society (COS) is representative of social service agencies established in the late 1800s in Europe, Canada, and the United States. These organizations were formed to prevent the poor from becoming dependent on charity services. Service providers distinguished between the deserving poor, those who should receive charity, and the undeserving poor, those who did not merit assistance. The undeserving poor were considered to have weak morals and were thought to be too lazy to look for work.

Community organizing strategy is an important part of advocacy at the cultural and structural levels. It brings individuals with common interests or concerns together in organizations. The organizations then work together to develop power and take action to bring about positive changes for the community they represent.

Context refers to the full scope of circumstances in which advocacy is taking place. It refers to the physical space or location, the political climate, the relations of power, interpersonal relations and dynamics, cultural norms, structural framework, and so on. In other words context is a complicated, changing space that requires acute continuous analysis.

Conventional social work practices are those that help services users to adjust to and cope with their circumstances such as unemployment, poverty, or mental illness rather than challenging the causes of these problems such as racism, sexism, biased legislation, or structural inequality.

Critical analysis is a disciplined process of analyzing underlying values, beliefs, assumptions, and causes of problems, situations, and contexts.

Cultural workers are politically engaged and culturally conscious and use social action to help raise awareness, develop alternative culture, and work for greater social justice for oppressed groups. They are advocates who fight against racism, sexism, classism, ageism, ableism, homophobia, and other forms of discrimination, all of which profoundly impact the people who come to advocates for assistance.

Dominant culture is a representation of society as it is created and reproduced by individuals and groups with greater influence and power. These dominant individuals and groups have influence and power because of their position, financial circumstances, or greater numbers and it is used to create a culture that reflects the powerful. The dominant culture is then popularized and reproduced in the media, arts and entertainment, and other means, through stereotyping and marginalization.

Generalist or **problem-solving approach** describes a model of social work and social work education. The approach has a knowledge base in the social sciences; a practice range of micro, mezzo, and macro; and a systematic approach to helping. The problem-solving approach is a common social work practice used when working with service users. The approach is a series of steps: engagement, assessment, planning, implementation, evaluation, termination, and follow-up.

Globalization is the increasing integration of economic, social, and political systems around the world. Positive viewpoints on globalization highlight the potential for greater sharing and understanding of cultural diversity and improvements in health and welfare of poorer nations. Negative viewpoints highlight, among other things, the concern that increased integration will lead to a decrease in cultural diversity and more poverty, especially in developing countries.

Inside advocates are service providers using administrative strategies to advocate for changes in the organization that employs them.

Legal strategy uses existing statutory conventions and institutions such as the criminal or civil legal systems to fight for the rights of individuals, groups, and communities. This type of advocacy practice requires specialized skills and knowledge of the legal and regulatory systems.

Legislative strategy is a type of advocacy, the broad intent of which is to champion, change, or defeat legislation at the municipal, provincial/territorial, or federal levels of government.

LGBTQ is an acronym for Lesbian, Gay, Bisexual, Transgender, and Queer. The acronym acknowledges sexual and gender diversity. Sometimes additional abbreviations are included, such as "2S" for *two-spirited* and "I" for *intersex*.

Low income cut-off (LICO) is a poverty measure used by Statistics Canada. According to this measure, people are considered to live in poverty if they spend 20 per cent or more of their income on necessities (food, clothing, and shelter) than the average family does. The LICO is calculated for different household and community sizes.

Managerialism is the use of business management practices in the social services, adopted because social services were considered to be lacking in professional management and therefore not using charity and tax dollars efficiently and effectively. Managerialism values hierarchical organization structures, tight supervision, accountability, and quantitative measurement.

Neo-liberalism is an approach that focuses on promoting capitalism unhindered by government policy restrictions. It is, for the most part, the approach favoured by conservative interests and the business elite, which seek to ensure that government regulation throughout the world is kept to a minimum.

Outside advocates are service providers using administrative strategy to bring about a change in social service agencies (for which they do not work) or in the social service system.

P/C/S analysis uses the P/C/S (personal/cultural/structural) model (see Thompson, 2001 or Mullaly, 2010) to analyze the oppression experienced by service users and others in society.

Poor bashing is negative impressions of and actions towards low-income people based on stereotypical beliefs, resulting in marginalization and discrimination. Poor bashing reinforces the systematic oppression of people with a low income by people with privilege, including service providers.

Poverty line is an income level below which people are considered to live in poverty. The generally accepted measure of poverty in Canada is Statistics Canada's low income cut-off (LICO) measure.

Privilege refers to unearned, sometimes invisible, advantages and benefits not available to members of oppressed groups.

Public education strategy is an approach aimed at bringing about a change in the public attitudes and beliefs that underpin institutions and legislation.

Reflexivity is a systematic process of reflection and self-assessment combined with an intense analysis of context and with a focus on action

Root-cause questioning is that which aims to develop an understanding and analysis of a problem by asking a series of why-type questions until there are no more why questions to answer.

Service user is a term increasingly used in the human services to refer to someone who is currently receiving benefits or services from a social service organization. The use of the term *service user* is a political choice for service providers, with the aim to reduce the power differences and as a reminder that everyone will be a service user at some time in their lives. Other terminology that is used in the field includes: clients, patients, consumers, survivors, participants, tenants, residents, and others.

Settlement House Movement (SHM) was a social movement started in the late 1800s in Europe and then Canada and the United States. Educated, wealthy, middle-class people, involved in the SHM, lived and worked with the urban poor. They believed that poverty was caused by social and economic conditions.

Settlement houses were establishments set up in poor urban neighbourhoods by the SHM, which provided services such as health care, education, childcare, and language classes.

Situational ethics do not follow specific rules, rather each case is considered distinct and requiring an exclusive solution. Ethical decisions, then, are flexible depending on the context. Some proponents consider the well-being of people and love to be the only guiding principles.

Small "p" and big "P" politics references the two spheres of politics in which advocates often work. Small "p" politics (sometimes called *personal politics*) is that of everyday lives and the seemingly trivial decisions and choices individuals make every day (the clothes you buy, the coffee you drink, etc.), which nonetheless form identity and cumulatively influence the personal, cultural, and structural levels in society. Big "P" politics is the official sphere, that of elections, politicians, political parties, and the workings of government at the municipal, provincial, national, and international levels.

Social action group is an organized group working together to bring about a change in an institution, legislation, or belief system. For example, the Black Lives Matter movement is fighting against racist police attitudes and actions such as carding.

Social location is an understanding of a person's location within the interconnecting systems of privilege and oppression. People are influenced by their social location but not predestined by it. Individuals are shaped by their social location but also have the capacity to change, transform, and act apart from their location.

Social policy legislation is federal or territorial/provincial legislation that forms the policy framework for social services, health care, and welfare programs.

Strategy is the overarching general or abstract approach to be taken to achieve an outcome.

Tactic is a small, specific step used in combination with other tactics. The sum of the tactics is designed to contribute to achieving the overall strategy.

Welfare is another term for social assistance. The amounts received by recipients in some provinces is as much as 60 per cent below the Statistics Canada low income cut-off. Welfare is a provincial/territorial responsibility in Canada and therefore there are 13 separate welfare systems. The policies and benefit levels vary from one province/territory to the next.

Workfare is a term used to describe a work-for-welfare policy. Most provinces in Canada require recipients of social assistance (welfare) to participate in a job search or training that will lead to employment (a type of workfare). Welfare recipients are penalized if they do not comply.

References

Alinsky, S. (1989). *Rules for radicals*. New York: Vintage Books.

Ambrose, M. (2015). Top scientists want tar sands development stopped. *Green Peace Blog Post*. Retrieved from www.greenpeace.org/canada/en/blog/Blogentry/10-reasons-top-scientists-want-a-moratorium-o/blog/53196/

Amnesty International. (2001). *José Eduardo Lopéz 20 Years Later It Is Time for Justice*. Retrieved from www.amnesty.org/en/library/asset/AMR37/002/2001/en/5f5188d8-d951-11dd-a057-592cb671dd8b/amr370022001en.pdf

Baines, D. (2007a). Anti-oppressive social work practice: Fighting for space, fighting for change. In D. Baines (Ed.), *Doing anti-oppressive practice: Building transformative politicized social work* (pp. 1–30). Halifax: Fernwood.

———. (2007b). Extending a radical tradition: Building transformative, politicized social work. In D. Baines (Ed.), *Doing anti-oppressive practice: Building transformative politicized social work* (pp. 191–5). Halifax: Fernwood.

———. (2011). An overview of anti-oppressive social work practice: Neoliberalism, inequality, and change. In D. Baines (Ed.), *Doing anti-oppressive practice: Social justice social work* (pp. 1–24). Winnipeg: Fernwood Publishing.

Baskin, C. (2011). *Strong helpers' teachings: The value of Indigenous knowledges in the helping professions*. Toronto: Canadian Scholars' Press.

Belenky, M., Clinchy, B., Goldberger, N., & Tarule, J. (1987). *Women's ways of knowing: The development of voice, and mind*. New York: Basic Books.

Benjamin, A. (2011). Doing anti-oppressive social work: The importance of resistance, history, and strategy. In D. Baines (Ed.), *Doing anti-oppressive practice: Social justice social work* (pp. 289–97). Winnipeg: Fernwood Publishing.

Bishop, A. (2002). *Becoming an ally: Breaking the cycle of oppression in people*. Halifax: Fernwood Publishing.

Borcea, D. (2006, August 24). The angry peacemaker. *The Hamilton Spectator*, p. A1.

Brown, J., & Hannis, D. (2008). *Community development in Canada*. Toronto: Pearson Education Canada.

Butler, A., Elliott, T., & Stopard, N. (2003). Living up to the standards we set: A critical account of the development of anti-racist standards. *Social Work Education 22*(3), 271–82.

Cable 14. (2014, October 16). Hamilton Talks with Larry Di Ianni [Video file]. Retrieved from www.cable14.com/hamilton-current-affairs-shows/hamilton-talks-october-16th-2014

Canada Mortgage and Housing Corporation. (2014). *Housing in Canada outline*. Retrieved from http://cmhc.beyond2020.com/HiCODefinitions_EN.html#_Adequate_dwellings

Canadian Association of Social Workers. (2005). *Code of ethics*. Retrieved from http://casw-acts.ca/sites/default/files/attachements/CASW_Code%20of%20Ethics.pdf

Canadian Bar Association British Columbia. (2014, March). *Conditional sentences, probation and discharges*. Retrieved from www.cbabc.org/For-the-Public/Dial-A-Law/Scripts/Criminal-Law/203

Canadian Housing and Renewal Association (CHRA). (2011). *Affordable housing*. Retrieved from www.chra-achru.ca/en/index.php/our-work/affordable-housing/

Canadian Internet Registration Authority (CIRA). (2014). *2014 fact book*. Canadian Internet Registration Authority. Retrieved from http://cira.ca/factbook/2014/the-canadian-internet.html

Carniol, B. (2000). *Case critical: Challenging social services in Canada*. Toronto: Between the Lines Press.

———. (2005). *Case critical: Social services and social justice in Canada*. Toronto: Between the Lines Press.

———. (2010). *Case critical: Social services and social justice in Canada*. Toronto: Between the Lines Press.

Carter, C., & Macpherson, D. (2013). Getting to tomorrow: A report on Canadian drug policy. *Canadian Drug Policy Coalition*. http://drugpolicy.ca/report/CDPC2013_en.pdf

Chapin, R. (2007). *Social policy for effective practice*. New York: McGraw Hill.

Chappell, R. (2006). *Social welfare in Canadian society* (3rd ed.). Toronto: Nelson.

———. (2014). *Social Welfare in Canadian Society*. Toronto: Nelson Education.

Chiefs of Ontario. (n.d.). 60s Scoop. Retrieved from www.chiefs-of-ontario.org/node/373

Coates, J., & McKay, M. (1995). Toward a new pedagogy for social transformation. *Journal of Progressive Human Services 6*(1), 27–43.

Conference Board of Canada. (2011). *Canadian income inequality.* Retrieved from www.conferenceboard.ca/hcp/hot-topics/caninequality.aspx

Council of Canadians with Disabilities. (2013). *Immigration and people with disabilities.* Council of Canadians with Disabilities. Retrieved from www.ccdonline.ca/en/socialpolicy/immigration

Dalrymple, J., & Boylan, J. (2013). *Effective advocacy in social work.* Washington, DC: Sage.

de Montigny, G. (1995). *Social working: An ethnography of front-line practice.* Toronto: University of Toronto Press.

Determine your elegibility – Refugee status from inside of Canada. (2012). *Government of Canada.* Retrieved from www.cic.gc.ca/english/refugees/inside/apply-who.asp

Diebel, L. (2011, February 1). Jason Kenney: The man who would be kingmaker. *The Toronto Star.* Retrieved from www.thestar.com/news/insight/2011/02/18/jason_kenney_the_man_who_would_be_kingmaker.html

Dietz, C. (2000). Reshaping clinical practice for the new millennium. *Journal of Social Work Education 36*(3), 503–20.

Dispatch: Hidden Colonial Legacy: 60s Scoop. (2015). CBC. Retrieved from www.cbc.ca/8thfire/2012/01/hidden-colonial-legacy-the-60s-scoop.html

Doctors for Refugee Care. (2015). *Day of action June15, 2015.* Retrieved from www.doctorsforrefugeecare.ca/day-of-action-june-15-2015.html

Dominelli, L. (1996). Deprofessionalizing social work: Anti-oppressive practice, competencies and postmodernism. *Social Work 26*, 153–75.

———. (2002). *Anti-oppressive social work theory and practice.* New York: Palgrave.

———. (2007). Contemporary challenges to social work education in the United Kingdom. *Australian Social Work 60*(1), 29–45.

———. (2011). Climate change, social workers' roles, and contributions to policy debates and interventions. *International Journal of Social Welfare 20*, 430–8. doi: 10.1111/ijsw.1468-2397.2011.00795.x

———. (2012). *Green social work: From environmental crisis to environmental justice.* Cambridge: Polity Press.

———. (2013). Environment justice at the heart of social work practice: Greening the profession. *International Journal of Social Welfare 22*, 431–9. doi: 10.1111/ijsw.12024

Dominelli, L., & McLeod, E. (1989). *Feminist social work.* London: MacMillan Education.

Egale. (2014, November 20). *Egale Calls on Senate to Pass Gender Identity Bill on 16th Transgender Day of Remembrance.* Retrieved from http://egale.ca/all/egale-calls-on-senate-to-pass-gender-identity-bill-on-16th-transgender-day-of-remembrance/

Employment Insurance: Ten Changes 2012–2013. (2013). *Government of Canada.* Retrieved from www.parl.gc.ca/Content/LOP/ResearchPublications/2013-03-e.htm#a6)

Ezell. M. (2001). *Advocacy in the human services.* Toronto: Brooks/Cole Thomson Learning.

Fay, J. (2011). Let us work together: Welfare rights and anti-oppressive practice. In D. Baines (Ed.), *Doing anti-oppressive practice: Social justice social work* (pp. 64–78). Winnipeg: Fernwood Publishing.

Finkel, A. (2006). *Social policy and practice in Canada: A history.* Waterloo, ON: Wilfrid Laurier University Press.

Fisher, A. (2014). Why Ted talks are better than the last speech you sat through. *Fortune.* Retrieved from http://fortune.com/2014/02/25/why-ted-talks-are-better-than-the-last-speech-you-sat-through/

Fletcher, J. (1966). *Situation ethics.* Philadelphia: The Westminster Press.

Food Banks Canada. (2015). *About hunger in Canada.* Retrieved from www.foodbankscanada.ca/Learn-About-Hunger/About-Hunger-in-Canada.aspx

Fook, J. (2002). *Social work: Critical theory and practice.* London: Sage Publications.

Fountain, H. (2015, March 14–15). Syria conflict is linked to climate change. *New York Times International Weekly,* p. A4.

Freeman, B. (2011). Indigenous pathways to anti-oppressive practice. In D. Baines (Ed.) *Doing anti-oppressive practice* (pp. 116–31). Winnipeg: Fernwood Publishing.

Freire Institute. (2014). Concepts used by Paulo Freire. Retrieved from www.freire.org/paulo-freire/concepts-used-by-paulo-freire

Freire, P. (1998). *Teachers as cultural workers.* Boulder: Westview Press.

———. (2003). *Pedagogy of the oppressed.* New York: The Continuum International Publishing Group.

Gaetz, S., Donaldson, J., Richter, T., & Gulliver, T. (2013). *The state of homelessness in Canada.* Retrieved from www.wellesleyinstitute.com/wp-content/uploads/2013/06/SOHC2103.pdf

Germer, C., & Siegel, R. (2010). Wisdom and compassion two wings of a bird. In C. Germer & R. Siegel (Eds.), *Wisdom and compassion in psychology: Deepening mindfulness in clinical practice,* (pp. 7–22). New York: Guilford Press.

Gil, D. (1998). *Confronting injustice and oppression.* New York: Columbia University Press.

Giroux, H. (2001). *Theory and resistance in education: Towards a pedagogy of opposition.* Westport: Bergin and Garvey.

———. (2006). *The Giroux reader.* Boulder: Paradigm Publishers.

Goffman, E. (1961). *Asylums.* Markham: Penguin Books Ltd.

Greenpeace. (n.d.) Tar sands. Retrieved from www.greenpeace.org/canada/en/campaigns/Energy/

Grenier, E. (2013, 29 August). Majority of Canadians want to loosen laws: Polls. *The Globe and Mail.* www.theglobeandmail.com/news/politics/majority-of-canadians-want-to-loosen-marijuana-laws-polls/article14010389/

Guest, D. (1980). *The emergence of social security in Canada.* Vancouver: University of British Columbia Press.

Hall, S. (1997). Introduction. In S. Hall (Ed.), *Representation cultural representations and signifying practices* (pp. 1–11). Thousand Oaks: Sage Publications.

Hanson, E. (2009). Residential schools. Indigenous Foundations University of British Columbia. Retrieved from http://indigenousfoundations.arts.ubc.ca/home/government-policy/the-residential-school-system.html

Healy, K. (2000). *Social work practices: Contemporary perspectives on change.* Thousand Oaks: Sage.

———. (2001). Reinventing critical social work: Challenges from practice, context and postmodernism. *Critical Social work* 2(1), Retrieved from www1.uwindsor.ca/criticalsocialwork/reinventing-critical-social-work-challenges-from-practice-context-and-postmodernism.

Healy, K., & Leonard, P. (2000). Responding to uncertainly: Critical social work education in the postmodern habitat. *Journal of Progressive Human Services* 11(1), 23–48.

Hennessey, R. (2011). *Relationship skills in social work.* Thousand Oaks: Sage Publications.

Hick, S. (2010). *Social work in Canada.* Toronto: Thompson Educational Publishing.

———. (2014). *Social welfare in Canada: Understanding income security.* Toronto: Thompson Educational Publishing.

Hoefer, R. (2012). *Advocacy practice for social justice.* Chicago: Lyceum Books.

Homan, M. (2004). *Promoting community change: Making it happen in the real world.* Belmont: Brooks/Cole Thomson.

———. (2008). *Promoting community change: Making it happen in the real world.* Belmont: Brooks/Cole Thomson.

hooks, b. (1989). *Talking back: Thinking feminist thinking black.* Toronto: Between the Lines.

Housing Connections. (2016, April). *Monthly statistical report.* Retrieved from www.housingconnections.ca/information/reports.asp

Housing Service Corporation. (2014). Canada's social and affordable housing landscape. Retrieved from www.hscorp.ca/wp-content/uploads/2014/06/Canada-Social-Housing-Landscape_FINAL.pdf

Idle No More. (2013). *Calls for change.* Retrieved from www.idlenomore.ca/

Immigrant and Refugee Protection Act Canada (S.C. 2001, c. 27) Part 2. (2001). *Government of Canada Justive Laws Website.* Retrieved from http://laws-lois.justice.gc.ca/eng/acts/I-2.5/index.html

Indigenous Foundations, University of British Columbia. (2009). What is Bill-C31? Retrieved from http://indigenousfoundations.arts.ubc.ca/home/government-policy/the-indian-act/bill-c-31.html

Institute for Intercultural Studies. (2009). *Frequently asked questions about Mead/Bateson.* Retrieved from www.interculturalstudies.org/main.html

International Telecommunications Union. (2014). *Mobile-broadband penetration approaching 32 percent.* Retrieved from www.itu.int/net/pressoffice/press_releases/2014/23.aspx#.VQc4FMJVikp

Ishtar Transition Housing Society. (2015). *History.* Retrieved from www.ishtarsociety.org/about/history/

James, C. (1998). Practical diversions and educational amusements: Evangelia house and the advent of Canada's settlement house movement, 1902–1909. *Historical Studies in Education 10*(1&2), 48–66. http://historicalstudiesineducation.ca/index.php/edu_hse-rhe/article/view/1552/1642

———. (2001). Reforming reform: Canada's settlement house movement, 1900–1920. *Canadian Historical Review 82*(1). 55–90. doi: 10.3138/CHR.82.1.55

Jansson, B. (2003). *Becoming an effective policy advocate*. Toronto: Nelson Thompson Learning.

Johnson, A. (2006). *Privilege, power and difference*. Toronto: McGraw-Hill.

Johnson, L., McClelland, R., & Austin, C. (2000). *Social work practice*. Scarborough: Prentice-Hall.

Kalaugher, L. (2013). Migration from drought to flooding? *Environmental research web*. Retrieved from http://environmentalresearchweb.org/cws/article/news/52223

King, H. (2012). Ghosts of indigenous activism past, present, future: #IdleNoMore's transformative potential. *Media Indigena Interactive Indigenous Insight*. Retrieved from www.mediaindigena.com/hayden-king/issues-and-politics/ghosts-of-indigenous-activism-past-present-future-idlenomores-transformative-potential

King, T. (2012). *The inconvenient Indian: A curious account of native people in North America*. Toronto: Penguin Random House Canada.

Kirst-Ashman, K. (2010). *Introduction to social work and social welfare*. Belmont: Brooks/Cole Cengage Learning.

Kirst-Ashman, K., & Hull, G. (2001). *Generalist practice with organizations and communities*. Toronto: Nelson Thompson Learning.

———. (2006). *Understanding generalist practice*. Toronto: Thompson Nelson.

Lee, B. (2001). *Case advocacy*. Scarborough: Nu-Spin Publishing.

———. (2011). *Pragmatics of community organization*. Toronto: CommonAct Press.

Lee, B., Sammon, S., & Dumbrill, G. (2014). *A glossary of AOP terms*. Toronto: CommonAct Press.

McGee, H. (2015). Mi'kmaq. *Historica Canada*. Retrieved from www.thecanadianencyclopedia.ca/en/article/micmac-mikmaq/

McIntosh, P. (1990). *White privilege: Unpacking the invisible knapsack*. Retrieved from www.cirtl.net/files/PartI_CreatingAwareness_WhitePrivilegeUnpackingtheInvisibleKnapsack.pdf

———. (2012). Reflections and future directions for privilege studies. *Journal of Social Issues 68*(1), 194–206.

McKnight, Z. (2011, November 9). The rate of criminal charges has risen dramatically in past decade. *Vancouver Sun*. Retrieved from www.vancouversun.com/news/Busted+Search+database+discover+many+busts+occurred+your+city+last+year/7521210/story.html

MacQueen, K. (2013, June 10). Why it's time to legalize marijuana. *Maclean's Magazine*. Retrieved from www.macleans.ca/news/canada/why-its-time-to-legalize-marijuana/

Mann, C. (2006). *1491 New revelations of the Americas before Columbus*. New York: Vintage Books.

Many implicated in manure dump at B.C. homeless site. (2013, July 23). *CBC News BC*. Retrieved from www.cbc.ca/news/canada/british-columbia/many-implicated-in-manure-dump-at-b-c-homeless-site-1.1325023).

Mental Health Rights Coalition. (2013). *The voices of experience project*. Retrieved from www.mentalhealthrights.ca/HTML/voe.html

Merriam and Webster. (2015). Situation ethics. Retrieved from www.merriam-webster.com/dictionary/situation%20ethics

Morgaine, K., & Capous-Desyllas, M. (2015). *Anti-oppressive social work practice*. Thousand Oaks: Sage.

Mullaly, B. (1997). *Structural social work: Ideology, theory and practice*. Toronto: Oxford University Press.

———. (2002). *Challenging oppression: A critical social work approach*. Don Mills, ON: Oxford University Press.

———. (2007). *The new structural social work*. Toronto: Oxford University Press.

———. (2010). *Challenging oppression and confronting privilege*. Toronto: Oxford University Press.

Myrie, E. (2014, December 11). Cold country offered a warm welcome: 40 years ago my siblings and I came to Canada from Jamaica. *The Hamilton Spectator*, p. A15.

National aboriginal organizations. (2005, November 16). *CBC News*. Retrieved from www.cbc.ca/news2/background/aboriginals/national_organizations.html

National Association of Friendship Centres. (2014). *Friendship centres*. Retrieved from http://nafc.ca/en/friendship-centres/

Neigh, S. (2012). *Talking radical resisting the state: Canadian history through the stories of activists*. Halifax: Fernwood.

Nolan, D. (2003, 6 June). Group set to fight fogging; Plans to take on city if it uses chemical to kill mosquitoes. *The Hamilton Spectator*, p. A05.

Ontario College of Social Workers and Social Service Workers. (2008). *Code of ethics*. Retrieved from www.ocswssw.org/professional-practice/code-of-ethics/

Ontario Healthy Communities Coalition. (n.d.) *What makes a healthy community?* Retrieved from www.ohcc-ccso.ca/en/what-makes-a-healthy-community

Pomeroy, S. (2005). *The cost of homelessness: Analysis of alternate responses in four Canadian cities.* National Secretariat on Homelessness. Retrieved from www.homelesshub.ca/sites/default/files/Cost_of_Homelessness_Pomeroy_English.pdf

Porter, J. (2014, September 8). 10 First Nations with more than 10 years of bad water: No safe drinking water in Neskantaga First Nation for nearly 20 years. *CBC News Thunder Bay.* Retrieved from www.cbc.ca/news/canada/thunder-bay/10-first-nations-with-more-than-10-years-of-bad-water-1.2755728.

Razack, N. (2002). *Transforming the field.* Halifax: Fernwood.

Rempel, S. (2009). *Critical social work field educators: Identity, context, resistance and pedagogy.* Unpublished doctoral dissertation, Ontario Institute for Studies in Education University of Toronto, Toronto, Canada.

Rice, J., & Prince, J. (2000). *Changing politics of Canadian social policy.* Toronto: University of Toronto Press.

Sands, R., & Nuccio, K. (1992). Postmodern feminist theory and social work. *Social Work* 37(6), 489–94.

Saul, J. (2009). *A fair country.* Toronto: Penguin Random House Canada.

———. (2014). *The comeback: How Aboriginals are reclaiming power and influence.* Toronto: Penguin Random House Canada.

Schneider, R., & Lester, L. (2001). *Social work advocacy: A new framework for action.* Toronto: Brooks Cole Thompson Learning.

Scrivener, L. (2008, June 1). The man who ripped up his degree. *Toronto Star.* Retrieved from www.thestar.com/news/gta/2008/06/01/the_man_who_ripped_up_his_degree.html

Secret Cold War Plan Included Mass Detentions. (2010, October 14). *CBC News.* Retrieved from www.cbc.ca/news/canada/montreal/secret-cold-war-plan-included-mass-detentions-1.962421

Shaw, R. (2001). *The activist's handbook.* Berkeley: University of California Press.

Smith, D. (1990). *The conceptual practices of power.* Toronto: University of Toronto Press.

Smith, K. (2007). Social work, restructuring and everyday resistance: "Best practice" gone underground. In D. Baines (Ed.), *Doing anti-oppressive practice* (pp. 145–59). Winnipeg: Fernwood.

Solomon, R., & Pitel, S. (2013). *Lives saved 1982–2010.* MADD Canada. Retrieved from www.madd.ca/madd2/en/about/about_history_and_impact.html

Spindel, P. (2000). *Advocacy as an empowerment strategy: Confronting systemic injustice.* Scarborough: Nu-Spin Publishing.

Stanbridge, K., & Ramos, H. (2012). *Seeing politics differently.* Don Mills: Oxford University Press.

Statistics Canada. (2012). *Canada internet use survey, 2012.* Retrieved from statcan.gc.ca/daily-quotidien/131126/ dq131126d-eng.htm

———. (2013). Persons in low-income after tax. *Government of Canada.* Retrieved from www.statcan.gc.ca/tables-tableaux/sum-som/l01/cst01/famil19a-eng.htm

Stepan, C. (2002, March 16). Temple arson sparked move to build peaceful community. *The Hamilton Spectator,* p. A04.

Steyaert, J. (2002). Inequality and the digital divide: Myths and reality. In S. Hick & J. McNutt (Eds.). *Advocacy, activism, and the internet* (pp. 19–31). Chicago: Lyceum Books, Inc.

Strega, S. (2007). Anti-oppressive practice in child welfare. In D. Baines (Ed.), *Doing anti-oppressive practice* (pp. 67–82). Winnipeg: Fernwood.

Swanson, J. (2001). *Poor-bashing: The politics of exclusion.* Toronto: Between the Lines.

Taylor, B. (2011). Glossary. In B. Taylor (Ed.), *Working with aggression and resistance in social work* (pp. 139). Exeter: Learning Matters.

Thompson, N. (2001). *Anti-discriminatory practice.* New York: Palgrave.

Tierney, W., & Rhoads, R. (1993). Postmodernism and critical theory in higher education: Implications for research and practice. In J. Smart (Ed.), *Higher education: Handbook of theory and research Vol. IX.* New York: Agathon Press.

Todd, S. (2010). Social work and sexual and gender diversity. In S. Hick. *Social work in Canada* (pp. 292–313). Toronto: Thompson Educational Publishing.

Truth and Reconciliation Commission of Canada. (2015a). *Honouring the Truth, Reconciling for the Future, Summary of the Final Report.* Retrieved from http://nctr.ca/assets/reports/Final%20Reports/Executive_Summary_English_Web.pdf

Truth and Reconciliation Commission urges Canada to confront "cultural genocide" of residential schools. (2015b, June 3). *CBC News.* Retrieved from www.cbc.ca/news/politics/truth-and-reconciliation-commission-urges-canada-to-confront-cultural-genocide-of-residential-schools-1.3096229

Tweddle, A., Battle, K., & Trojman, S. (2013). *Welfare in Canada 2012*. Ottawa: Caledon Institute of Social Policy. Retrieved from www.caledoninst.org/Publications/PDF/1031ENG.pdf

Union of British Columbia Municipalities. (2010). *Local government elections task force discussion document: Local election cycles discussion paper*. Retrieved from www.localelectionstaskforce.gov.bc.ca/library/Local_Election_Cycles_Discussion_Paper.pdf

United Nations General Assembly, Human Rights Council 17th Session. *Promotion and protection of all human rights, civil, political, economic, social and cultural rights, including the right to development: Report of the Special Rapporteur on the promotion and protection of the right to freedom of opinion and expression, Frank La Rue*, (A/HRC/17/27) 16 May 2011. Retrieved from www.article19.org/data/files/pdfs/reports/report-of-the-special-rapporteur-on-the-promotion-and-protection-of-the-righ.pdf

United States Holocaust Memorial Museum. (2014). *Holocaust encyclopedia pogroms*. Retrieved from www.ushmm.org/wlc/en/article.php?ModuleId=10005183-title=Pogroms

University of Michigan. (2010). *Thoughts on problem solving*. Retrieved from www.umich.edu/~elements/probsolv/strategy/crit-n-creat.htm

Vaughn, L., & MacDonald, C. (2013). *The power of critical thinking*. Don Mills: Oxford University Press.

Waldie, P. (2013, July 18). U.K. ill-prepared for scorching summer; heat wave blamed for hundreds of deaths. *The Globe and Mail*. Retrieved from www.theglobeandmail.com/news/world/hundreds-dead-in-uk-heat-wave/article13314670/

Ward, L. (2002, 8 July). Africville—The lost town. *CBC News*. Retrieved from http://hrsbstaff.ednet.ns.ca/waymac/African%20Canadian%20Studies/Unit%208.%20Afro-Canada/africville.htm

Wealthiest 1% earn 10 times more than the average canadian. (2013, Sept 11). *CBC News*. Retrieved from www.cbc.ca/news/business/wealthiest-1-earn-10-times-more-than-average-canadian-1.1703017

Wharf, B. (1990). *Social work and social change in Canada*. Toronto: McClelland and Stewart.

Who are Canada's top 1%? (2013, September 15). *CBC News*. Retrieved from www.cbc.ca/news/canada/who-are-canada-s-top-1-1.1703321

Wilks, T. (2012). *Advocacy and social work practice*. Maidenhead: Open University Press.

Withnall, A. (2014, February 24). Where in the world is the worst place to be gay? *The Independent*. Retrieved from www.independent.co.uk/news/world/politics/and-you-thought-uganda-was-bad-map-shows-where-in-the-world-it-is-worst-to-be-gay-9152558.html

Wood, B. (2014). *Employment insurance (EI) changes*. Sherman Hub News. Retrieved from https://hubnews.wordpress.com/2014/11/05/employment-insurance-ei-changes/

World Health Organization. (2012). *Atlas of health and climate*. Retrieved from http://issuu.com/climateandhealth/docs/who-wmo_-_atlas_of_health_and_clima;

———. (2014, March 25). *7 million premature deaths annually linked to air pollution*. Retrieved from www.who.int/mediacentre/news/releases/2014/air-pollution/en/

Zastrow, C. (1981). *The practice of social work*. Homewood, IL: The Dorsey Press.

Zinn, H. (2002). *You can't be neutral on a moving train: A personal history of our times*. Boston: Beacon Press.

Index